A Practical Introduction to
Measurement and Evaluation

EDUCATION FOR LIVING SERIES

under the Editorship of

H. H. REMMERS

SECOND EDITION

A PRACTICAL INTRODUCTION TO

MEASUREMENT

AND EVALUATION

H. H. REMMERS
Professor of Education and Psychology, Emeritus
Purdue University

N. L. GAGE
Professor of Education and Psychology
Stanford University

J. FRANCIS RUMMEL
Professor of Education
University of Oregon

HARPER & ROW, PUBLISHERS, NEW YORK

Contents

v

PART FOUR:

Appraisal of Personality Aspects

Figures

Tables

Preface to the Second Edition

What we said in the Preface to the first edition of this book holds fundamentally for this second edition. That teachers are busy people, that measurement and evaluation, while highly significant as an integral part of teaching, are not all of education, that a single semester sets limits to what prospective teachers can learn of these matters, and the consequent need to provide a practical book—all of this is at least as relevant as it was six years ago, when the first edition was published. That we were not wholly unsuccessful in achieving our aim we judge from the reception of the first edition by those who used the book—prospective and practicing teachers, counselors, and administrators.

We have, therefore, retained the original organization of the book. What we have done is to recognize the changing educational scene by updating references, techniques, and to add certain emphases. Among these, in addition to including additional end-of-chapter references and deleting a few judged less or no longer relevant, are current corrected references to test publishers, noting recent attacks on tests and testing, a new section on the classification of educational objectives in the affective domain, a new section on the standard error of a score with a simple shortcut for estimating it, and a simple procedure for analyzing test items to evaluate how well they function and to provide "feedback" for the teacher and students.

We can only reemphasize our counsel to the teacher student to go beyond this text by investigating fairly thoroughly one major kind or area of tests, by examining the tests and test manuals and, so far as may be, the research literature, publishers' catalogues, and the

Mental Measurement Yearbooks. This book is truly only an introduction to the fascinating science and technology of measurement and evaluation.

H. H. REMMERS
N. L. GAGE
J. F. RUMMEL

December, 1965

Preface to the First Edition

Why another textbook in educational measures and evaluation? In this book we have tried to keep especially in mind the conditions under which teachers do the measurement and evaluation part of their work. From much experience in working with teachers, we are keenly aware that they have a lot to do besides measuring and evaluating. We need not enumerate here the myriad other important ways in which teachers must spend their time. Despite our obvious feeling that measurement and evaluation are highly significant in education, they are not all of education. We have tried not to let love of our subject blind us to these realities of the teacher's situation. It is this realization that there are other things in the teacher's life besides measurement and evaluation that has led us to offer a book like the present one. Whether we have done well—keeping the book relatively short, choosing topics within these boundaries, and writing clear sentences and chapters—will be for the busy student and teacher to judge.

Accordingly, this book is intended to be practical. By "practical" we mean two things: what it is practical for a student to try to *learn from a textbook* in a single semester's course and what it is feasible for a teacher to try to *use in his own classroom and school.*

Although the classroom teacher is the major focus of the book, obviously its content is also focally relevant to the professional role of the counselor and the administrator. They and the teacher are the major elements in the professional team that orchestrates the educational theme in the classroom, the school, and the school system.

In seeking practicality, we have had to square our enterprise with the well-known and sound idea, "There is nothing more practical than a good theory." For this reason we have not slighted powerful theoretical concepts (such as *validity* and *reliability*) and principles (such as gearing tests to *objectives*). The underlying philosophy of the text is that the learner is a whole person, not just the academic to-be-taught-subject-matter person. Keeping the book relatively short required us regretfully to compromise on what we judge to be all the relevant factors involved, notably community aspects and characteristics of school personnel.

Like any textbook, this one reflects a certain conception of the course. What kind of course do we have in mind? As indicated in Chapter 1, we see the present book, or any textbook, as providing only a part of the ideal course. Properly, the student will also investigate fairly thoroughly one major kind or area of tests by examining the tests and test manuals themselves and to some extent by looking into their research literature. He will carry out simple laboratory exercises in the statistical handling of data, of the kind he will confront as a teacher. He will not get through the course without some reading of publishers' catalogues and the *Mental Measurements Yearbooks*. Finally, depending on what he teaches at what grade level, he will try to identify and begin solving at least one of the real problems of measurement and evaluation that he faces as a teacher in his own classroom or school. In other words, we do not see this book as the student's whole world. We hope he will go beyond this book, or any book, into the fascinating larger realm of materials and activities actually involved in measurement and evaluation.

Our text is therefore shorter than most; yet, we hope it offers a balanced and solid introduction to the field. Longer books could be used for the kind of course we have in mind if the instructor simply omitted parts of them. But it is hard to shorten by omission without losing proportion and continuity. So we have tried to do the reducing job in advance, to make room for nontextbook learning, and in this way to give the student a practical introduction to measurement and evaluation.

If the reader is familiar with *Educational Measurement and Evaluation* by H. H. Remmers and N. L. Gage (revised edition, Harper & Row, 1955), he will recognize much in the present volume which has been taken from that book. The remaining material in this book has been prepared by Dr. Rummel, who also developed the orientation and outline of the present book. In essence, Dr. Rummel did most of the rearranging and wrote most of the new material, with Dr. Remmers and Dr. Gage acting as editors.

H. H. REMMERS
N. L. GAGE
J. F. RUMMEL

November, 1959

PART ONE
Orientation

CHAPTER 1

Purpose and organization of this book

Wilhelm Wundt, in 1879, made one of the earlier attempts to study human behavior objectively when he established an experimental laboratory in Germany and developed tests which measured sensory-motor abilities. In 1897, Hermann Ebbinghaus investigated the problem of fatigue in learning by means of a "completion test"; this was probably the first intelligence test. In the same year, Joseph M. Rice published a report of an experiment on the effectiveness of spelling drills in American schools. He devised a test to measure achievement in spelling which may be considered the first modern formal objective achievement test.

Developments in the field of educational measurement and evaluation have been so rapid and extensive since these early beginnings that now colleges and universities offer as many as six to a dozen different courses of instruction for the training of specialists. The published literature in the field runs into hundreds of volumes.

This textbook is designed for an introductory course in measurement and evaluation for prospective elementary and secondary teachers and school administrators. It is basically an orientation to measurement and evaluation for students who have had little or no systematic study of principles and practices in this field, and who have no related background other than the usual introductory courses in education.

We believe that the soundest approach to an understanding of educational measurement and evaluation is through emphasis on principles and practices, especially those basic to and nearly the same in evaluation in all areas of concern to teachers and administrators. These are supplemented by descriptions of appropriate specific instruments, procedures, and sources of information.

The book has four major sections: orientation, the school testing program, evaluation of classroom instruction, and appraisal of personality aspects.

Part One: Orientation. Part One provides a synoptic presentation of the areas of evaluation, the instruments of evaluation, and the interpretation and uses of evaluative devices to give students a general background for integrating principles and practices discussed more fully in the subsequent chapters. Too often students get so lost in the maze of details about specific aspects of measurement and evaluation that they fail to see the whole picture clearly. We believe that this initial survey of evaluation in the school program will lead to a more meaningful understanding on the part of the student.

This part includes a chapter that presents the basic statistical concepts used in measurement, since discussion of many aspects of measurement requires some statistical knowledge. We do not expect that prospective teachers and administrators who will be using their own or commercially developed instruments of evaluation will be interested in becoming expert statisticians. However, all will find it worth while to understand some of the basic concepts and techniques of computation used in interpreting the results of standardized tests and other measurements. The chapter is presented in a "how-to-do-it" manner with emphasis on the application of statistical tools in dealing with test scores.

Part Two: The School Testing Program. Nearly every teacher and school administrator will be concerned with a basic testing program. Part Two is devoted to the development and administration of the program, the selection of good measurement instruments, and the techniques of administering, scoring, and interpreting test results. It is important that those concerned with the testing program know what materials are available and how to select those that will best meet their needs. This part does not make an exhaustive survey of available instruments, but it does discuss numerous examples for a beginner.

Part Three: Evaluation of Classroom Instruction. Part Three is designed to assist teachers and others who devise their own tests and evaluation devices. It provides the basic principles and "know-how" for the identification of educational objectives, the construction of teacher-made tests with examples of good and poor items, and the techniques of assigning grades and reporting pupil progress.

Part Four: Appraisal of Personality Aspects. Since several other courses required of prospective teachers usually include discussions of personality and the teacher's role in its development, Part Four is concerned primarily with the measurement of interests and attitudes and the evaluation of personal and social adjustment. The more complex techniques of personality appraisal, included in many textbooks used for an introductory course, are omitted here in the belief that they require a background of training and an extensiveness of treatment not possible in a first course in measurement.

Supplements to This Book. We recommend that this book be supplemented by some laboratory sessions, especially (1) in the elementary statistical techniques, (2) in the study of various types of standardized tests and their administration and use, and (3) in the writing of items for teacher-made tests. Accordingly, we include laboratory exercises, discussion questions, and suggestions for additional independent study at the end of some chapters.

The detailed outlines at the beginning of the chapters provide a guide to study and review. By making questions of these topic headings a student can test himself on the more important aspects of measurement and evaluation.

A glossary of technical terms used in educational measurement is presented in Appendix B. The terms defined are the more common or basic ones such as occur in test manuals and research reports. The student should refer to this Glossary whenever he meets an unfamiliar technical term in the book.

Survey of evaluation in the school program

What Is Evaluation?

How Do We Go About It?
    What Is To Be Evaluated?
    What Are the Purposes of Evaluation?
    What Do We Use?
    Can We Do It Ourselves?
    What Are These Scores About?

Areas of Evaluation
    Scholastic Aptitude
    Scholastic Achievement
    Special Abilities
    Creativity
    Personal Interests and Plans
    Health and Physical Status
    Home and Family Relationships
    Emotional and Social Adjustment
    Attitudes
    Work Experience

Instruments of Evaluation
    Measures of Intelligence
        Individual and Group Measures. Language and Nonlanguage
        Measures. Multiscore Measures. Group Tests

Measures of Achievement
General Educational Development. Subject-Matter Tests. Manipulative-Performance Tests. Reading Tests
Measures of Interest
Reasons for Determining Interests. Advantages and Limitations of Interest Inventories. Typical Interest Tests
Measures of Adjustment
Physiological Measurement. Free Association and Projective Techniques. Rating Scales. Questionnaires and Self-Inventories

Interpretation and Use of Evaluating Devices
Descriptive Types of Information
Relevance of Norms
General Level and Pattern of Pupil Development
Uses of Evaluative Devices.
Instructional Uses. Use of Results in Counseling. Uses in General Administration
Misuses of Evaluative Devices

Chapter 2 deals with the nature of evaluation, the general problems faced in going about it, the areas of evaluation, the kinds of instruments used and the interpretation and use of evaluation devices.

WHAT IS EVALUATION?

There is nothing new in the idea of evaluating the public schools. Everyone who has ever been in a school—and who has not?—finds it easy to say what is good and bad about it. Members of men's clubs know exactly how the schools should "be run along sound business lines." Housewives frequently compare current educational practices with those of the "good old days," often to the disadvantage of the modern school. There is no lack of evaluation.

Recently, indeed, a rather extensive stream of negative criticisms has been published, aimed at testing in general and at objectively scored standardized tests in particular. Books with catchy titles such as "The Tyranny of Testing," "The Brain Watchers," and "They Shall Not Pass" have been aimed at the general public. A number of newspapers have further publicized the controversy.

This pressure has constrained the President and a Project Director of Educational Testing Service, the largest testing agency in this country, to publish a book "intended to provide teachers, interested school board members, and parents with a broad picture of what the testing in schools and colleges is all about."[1] It is a sane, lucidly written, authoritative, and balanced discussion of what tests as aids in teaching can and cannot do.

Responsible criticism, be it said, even if wholly negative, is never inappropriate. Unfortunately, the recent criticisms have produced more heat than light. That there are sometimes bad test items and indeed some bad tests marketed by unscrupulous or incompetent individuals, that tests are powerful tools that can do serious harm in the hands of incompetent users—all of this is better known by the responsible scientists concerned than generally by the critics. There is overwhelming evidence that the alternative advocated by at least one vocal critic—teachers' recommendations and screening interviews —are expensive and less valid than scientifically constructed objective tests.

That any measurement always contains some error is also well known. The measurement expert, indeed, can indicate the amount of error in a test score. We discuss the technical aspects of this tremendously important concept in the last part of Chapter 8. To quote an unknown Renaissance scholar, "He who knows not mathematics cannot know any other science, and he cannot, moreover, become aware of the extent of his own ignorance." The error of a score is a measure of the extent of one's ignorance concerning what has been measured. Measurement in the schools is inevitable. To quote a famous recent scientist, Lord Kelvin, "Until you've measured it you don't know what you're talking about." Just as a mother is not accused of lacking mother love because she weighs her baby often, so testing can be effective in measuring and evaluating pupil achievement and progress.

Since evaluation goes on inevitably, it is of vital importance that its principles, techniques, and uses be understood. To clarify these points is the purpose of this chapter.

Evaluation and *measurement* are terms often used with little regard for their meanings. *Measurement* refers to observations that can be

---

[1] Henry Chauncey and John E. Dobbin, *Testing: Its Place in Education Today,* New York: Harper & Row, 1963.

expressed quantitatively and answers the question "how much." *Evaluation* goes beyond the statement of how much, to concern itself with the question "what value." It seeks to answer the pupil's and teacher's question, "What progress am I making?" Evaluation, therefore, presupposes a definition of goals to be reached—objectives that have been set forth.

In the development of objectives, certain principles are important:

1. Objectives must be twofold. That is, they should set forth what the institution is trying to accomplish and what the students should attain or work toward.
2. Objectives should generally be developed cooperatively. If the administration alone attempts to establish the objectives and the role of the teacher is merely to carry out its directives, the results are often questionable. Such a policy tends to breed resentment and dissatisfaction.
3. Objectives should be broad and general. However, these broad objectives must be so stated that they are subject to specific implementation.
4. Further objectives should grow out of the task of appraising students' performances.

Methods must be developed for obtaining evidence as to how closely the school is realizing its objectives, and sources of this evidence must be identified. This point will be developed more fully in the discussion of the school testing program (Chapter 4) and of evaluation in classroom instruction (Chapter 7).

Finally, we interpret the results in the light of our objectives.

The processes of evaluation are wasted effort unless the discovered weaknesses are corrected. Who should correct them? Obviously, the students must correct the weaknesses revealed in themselves, and the faculty must correct deficiencies revealed in the educational program.

In summary, we evaluate because we must always be concerned with whether we are reaching the goals of our teaching efforts. By analyzing methods and results we hope to find ways of improving them. Evaluation is not an extra chore imposed upon instruction— a distasteful task to be completed as quickly as possible; it is an integral part of what a good teacher does to make his teaching more effective. To evaluate what he does is as important as doing it.

Evaluation is not just a *testing program*. Tests are but one of the many different techniques (such as observation, check lists, questionnaires, interviews, etc.) that may contribute to the total evaluational program. A school should use tests only if they yield useful information about progress toward the objectives of the educational program. It is clearly not a question of *either* evaluation *or* testing, but of intelligent use of appropriate tests *in* evaluation.

Evaluation is not a culminating activity. The primary purpose of evaluation is to answer questions about the program such as:

What progress is the teacher making toward the objectives of the educational program?

Are his methods effective?

Is he actually changing student behavior in the desired direction?

Are his objectives achievable? Are they worth while?

Each of these questions is concerned with an *ongoing* educational program, not with a finished one. Continual evaluation, then, is essential.

HOW DO WE GO ABOUT IT?

Planning a program of evaluation raises at least five basic interlocking questions: What is to be evaluated? What are the purposes of evaluation? What do we use? Can we do it ourselves? What are these scores about?

What Is to Be Evaluated?

First it is necessary to consider the areas in which evaluation of pupil growth and development may be made. We can group these areas in general as intelligence, interest, achievement, physical, and emotional. The task of deciding what areas are to be evaluated is far from an easy one. In how many areas should we attempt evaluation? What specific types of evaluation should we make? The decisions—a cooperative enterprise on the part of administrators, teachers, pupils, and parents—should be made in keeping with the purposes of evaluation and the objectives of education.

What Are the Purposes of Evaluation?

How am I doing? Is this a good school for children? Are the schools accomplishing what they are supposed to accomplish? These are but a few of the many questions that every educator should be able to answer for his individual unit, whether this unit is the entire school system, a single school, a single class, or an individual pupil.

One of the most important purposes of evaluation is to *adapt instruction to the differing needs of individual pupils.* Evaluative techniques lead to identification of pupils needing specialized work and to the kind of specialization required. Without these techniques teachers may overestimate or underestimate the extent to which they should differentiate their treatment of pupils. All teachers make some adaptations to individual differences. Although the influence of evaluation may not result in different types of activities, it can lead to better-directed and more effective methods of carrying on activities.

Another use of evaluation is in *educational guidance.* Evaluation leads to information revealing how much aptitude a pupil possesses for scholastic work in general, as well as the broad areas of scholastic work in which he is most likely to succeed. It provides a basis for long-range counseling, placement, and follow-up work as well as assistance in dealing with the many immediate problems of pupils.

In *personal guidance,* evaluation is used to identify the most troublesome problems—educational, vocational, social, or emotional —that pupils face.

In addition to purposes pointed directly toward pupil needs, pupil evaluation is important in the overall *appraisal of the total school program.* It reveals specific strengths and weaknesses in the program. It provides bases upon which to compare one school's program with another's. It makes possible a study of the progress of a program between different dates, the development of school standards and school norms, and the nature of needs in curriculum improvement.

Pupil evaluation may also be used as a basis, through reports to parents and school patrons, for the improvement of *public relations* and the mobilization of public opinion.

What Do We Use?

A third consideration basic to evaluation is the selection of appropriate methods and instruments of evaluation. We could use several different techniques to get the same type of information. For example, we could estimate a pupil's vocational interest by an interview, by his responses to single items on a questionnaire, by an analysis of his hobbies or out-of-school activities, by his scores on an interest test, and so forth. Which of these techniques is best? Should we use all of them? Is this unnecessary duplication? Couldn't we get all the answers from a comprehensive testing program? From the viewpoint of economy, it is clear that we should select *the methods and instruments which yield information especially valid for the specific purposes set forth.*

Can We Do It Ourselves?

For one reason or another, the idea has developed that only individuals who have been specially trained in techniques of guidance and psychometric methods are capable of using evaluative instruments. It is true, of course, that the results of tests and inventories are worse than meaningless if there have been errors in administering and scoring them, or if there has been inaccurate recording of results. However, nearly all teachers can become good examiners and scorers with a little help from manuals and trained counselors.

In most schools, classroom teachers can and should administer tests designed for groups of pupils. By reason of specialized training, a counselor is ordinarily in the best position to administer tests that can be given to only one pupil at a time. Sometimes, however, a classroom teacher may be able to do a better job than the counselor in administering a particular type of test to a certain individual. This is likely to be the case if the counselor has already failed in an attempt to establish rapport with the pupil. These points are discussed in Chapter 4.

In the same way, should the teacher make his own tests or use those that he can buy from test publishers? For some purposes, as we shall see, his own tests will probably be best, but in other cases he will have to use standardized, commercially published tests.

What Are These Scores About?

The fifth consideration involves interpretation of the scores or results of evaluations. Interpreting the results provides answers to the first two questions—what is to be evaluated and what are the purposes of evaluation. Interpretation applies the information obtained from the methods and instruments of evaluation to problems in education. It provides a reason for careful consideration of details in test administration. The methods by which data from evaluative instruments are interpreted and used give meaning to the entire program and translate the results into practical application.

Evaluation and good teaching go hand-in-hand. In fact, a description of the processes a good teacher tries to follow shows that evaluation is present throughout. Good teaching follows these five steps:

1. The teacher analyzes the individual pupil's capacities, knowledge, past experience, interests, and needs.
2. The teacher analyzes the pupil's goals and helps and encourages him to revise his goals in accordance with his capacities.
3. The teacher harmonizes the educational process with the pupil's capacities and goals.
4. The teacher evaluates the pupil's progress in terms of his capacities and goals.
5. The teacher and the pupil, working together, reconsider the revised goals in light of the progress achieved and strive to correct weaknesses which would interfere with the attainment of reasonable goals.

A good teacher is evaluating when he takes into consideration the many factors inherent in student growth. These factors include acquiring proper attitudes toward others, safety habits, manipulative skills, knowledge, appreciation, understandings, and so forth. Some of these factors can be measured with rather precise methods and instruments. Others require careful exercise of judgment based on effective observation.

AREAS OF EVALUATION

A comprehensive program of evaluation provides an effective means of securing a developmental and cross-sectional picture of the characteristics of each pupil in the school. These data are a means to an end, not ends in themselves. Their greatest value lies in their effective use by administrators, counselors, and teachers as a basis for instruction and guidance. To understand students in all dimensions of their personality and environment requires a comprehensive sampling of facts about each student.

Described below are ten areas within which the teacher needs information for adequate pupil evaluation. The importance of each of these areas depends on the specific purposes of evaluation; the order in which they are listed is not intended to indicate their relative importance.

Scholastic Aptitude

Scholastic aptitude is usually evaluated by means of the grades a pupil has earned in preceding courses or of tests of ability and achievement. The best single predictor of ability to succeed in future schooling is some measure of past school achievement. This information is not always available and in some instances is far from reliable. Originally tests designed to fill this need were called intelligence tests. Since many such tests have been validated on the basis of their ability to predict success in school, the more descriptive title, scholastic aptitude test, is becoming widely employed.

Scholastic Achievement

There are several means of appraising the scholastic achievement of individuals. These include the scholastic marks earned in earlier grades, various standardized and teacher-made achievement tests, survey and diagnostic tests of basic skills, school activities, and some work experiences. The distinction between scholastic aptitude and scholastic achievement is not always clear-cut. Achievement may be described as what a person has learned, whereas aptitude may indicate how well he may learn in the future. Obviously, how well a pupil has learned may often be a good basis for predicting how well he will learn in the future in similar areas. Thus, means of appraising achievement may in many cases be put to the same uses as means of appraising aptitude. For example, the grades a student has received in junior high school may serve as a fair basis for predicting his subsequent success in senior high school.

Special Abilities

Special abilities include clerical, mathematical, artistic, musical, mechanical, and many other abilities of a relatively specific nature. Special abilities may be subdvided into broad general categories such as musical memory, mechanical ingenuity, or scientific reasoning, or into special occupational fields such as nursing, woodworking, fork-lift operating, or law. The various means of appraising these abilities include printed paper-and-pencil tests, products made by students, oral interviews, and evaluation of previous achievement or performance. Because of the many factors influencing success in special ability areas, no single method of appraisal is sufficient. Such factors as ambition, habits of work, interest, and other personal qualities tend to reduce the accuracy of any prediction of success based merely on appraisal of ability.

Creativity

During the past few years we have heard much discussion about the development of creativity in the educative process and the need for instruments to identify and measure it. But present research knowledge about creativity is scanty, and no demonstrably satisfactory instruments for its evaluation are available. Many of the researchers working on the problem have focused on understanding the nature of creativity and of the creative person, rather than hurriedly trying to build a test of creativity to market for widespread use. As a result, a great variety of characteristics have been studied by means of measuring instruments designed for research purposes only.

Evidence is gradually accumulating that the traditional intelligence and achievement tests, at best, reveal only minor variations in some aspects of creative performance. They do not directly involve the abilities to create new ideas or new things. In fact, nearly all research attempts to measure and study creativity have focused upon nonverbal intellectual tests, nonintellectual tests, biographical inventories, and environmental factors.

But until we develop a definition of creativity which is generally acceptable, and until researchers have been able to identify its component factors in terms of empirically observable acts of behavior, we must be very cautious and avoid drawing anything but tentative conclusions from the results of any instruments which presume to be measuring creativity. Creativity is not yet ready for routine measurement in the schools.

Personal Interests and Plans

We know that information concerning the degree to which the interests of an individual agree with those of persons successfully engaged in a given field is definitely valuable, in conjunction with other bits of information, in predicting whether he will stay in that field. Some evaluation methods in this area deal with the expressed likes and dislikes of the pupil, whereas other methods attempt to determine latent interests. The means of appraising personal interests and plans of individuals include autobiographies, interest inventories or tests, stated interests, interviews, previous achievement, and both work and leisure activities.

Health and Physical Status

Since health and physical status are so important in themselves, no evaluative procedures would be complete that did not consider such factors. Among the means of appraising health and physical status are physical examinations, health histories, observations, attendance records, follow-ups by nurses, and family consultations.

Home and Family Relationships

Emotional and Social Adjustment

Attitudes

Home and family relationships, emotional and social adjustment, and attitudes may be grouped together since they are so closely interrelated. These areas are sometimes included in one category loosely described as personality. Evaluation in these areas is difficult because of lack of agreement concerning the nature of personal qualities. Since individuals possess a variety of traits, habits, and attitudes, some of which are largely specific in certain situations, it becomes necessary to evaluate these characteristics in a number of ways. Thus the means of appraisal include observation, records of anecdotes, self-rating scales, interviews, themes, autobiographies and other documentary information, student questionnaires, opinion polls, check lists and adjustment inventories, reports from employers and group workers, and parent conferences. Appraisal of these areas is the focus of attention in Chapters 10 and 11.

Work Experience

Evaluation of work experience helps in understanding students in some dimensions of their personality and environment and also provides information of value for instruction and guidance. The usual means of appraisal in this area include records of employers, reports of vocational counselors, interviews, and student questionnaires.

Methods of evaluation are primarily concerned with the techniques best suited for collecting the information needed. In connection with the foregoing list of areas of information, we repeatedly mentioned techniques for collecting information. These techniques included questionnaires, interviews, observations, rating scales, behavior descriptions, objective tests, anecdotal records, and cumulative records. Some of the other techniques, used less frequently, include the sociometric method, products made by students, reports by parents, teacher-parent conferences, self-rating scales, diaries, themes, and opinion polls.

Obviously the teacher needs a considerable amount of information about individuals for a proper evaluation of pupil growth and development. Where they are applicable, objective techniques are preferable, for they provide data whose reliability and impersonal quality are highly desirable as a starting point in evaluation. Measurement instruments used in connection with these techniques fall into four general categories: measures of intelligence, measures of interest, measures of achievement, and measures of adjustment. We shall discuss these instruments of evaluation in considerable detail in subsequent chapters.

INSTRUMENTS OF EVALUATION

Selecting instruments of evaluation is basically a twofold process: (1) determining as exactly as possible what is to be measured, and (2) obtaining an instrument that will best do the measuring. This process can be further summarized by the words "what" and "how." All persons making evaluations should constantly consider these words, and all they imply. The desirable accuracy of evaluation is closely related to its purpose. Approximate measurements sometimes suffice. At other times it is necessary to have a measurement that is as precise and accurate as possible. This section reviews briefly the several types of instruments usable in evaluating intelligence, achievement, interest, and adjustment. However, you should be cautioned that many published instruments of evaluation do *not* conform adequately to all of the principles presented in this text. Satisfactory instruments have not been devised in some areas of evaluation. The principles presented throughout this book will be helpful in developing better instruments in the future.

Measures of Intelligence

Perhaps the most important factor related to success in school work is the ability to do abstract thinking. This may be interpreted as the ability to understand and manipulate abstract symbols such as mathematical symbols, word meanings, and verbal relationships. Although this is not the only factor, it is probably the most important *single* factor. For this reason most tests that have been developed for predicting school success or ability to learn have endeavored primarily to measure the pupil's abilities in these respects. Such tests have commonly been called "intelligence" tests, although the present trend is to use the terms "scholastic aptitude" or "educational aptitude" tests.

Individual and Group Measures. Scholastic aptitude tests may be suitable either for individuals or for a group. Individual tests can be administered to only one person at a time. Administration and interpretation of this type of test require people thoroughly trained in the methods used, and generally also a considerably longer time for administration than do group tests. Although some of the best scholastic aptitude tests are designed to be administered to one individual during an interview by persons with special training, teachers without this special training can sometimes get satisfactory results with such tests. Group tests are much less expensive, as far as time and money are concerned, than individual tests because they can be given to several pupils at one time and can be scored rapidly.

Language and Nonlanguage Measures. A growing tendency is toward using tests that are to some extent diagnostic. For example, information concerning a pupil's aptitude in language and non-language, or verbal and nonverbal abilities, is often helpful in evaluation. Thus some tests provide separate measures of language and nonlanguage ability as well as the total measure.

Multiscore Measures. Further breakdowns of ability are made by scholastic aptitude tests which yield several scores on different types of test materials. These tests have been constructed on the theory that better decisions can be made if several specific strengths and weaknesses are known. However, it is not definitely known what significance can be attached to many of the various scores provided by such tests. Among the measures provided by multiscore tests are measures of ability to do tasks involving number, word meaning, space, word fluency, reasoning, and memory.

Since it is impractical to discuss adequately all the various instruments for measuring scholastic ability available at the present time, we shall mention only representative tests. (For a more adequate description of specific tests refer to Buros' *Mental Measurements Yearbooks*[2] and the latest edition of *Tests in Print*,[3] a comprehensive bibliography of tests for use in education, psychology, and industry, edited by O. K. Buros. The most widely used individual tests are probably the Revised Stanford-Binet Tests of Intelligence (16)[4]

[2] O. K. Buros (ed.), *Mental Measurements Yearbooks*, Highland Park, New Jersey: Gryphon, 1938, 1940, 1953, 1959.

[3] O. K. Buros (ed.), *Tests in Print*, Highland Park, New Jersey: Gryphon, 1961.

[4] The numbers in parentheses, following the titles of tests, refer to the publishers listed in Appendix A.

and the Wechsler Intelligence Scale for Children (WISC) (20). The Stanford-Binet consists of a series of subtests arranged in age levels from 2 to 18 and requires approximately two hours for administration. It was devised to estimate a student's probable rate of progress in school and to pick out pupils unlikely to profit from formal school instruction. It yields a single score of mental ability. The test was originally developed in 1905 by the Frenchmen, Binet and Simon; the latest revision was made by Terman and Merrill in 1960. The WISC consists of ten subtests yielding scores for performance and verbal ability as well as a total score.

Another individual test widely used for adolescents and adults is the Wechsler-Bellevue Intelligence Scale (20). It yields a verbal score, a nonverbal or performance score, and a full scale or total mental ability score. Administration time for this test is approximately one hour.

The greatest limitation of individual tests of scholastic aptitude lies in their administration and interpretation, since few schools have the time, trained personnel, and clerical assistance to use them with all pupils. In the usual school situation these tests should be reserved for testing special and doubtful cases. It is necessary and desirable to use group tests for measuring scholastic aptitude of the entire school population.

Group Tests. There are several group tests of scholastic aptitude. Two of the simplest and very widely used intelligence tests are the Otis Self-Administering Test of Mental Ability (14) and the Otis Quick-Scoring Mental Ability Test (14). The second is a revision of the first, including a few more items and covering a wider range of grades; and it is more easily scored. The Kuhlmann-Finch Tests (12), a series of overlapping batteries extending from kindergarten to the adult level, are in some respects preferable to the Otis tests, for they have a somewhat better balance of verbal, numerical, and spatial material. However, these tests are comparatively more difficult to administer and score. Among other widely used tests of general scholastic aptitude are the Kuhlmann-Anderson Tests (21), Differential Aptitude Tests (20), School and College Ability Tests (SCAT) (9), the Lorge-Thorndike Intelligence Tests (16), Henmon-Nelson Tests of Mental Ability (16), the Pintner General Ability Tests (14), the Terman-McNemar Test of Mental Ability (14), the California Test of Mental Maturity (6), the SRA Primary Mental Abilities Tests (25), the SRA Tests of Educational Ability (25), and the Academic Promise Tests (20).

Measures of Achievement

Achievement measures appraise a pupil's educational growth and development. As previously mentioned, tests of intelligence or scholastic aptitude purport to predict a student's performances; tests of achievement assess what he has learned in school or other situations where learning and teaching are intended to go on. But scores on achievement tests are also excellent bases for predicting future educational success in the areas measured by the tests. For example, the student high in verbal and perceptual aspects of intelligence tests usually shows high reading achievement, and the student low in the quantitative aspects of intelligence tests is usually low in mathematical achievement. Thus, tests of achievement probably should form the core of a systematic program in every school that hopes to do a thorough job of evaluation.

Achievement tests are designed to measure relative accomplishment in specified areas of work. They are of two main types: general and diagnostic. These are closely related; there is no fine line of demarcation between them. The general achievement test may be defined as one designed to express in a single score a pupil's relative achievement in a given field of work. The diagnostic achievement test is designed to reveal a person's strengths and weaknesses in one or more areas of the field being tested. Some of the more extensive and comprehensive general achievement tests are made up of several subtests so that the composite score may be used as a measure of general achievement and the subtest scores may be used as diagnostic measures. These tests are usually referred to as achievement test batteries.

There are many varieties of achievement. Since acquiring knowledge is one of the objectives of nearly all school "subjects," many achievement tests attempt to measure how much of this knowledge a pupil has acquired. However, achievement is complex; and the more carefully the test is planned in terms of the aspects of achievement to be tapped (such as the ability to organize ideas, to make inferences, to draw valid conclusions), the more valuable will it be in the evaluation program. Among the several varieties of subject-matter achievement tests, some of the more useful are tests of general educational development, tests of specific subject areas, and manipulative-performance tests.

General Educational Development. Since an important purpose of education is to develop the individual's ability to apply facts and principles he has learned, many achievement tests are aimed at measuring applicable understandings in a cultural area, rather than proficiency in a given "subject." Thus, tests of "general educational development" stress understanding rather than knowledge of factual material. They cover such areas as the mechanics and effectiveness of expression; interpretation of materials in the physical sciences, social studies, and literary areas; and skill in quantitative thinking.

Typical tests include the following: the Co-operative General Culture Test (9), USAFI Tests of General Educational Development (14), the Iowa Tests of Educational Development (25), SRA Achievement Series (25), and the Sequential Tests of Educational Progress (STEP) (9). The Co-operative test measures understanding of current social problems, history and social studies, science, fine arts, and mathematics. The USAFI (United States Armed Forces Institute) tests include measures of correctness and effectiveness of expression; interpretation of reading materials in social studies, natural sciences, and literature; and general mathematics ability. The Iowa tests measure understanding of basic social concepts; general background in natural sciences; correctness and appropriateness of expression; quantitative thinking; interpretation of reading materials in the social studies, natural sciences, and literature; general vocabulary; and uses of sources of information. These Iowa tests are the most comprehensive tests of general educational development for secondary schools commercially available at present. The SRA Achievement Series—for Grades 2–9—is an integrated program for measuring the educational development of elementary and junior high-school pupils in the broad curricular areas of reading, language arts, arithmetic, and work-study skills. The Sequential Tests of Educational Progress (STEP) are designed to measure critical skills in the application of learning in several major academic areas of school and college instruction: listening comprehension, reading, writing, mathematics, science, and social studies. The four levels of STEP range from Grade 4 through the sophomore year of college. For a more extensive and detailed description of these and similar tests, consult Buros' *Mental Measurements Yearbooks*.

Subject-Matter Tests. Since specific subject-matter tests have been the concern of test makers for many years, hundreds of such tests are currently available. We shall make no attempt to list any as typical because of the large variety available. One has but to obtain catalogues from any test publisher to find tests in most areas. Appendix A contains a list of these publishers.

Subject matter is the one measurement area in which classroom teachers may and should particularly develop tests. We highly recommend that teachers develop objective tests for use as quizzes, midterm and final examinations, and general guideposts for their teaching. Such test development will increase their understanding of a more general type of testing program, aid their evaluation of student progress, and provide a frame of reference for revision of course objectives, subject matter, and methods.

Teachers usually need not use standardized tests in subject-matter areas; in many instances, the use of the norms provided by such tests is neither desirable nor valid. In the first place, the objectives for a specific course vary so much from teacher to teacher that published tests in a subject-matter area may not fit the objectives of the course being taught by the local classroom teacher. In the second place, standardized subject-matter tests often do not provide sufficient information with respect to the development of the norms to enable a teacher to determine whether or not his class is comparable to the group on which the tests were originally standardized.

Manipulative-Performance Tests. Written tests are usually not valid for measuring manipulative skills. For example, a pupil may be able to give satisfactory answers on a written test on the various working parts of a lathe, and the procedures to use in certain operations with the machine, but fail completely in actually cutting a machine screw or turning out an acceptable lamp column. A manipulative-performance test measures a student's skill in the actual performance of selected operations under controlled conditions. As a student completes certain operations, the teacher carefully observes the performance and records on a previously constructed check list the extent to which the student meets certain standards. The performance test provides a basis for appraising the overall performance and evaluating elements in that performance. It is impossible to obtain commercial tests of this type, although check lists for a few specific manipulative skills are available. Hence these tests must generally be teacher-made.

Reading Tests. Since the typical school situation and, in fact, many of life's situations require individuals to do considerable reading, reading skill has received the special attention of teachers and administrators. The improvement of reading is one of the generally accepted objectives of education. Hence special attention has been given to the evaluation of reading.

Reading achievement is usually sampled in both subject-matter and general achievement tests. In addition, a large number of specific reading tests have been developed. Some of these tests provide scores on rate of reading, reading comprehension, and special skills in reading maps, directories, tables, or advertisements. Reading ability is very highly correlated with other measures of scholastic aptitude and academic achievement. The correlation is so high that the question is often raised as to whether or not all tests are reading tests. There is some merit in this question. However, most other tests reveal abilities other than reading ability alone.

General reading ability can usually be measured with tests of general educational development. However, specific abilities in reading should be evaluated by means of diagnostic reading tests. Some of the most widely used diagnostic tests of reading ability include the Durrell-Sullivan Reading Capacity and Achievement Tests (14), Gates Reading Diagnostic Tests (5), SRA Reading Record (25), and the Stroud-Hieronymus Primary Reading Profiles (16). Since many tests have been developed to measure specific skills in reading, we recommend that you consult Buros' *Mental Measurements Yearbooks* before selecting a test for diagnostic use.

Measures of Interest

Another major area of evaluation for which information is desirable is *interest*. An interest inventory provides some information about a person's likes and dislikes, or preferences and distastes, for certain types of activities. How a person feels about an activity is an important factor in whether he will continue it. Common experience and some research data indicate that certain aspects of interest are remarkably persistent and stable. It is in the search for these more permanent aspects of interest, particularly those important for adjustment in various vocational fields, that interest inventories have been developed.

Reasons for Determining Interests. One reason for appraising an individual's interests is to determine whether he will be satisfied in doing a particular type of work. Another is to ascertain whether he is likely to be interested in the same things as other people engaged in that activity. If so, his personal relationships with others in that field are likely to be congenial. Then, too, educational psychologists claim that individuals tend to do better at things which interest them most. However, a high degree of interest does not necessarily indicate ability to be successful in such activities. A final reason for appraising interest is that the process may call the individual's attention to a field of activity to which he has previously given little or no thought.

Advantages and Limitations of Interest Inventories. The types of information available from interest inventories vary a great deal. Some inventories yield scores related to several specific occupations, whereas others provide scores in broad fields of interest such as mechanical or computational, rather than in specific occupations. Interest inventories are relatively easy to administer, but some of them are difficult to score and must be handled by a trained person. They can give considerable important information about individuals that would not be otherwise available.

Typical Interest Inventories. Among the more widely used interest tests and inventories are the following: the Kuder Preference Record, separate versions entitled Personal, Vocational, and Occupational (25), Strong's Vocational Interest Blank (separate blanks for men and women) (20), Thurstone's Vocational Interest Schedule (20), Brainard Occupational Preference Inventory (20), Lee and Thorpe's Occupational Interest Inventory (6), and Vocational Interest Analyses (6). For detailed descriptions and reviews of these tests and others, see Buros' *Mental Measurements Yearbooks*.

Measures of Adjustment

Accurate objective information with regard to aptitude, achievement, and interest is very important in any program of evaluation, but gives only part of the picture for each individual pupil. Most teachers and administrators are aware that adjustment or personality factors are fully as important as the more easily measured aspects of pupil growth and development. There is an insistent demand for valid and reliable records of personality development to assist the school in its evaluation program.

There are numerous approaches to the study of personality and adjustment—physiological measurement, free association and projective techniques, rating scales, questionnaires, interviewing, and others. One obstacle to personality measurement is that there is little general agreement on a definition of personality, or on the number and nature of the traits which compose it. Perhaps the simplest approach to an introductory understanding of personality tests is to consider them as instruments that endeavor to measure the personal and social adjustment of an individual as revealed by his emotions, attitudes, and values. Personality measurement, however, is a complex matter and cannot at present be carried out by a single test or similar device. Instruments for evaluating various components of personality are for the most part still in an experimental stage of development.

Physiological Measurement. In an emotional situation, certain measurable physiological changes occur—in blood pressure, pulse rate, amplitude of breathing, galvanic skin reactions, palm sweating, and many others. In general, these changes are only one phase of emotional adjustment and are not predictive of success or failure in life situations. Furthermore, their measurement requires such complex apparatus and specially trained personnel that it has to be restricted to clinical use and is therefore not suitable for typical school use.

It is encouraging, however, that experimental work is now being carried on which may be of extreme value to the future development of evaluation programs.

Free Association and Projective Techniques. One method being used by an increasing number of psychologists involves exposing an individual to some more or less vague stimulus to which he can respond with considerable leeway. That is, he is given an unfamiliar task to which he presumably reacts in the same way as he would approach an unfamiliar situation in actual life. Each task is apparently meaningless, although the individual being tested is asked to give a meaning in his own way. When this is done, the trained clinician is able to interpret each person's reactions in terms of established personality patterns.

Typical instruments of this type include the Kent-Rosanoff Free Association Test (29), the Rorschach Inkblot Test (20), and the Thematic Apperception Test (20). However, like the physiological measures, these tests require trained personnel to administer and interpret them and hence are best confined to clinical studies and application.

Rating Scales. Rating scales have long been used as instruments for appraising pupil adjustment. Ratings involve judgments as to where the individual stands on a scale with respect to certain traits. Although research indicates that the ratings on such scales are often faulty, they sometimes do provide a useful method of quantifying impressions about a student and thus may be of some value in the evaluation program.

Of the many devices available in this field, illustrative ones used include the Vineland Social Maturity Scale (12), the American Council on Education Personality Report (2), and the Haggerty-Olson-Wickman Behavior Rating Schedule (14).

Questionnaires and Self-Inventories. Although the questionnaire method has serious limitations, personality measurement in recent years has tended to move in the direction of the standardized questionnaire or self-inventory. The best use for adjustment questionnaires is in locating the extremely maladjusted individual and following up such cases with individual counseling and therapy. Typical instruments of this type include the Bell Adjustment Inventory (8), the Mental Health Analysis (6), Mooney Problem Check List (20), SRA Youth Inventory and SRA Junior Inventory (25), California Psychological Inventory (8), and the Syracuse Scales of Social Relations (14).

INTERPRETATION AND USE OF EVALUATING DEVICES

As a basis for discussing the interpretation and use of evaluating devices, it is desirable to look briefly at the measurement process and the specific functions of test scores. The measurement process is essentially a means of obtaining accurate descriptive information about individuals. It is necessary to be concerned with two fundamental problems: (1) the purposes for which this descriptive information is obtained, and (2) the types of information necessary for these purposes. The first problem has been the focus of attention in preceding sections of this chapter. The second is the source of the concepts to be discussed in the present section. These concepts are treated in greater detail in Chapters 6 and 9.

Considerable progress has been made in developing instruments for evaluating pupil growth and development. But it is still true that even the best instruments available are crude and ambiguous in comparison with ideal instruments. For this reason the interpretation of evaluating devices is complicated and, because certain essential facts are not provided, frequently inaccurate. Hence school personnel are handicapped in getting the facts concerning the educational growth and development of pupils. However, if those concerned with evaluation understand some of the concepts involved in the interpretation of evaluating devices, these devices can be extremely valuable despite their limitations. Perhaps a brief review of the information usually required in interpreting an individual test score will clarify the significance of that score for various testing purposes.

Descriptive Types of Information

One type of information descriptive of an individual's performance may be expressed in terms which are *absolute with respect to specific functions and materials included in a test.* For example, let us suppose that an individual knows the answers to 63 items on an examination. This information in itself is obviously of very limited significance. However, if we express this score as the percentage of the total number of questions asked, or the maximum possible score, it may have more meaning. If there were 76 items in the test, the raw score of 63 would equal 83 percent. The percentage score is still relatively meaningless. It may indicate quite high ability if the items in the test are "difficult," or quite low ability if the items are "easy." Whether items are "easy" or "difficult" we can determine only with respect to other scores, groups of scores, or norms for various groups of individuals.

Another type of information is descriptive of an individual's performance *relative to the performance of other individuals and groups.* If we know that a raw score of 52 is the average score of the class of which this individual is a member, the score immediately takes on new meaning. We could make a still more meaningful interpretation if we knew that the score of 63 corresponds to a rank of 2 in a class of 30 students, or a percentile rank (to be defined later) of 93 in that class. Yet we need still more information to obtain the full significance of this score. It is important to know how this score compares with those made by individuals in other groups, such as other similar classes in the same school, other schools, groups with various amounts of instruction, groups in various sections of the country, and the like. Such comparisons are usually made by noting the percentile rank which corresponds to the raw score of 63 in these various groups, that is, how the score compares with norms of other groups.

A third type of information describes an individual's performance *relative to his own previous performances.* For many purposes it is desirable to know what progress the student has made over a given period. This information may show his "growth," and may be expressed in either absolute or relative terms. For example, if he made a score of 48 a year ago on the same test or on a comparable form of the test, his new score of 63 gives some indication that he has made a gain in whatever is being measured. If we transfer these raw scores into "grade scores" (to be defined later), the increase from 48 to 63 in one year might permit the statement that the latter score is 1.6 grades higher than that made a year previously.

A fourth type of information describes an individual's performance *in comparison with his performance on tests in other areas* or in other "subjects." The information that he made a score of 63 on a particular test and a score of 94 on another test has little meaning as to comparative performance. However, if we transform both scores into terms of relative performance, such as percentile scores, or of other norms (to be defined later), they will provide a meaningful basis for interpretation.

From the foregoing discussion obviously two things are essential if the interpretation of test results is to contribute to understanding the individual. The test must be appropriate for the purpose of the testing, and it is necessary to know how others have performed on the test. Norms provide for this second essential. Even if a test is appropriate, reliable, and valid, a score obtained from it is relatively meaningless until it is compared with other scores. Furthermore, the other scores will also be meaningless and misleading for purposes of comparison, if they are not based on groups of people with whom it is sensible to compare the individuals being evaluated. In other words, norms must be relevant.

Relevance of Norms

Because tests are given for a variety of reasons, a variety of norms is needed. For example, assume that the individual previously mentioned is a senior high-school boy in a mechanical arts course and that his score of 63 was made on a test of mechanical aptitude. Assume further that, in addition to (1) the norms tables provided by the test manual, the school has accumulated norms over several years (2) for all senior boys in the high school, (3) for all senior boys in mechanical arts courses, and (4) for new employees of two local machine shops which provide vocational opportunities for qualified boys from this high school. In the class of which this boy is a member his score corresponds to the 93rd percentile. Comparisons with the other available norms provide the information found on page 31.

In comparison with high-school senior boys *in general*, his rank is

From the manual norms 99

On local senior norms 97

In comparison with high-school senior boys in *mechanical arts*, his rank is

From the manual norms 78

On norms of local seniors in mechanical arts 85

In comparison with *new employees*, his rank is

On Firm X's new employee norms 56

On Firm Y's new employee norms 24

It is obvious that the score this boy has made may be interpreted in many ways. The major principle in interpretation is that norms should be meaningful for the particular purpose of the testing.

General Level and Pattern of Pupil Development

In the foregoing discussion the scores and norms referred to only one aspect of an individual's ability. Any adequate program of evaluation will, of course, include estimates of pupil growth and development in many areas. Instruments of evaluation should provide a basis for judging the general level of the pupil's development. In addition, the pattern of his profile (see Glossary) of development should help in identifying his strong and weak areas. Because profiles are simple to construct and relatively easy to interpret, they are a popular method of summarizing the results of measurement in several areas. They have the added advantage that the graphic presentation enables one to secure an overall picture of the pupil's general development and the relationships among the several specific areas of development.

The use of pupils' profiles is based on at least three premises. (1) Different spheres of work require different patterns of intelligence, interests, achievements, adjustments, and the like. (2) The pupil has his own individual pattern for a set of such traits. The profile of these traits reveals his pattern. (3) The kind of education and guidance he receives will be most effective if it gives him an awareness of his various strengths and weaknesses, if it helps him to develop the knowledge and skills useful in solving his problems, if he knows the kinds of traits required for success in various activities, and if he can be prepared for the types of activities in which he has the greatest potentiality for success and satisfaction.

Uses of Evaluative Devices

The discussion of the interpretation of evaluative devices has implied numerous possible uses. Interpretation and use are so closely related as to be inseparable at times. Although we have already suggested some of the uses, this section presents a brief summary of the more important possible uses of evaluative devices.

Instructional Uses. The most important single use of evaluative devices is in adapting instruction to the differing needs of pupils. The teacher must interpret the results yielded by these instruments and translate the information obtained into specific actions. He may use the results to discover the scholastic aptitudes of pupils and adapt instruction to their individual levels of aptitude. By knowing in detail the general educational level and pattern of pupil achievement, he has a guide for developing all types of achievement in the school curriculum according to the abilities of his pupils. He has the information needed for discovering exceptionally able students and can make special provision for them. He also has information by which he can diagnose individual pupil weaknesses in different areas and he can develop remedial treatment based upon this diagnosis. The teacher's activities can be better directed and more effective, since they are based upon a more dependable acquaintance with each pupil's educational level.

Use of Results in Counseling. The use of evaluative devices in counseling depends entirely upon the guidance functions carried on in the school. Although these functions vary considerably from one school to another, a number appear to be common to most guidance programs. Results of evaluation are useful in conferring with pupils from time to time about achievement and problems of adjustment, and with parents about their children. In educational counseling, such results provide a basis for guiding pupils into or away from certain courses and thus for reducing the frequency of failure. In vocational counseling, the results of evaluation procedures may be used to help pupils and parents make plans for pupils' careers after graduation; they are also valuable in making reports to colleges and prospective employers.

Uses in General Administration. The school administrator needs information both for evaluating the total educational offering of the school, and for his policy-making decisions. By knowing the status of the school as a whole, and of subgroups within it, in comparison both with its previous status and with other schools in similar situations, he is in a better position to translate educational philosophy into administrative action. These administrative uses of evaluation can be far-reaching indeed, affecting curriculum planning and revision, methods and materials of instruction, standards for employment of personnel, and the placement and grouping of students.

Misuses of Evaluative Devices

No discussion of evaluative devices would be complete without a word of caution. There have been, and still are, many possible misuses of these instruments.

Many users of tests and other evaluative devices have sometimes allowed themselves to be misled by the labels or names attached to the instruments. This has not always been the fault of the user, because some instruments unfortunately have been named incorrectly. This has been due, in some instances, to the various connotations of labels under different conditions and in different situations. For example, achievement tests and aptitude tests have often been interpreted as measuring very different things even when their content is very similar, and they have often been interpreted as measuring the same thing when their content has varied to a wide extent.

In some instances, tests are out of line with the objectives of the teacher or school using them, and thus do not provide valid measurement in the areas in which they are used. Users of evaluative instruments have the responsibility of carefully examining each instrument they contemplate using to decide whether or not it fits objectives and pupils.

Another frequent misuse of tests stems from placing too much confidence in scores obtained for individual pupils and in limited evaluations. No test is perfectly reliable, and there is always a certain amount of error in even the best test administered under ideal conditions.

A very serious misuse is to judge the effectiveness of an individual teacher on the basis of test scores made by his class. To do this ignores the effects of class ability, previous educational experiences, adequacy of instructional and resource materials, effectiveness of supervisory assistance, and attitudes of pupils and parents toward school achievement. Class achievement is not dependent only upon the teacher who has the class at the time of the test; it also depends upon preceding teachers, the total school program, and the home and community environments.

Closely allied with the above misuse is the practice of coaching pupils specifically on items the teacher expects to appear on the tests. In many instances this practice results from an administrative policy of judging a teacher's effectiveness by the test scores of his class. It is perfectly legitimate and desirable, however, for teachers to be interested in the types of test items used and in the development of the types of abilities to be evaluated. If worthwhile objectives are the basis for teaching, then tests should be selected to evaluate these objectives.

SUGGESTED REFERENCES

Adkins, D. C., Measurement in relation to the educational process, *Educ. Psychol. Meas.*, 1958, *18*:221–240.
> Presents a meaningful analysis of the relation of measurement to education and a plea for a more orderly curriculum and a more highly organized plan for measurement that are closely geared at every stage of the educational process.

Chauncey, Henry, and Dobbin, John E., *Testing: Its Place in Education Today*, New York: Harper & Row, 1963.
> In this book the President and a Project Director of Educational Testing Service present a lucid nontechnical discussion of what Testing is all about.

Downie, N. M., *Fundamentals of Measurement*, New York: Oxford, 1958.
> Chapter 1 presents the purposes of evaluation and the philosophy

and psychological principles underlying evaluation and measurement.

Gerberich, J. R., Greene, H. A., and Jorgenson, A. N., *Measurement and Evaluation in the Modern School*, New York: McKay, 1962.

Chapters 1 and 2 discuss the general meaning of measurement and evaluation for the elementary and secondary classroom teacher, and present a good review of the historical development of educational and mental measurement from prior to 1800 to date.

Lindquist, E. F. (ed.), *Educational Measurement*, Washington: American Council on Education, 1951.

Chapters 1 to 4 discuss the functions of measurement in the facilitation of learning, the improvement of instruction, counseling, and educational placement.

Stanley, Julian C., *Measurement in Today's Schools*, Englewood Cliffs: Prentice-Hall, 4th ed. 1964, pp. 2–51.

The first of the two chapters discusses how measurement and evaluation permeate schools; the second is an excellent brief, historical review of the development of measurement.

Wrightstone, J. W., *What Tests Can Tell Us About Children*, Chicago: Science Research Associates, 1954.

A brief survey of the field of measurement which should be required reading for every elementary- and secondary-school teacher.

————, Justman, J., and Robbins, I., *Evaluation in Modern Education*, New York: American Book, 1956, pp. 3–13.

Excellent discussion of origins and trends in measurement and evaluation.

CHAPTER 3

Statistical concepts used in measurement

Ranking: A First Step in Test Score Interpretation

Grouping and Frequency Distributions

Graphic Representations of Frequency Distributions

Measures of Central Tendency
The Arithmetic Mean
The Median

Measures of Variability
The Range
The Quartile Deviation
The Standard Deviation

The Normal Curve
Interpreting the Standard Deviation
Area Relationships

Making Test Scores Comparable
Standard Scores
T-Scores
Percentiles
Stanines

36

Derived Scores
 Age Norms
 Grade Norms
 Percentile Ranks
 Standard Scores
 Quotient Norms

Measures of Relationship—Correlation
 Closeness and Direction of Relationships
 Data Required for Determining Relationships
 Rank Correlation (ρ)
 Scatter Diagrams
 Pearson Product-Moment Coefficient of Correlation (r)

The comparisons necessary if raw scores are to have meaning may be made either against absolute standards or against norms based on other pupils. Absolute standards enable the teacher to consider a pupil qualified regardless of the relationship between his performance and that of other students. Thus if it is considered desirable and satisfactory for a pupil to be able to write his own name legibly, a test item that requires this and is answered correctly by the pupil can easily be interpreted. If a job requires the ability to lift 100-pound weights at a given rate of speed, the individual's success at this can be readily interpreted regardless of the performance of other people. Standards define the minimum degrees of excellence acceptable in the performance of given tasks. Whenever absolute standards are available, even a single test score can be readily interpreted simply by comparing it with the standard. These interpretations are valuable even in such simple forms as those that denote a pupil's performance as "successful" or "failing."

Absolute standards are unavailable for achievement of instructional objectives, general and special mental abilities, attitudes and interests, and other highly important aspects of pupils. Hence norms are widely used in the interpretation of raw scores. It is impossible to set up definite levels or kinds of performance in these pupil aspects without *relating* the performance of pupils one to another. The spelling ability of a pupil of a given chronological age or school grade cannot be interpreted meaningfully as successful or failing by an absolute standard. We can know the degree to which this ability is creditable only by comparing it with the spelling ability of other pupils. This is so because for such aspects of pupils there can never be any external yardstick independent of other pupils. It is impossible to define levels of performance on most tests without relating the scores to those of other pupils. Hence, the need for norms, which provide a way to make such comparisons. And statistical methods provide the techniques necessary for interpreting the raw scores of individual pupils.

RANKING: A FIRST STEP IN TEST SCORE INTERPRETATION

If instead of a single score the teacher has the scores of two pupils, he can take the first step in interpretation by noting which of the two scores is higher. It is then probable (but not certain) that the pupil with the higher score has more of the achievement, ability, or whatever the test measures. As the number of pupils (or raw scores) increases, interpretability also increases because the teacher has more scores with which to compare each single score. A simple ranking enables him to interpret each raw score as an indicator of test performance. The process of test score interpretation is evident from this procedure—for the impossibility of stating whether a given score is successful or failing, he substitutes the possibility of determining which score is best, better, worse, and worst.

GROUPING AND FREQUENCY DISTRIBUTIONS

A fairly large number of test scores, say 30 or more, can usually be interpreted more readily when put into groups. The result of this grouping is a *frequency distribution*. Grouping and frequency distributions are probably best clarified by an example. Table 1 gives the raw scores obtained by 80 fourth-grade pupils on a 50-word spelling test.

As these scores stand, it obviously is difficult to interpret them. Ranking them is the first step in interpretation. However, grouping the scores in a frequency distribution results in a form of ranking—

Table 1. Scores of 80 Fourth-Grade Pupils on a 50-Word Spelling Test

22	25	16	44	43	6	42	39
49	46	39	37	35	32	29	26
17	22	28	30	32	35	27	38
45	41	16	21	25	38	37	35
31	30	28	40	38	36	13	24
27	30	31	35	31	31	30	30
40	37	36	34	20	24	27	30
18	22	36	29	37	36	33	11
45	40	19	23	27	29	36	34
19	23	27	29	39	37	36	33

it condenses the data into a smaller and more comprehensible number of categories. The steps in grouping the spelling test scores into a frequency distribution are as follows:

1. *Determine the range of the scores.* The *range* is 1 plus the difference between the highest and the lowest score. Look through the list of scores and find the highest and lowest. Subtract the lowest from the highest. The highest score is 49, the lowest is 6. The range is 1 plus the difference between 49 and 6, or 44.

2. *Determine the size of the class interval to be used.* A *class interval* is one of the groups in which scores are tabulated. The number of intervals should usually be between 10 and 20. Dividing the range by 15 gives some idea of the size of interval to use. Dividing 44 by 15 gives 2.9+. If we use intervals of *odd* numbers of units, the computation required in obtaining subsequent statistical measures is easier; hence the size of the class interval should be an odd number near the value obtained by the above division. We choose a class interval of 3 for this example of 80 scores.

3. *List the class intervals in a column beginning with the highest.* The midpoint of a class interval should be an integral multiple of the size of the class interval. In this example the intervals will include three scores, of which the middle score is a multiple of 3. The highest score, 49, will thus be in the interval of scores 47–48–49.

At this point we need to discuss the limits of a single raw score. Any single score, say 35, represents a distance stretching all the way from somewhere above 34 to somewhere below 36. At what points between 34 and 35, and between 35 and 36, shall we set the *limits* of 35? We may say that 35 represents a midpoint whose limits are

34.5 and 35.5; or 35 is the most representative score for all pupils with scores between 34.5 or more and 35.5 or less. Thus, in listing the column of class intervals, we might write for the upper *real limit* of each interval a number that is half a unit greater than the highest score in that interval, and for the lower *real limit* a number that is half a unit less than the lowest score falling therein. Inspection of Table 2 shows that the real limits of the highest interval are 46.5 and 49.5. This consideration applies to the computation of various statistical measures described later in the chapter. The column of class intervals in Table 2 show the *integral* limits rather than the real limits, in accordance with common practice. The highest class interval is 47–49, the next 44–46, and so on down to the lowest interval, 5–7.

Table 2.   The Scores in Table 1 Grouped into a Frequency Table, Including Cumulative Frequencies Used in Making an Ogive

Scores	Tabulation	f	cf
47–49	/	1	80
44–46	////	4	79
41–43	///	3	75
38–40	ЦЖГ ////	9	72
35–37	ЦЖГ ЦЖГ ЦЖГ	15	63
32–34	ЦЖГ /	6	48
29–31	ЦЖГ ЦЖГ ////	14	42
26–28	ЦЖГ ///	8	28
23–25	ЦЖГ /	6	20
20–22	ЦЖГ	5	14
17–19	////	4	9
14–16	//	2	5
11–13	//	2	3
8–10		0	1
5– 7	/	1	1
		$N = 80$	

4. *Tabulate each raw score.*   Make a mark after the appropriate interval for each raw score which falls within it. For every fifth score in an interval make a diagonal mark connecting the preceding four. After you have tabulated all the 80 scores, total the number of marks in each interval and write it in the column labeled *f*, or

frequency. The frequency in each class interval is thus the number of scores that fall within it. The sum of the frequencies in all class intervals is obviously the same as the total number of pupils whose test scores you are interpreting. Write this total frequency, or N (for number), at the bottom of the frequency column.

GRAPHIC REPRESENTATIONS OF
FREQUENCY DISTRIBUTIONS

Often a frequency distribution of test scores can be comprehended better when shown graphically. For this purpose three major types of graphs are used: the *frequency polygon*, the *histogram*, and the *ogive*. In the frequency polygon and histogram, the horizontal axis represents the scale of magnitude of scores, and the vertical axis represents the frequency or number of scores at each of the points along the scale of magnitude. We point off the horizontal axis in the same class intervals as those used in the frequency distribution, beginning at the left with the lowest one and proceeding to the right with as many intervals as are necessary to include the complete range. We point off the vertical axis similarly, beginning with zero at the bottom and proceeding upward to the largest frequency. For a frequency polygon, we connect these points by *straight lines*, as shown in Fig. 1. In the histogram, on the other hand, we indicate the

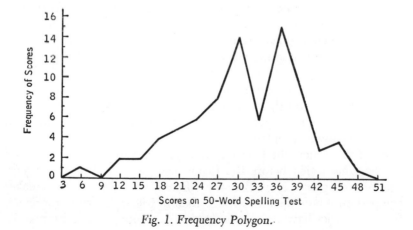

Fig. 1. Frequency Polygon.

frequency in each class interval by a *rectangle* whose base is the width of the class interval and whose altitude shows the frequency within that class interval. This is illustrated in Fig. 2. Note that the intervals on the score scale, the horizontal axis, are indicated in these two figures by the midpoint of the class intervals instead of the range of scores for each interval, as in Table 2. This procedure has the same meaning and makes it easier to label the graphs.

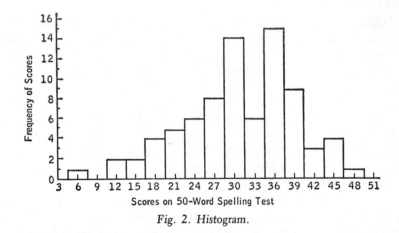

Fig. 2. Histogram.

Sometimes it is desirable to convert the frequency scale into a percentage scale. This conversion is useful when we wish to superimpose frequency polygons of test scores for two or more groups containing different numbers of persons. For example, suppose we want to compare frequency distributions of the spelling test scores for two fourth-grade classes, one with 28 pupils and the other with 52. To put these on the same frequency scale, we would convert the f's in both groups to percentages of the given group, as shown in the accompanying tabulation.

Fig. 3 shows how the two frequency polygons look, if superimposed on the same scales, before the frequencies are converted to percentages of each group. Note that the different size of the groups makes comparison more difficult in Fig. 3 than in Fig. 4. In the latter figure, the frequencies have been converted to percentages (not cumulative

Scores	Class A		Class B	
	f	%	f	%
47–49	1	4		
44–46	4	14		
41–43	3	11		
38–40	7	25	2	4
35–37	5	18	10	19
32–34	3	11	3	6
29–34	2	7	12	23
26–28	2	7	6	12
23–25	1	4	5	10
20–22			5	10
17–19			4	8
14–16			2	4
11–13			2	4
8–10			0	0
5– 7			1	2
Total	28	101[a]	52	102[a]

[a] Different from 100 because of rounding errors.

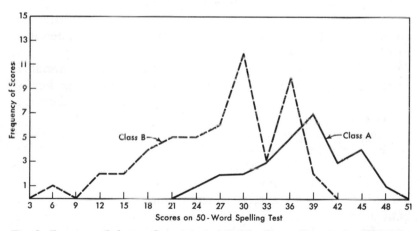

Fig. 3. Frequency Polygons Superimposed Before Group Frequencies Are Converted to Percentages of Total Group.

percentages, as in an ogive; see below). This conversion makes the areas of the two polygons the same and hence their shapes are easier to compare.

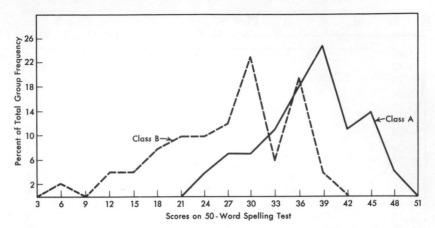

Fig. 4. Frequency Polygons Superimposed After Group Frequencies Are Converted to Percentages of Total Group.

The ogive differs from the frequency polygon and the histogram mainly in that the vertical axis is pointed off in *cumulative frequencies*. Beginning with the lowest interval in Table 2, we write its frequency, 1, in the table column headed *cf.* (or cumulative frequency). We then add the frequency for the next higher interval, 0, to the previous value; this gives a cumulative frequency of 1 again. To this value we add the frequency of the next higher interval, 2, for a cumulative frequency of 3. We continue thus to the highest interval; the cumulative frequency here should equal the total number of cases, 80.

In making an ogive or cumulative frequency curve, we mark off the horizontal axis as we did for the frequency polygon and histogram. We point off the vertical axis to include the *total* number of frequencies in the distribution. Beginning with the lowest interval, 5–7, whose midpoint is 6, we place a point above the *upper real* limit of the interval, at 7.5, at a height corresponding to the cumulative frequency for the interval on the vertical axis. We plot similarly the cumulative frequencies for each higher interval, plotting the final cumulative frequency, 80, above the *upper real* limit of the highest interval, at 49.5. The ogive for the values in Table 1 is shown in Fig. 5.

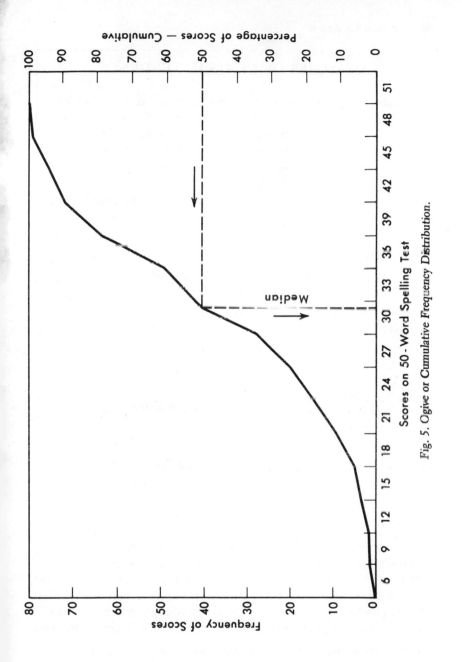

Fig. 5. Ogive or Cumulative Frequency Distribution.

MEASURES OF CENTRAL TENDENCY

In many frequency distributions the scores tend to be "bunched" near the middle of the range and to become relatively less and less frequent toward either end of the range. Determining the point of "central tendency," or the point around which the scores tend to center, is a convenient way of locating the single most representative score. Several measures of central tendency, or averages, are used for this purpose; the ones most used are the *arithmetic mean* and the *median*.

The Arithmetic Mean[1]

The arithmetic mean is already familiar to the reader, because it is the measure commonly referred to as the "average." It is computed by adding all the scores in a group and dividing the sum by the number of scores. This may be expressed in a formula as follows:

$$M = \frac{\text{Sum of scores}}{\text{Number of scores}} = \frac{\Sigma X}{N}$$

where X = each score in turn

Σ = the sum of the (upper-case Greek letter sigma, meaning to add)

N = number of scores

In Table 1 above, the sum of all the scores is 2468. Dividing this sum by 80, the number of pupils, gives a mean equal to 30.85.

The Median

The median is defined as the point in a rank ordering of scores on either side of which lie 50 percent of the scores. It is, then, the midpoint of the distribution of scores, or the $N/2$ measure in the rank order. Computing this average sometimes requires less labor than computing the arithmetic mean. It is a good measure to use when we do not want to weight the scores in proportion to their

---

[1] For the computation of the mean of grouped measures, refer to p. 51

deviation from the average. If the scores are not grouped in a frequency distribution, we obtain the median by arranging them in the order of magnitude, or ranking them, and counting from either end until the $N/2$ measure is reached. If there is an even number of scores, there will be no single middle score, but rather two. In this case the median is the arithmetic mean of the two middle scores.

Suppose 18 raw scores are arranged in order of magnitude, as follows:

| 33 | 32 | 32 | 30 | 29 | 28 | 27 | 26 | 26 |
| 24 | 22 | 21 | 20 | 20 | 18 | 17 | 16 | 15 |

Since there are 18 scores, $N/2$ is equal to 9. Counting the ninth score from either end shows that 26 and 24 are the two middle scores. The arithmetic mean of these two is 25, or $(26 + 24) \div 2$.

For grouped data, the following steps are necessary. These steps provide the median for the scores in Table 2.

1. *Divide N by 2.* In this case $80 \div 2 = 40$.

2. *Determine the interval that contains the median.* The *cf* column in Table 2 shows that there are 28 pupils below the interval 29–31, and that the 40th pupil must be within that interval.

3. *Interpolate within the interval for the median value.* The lower real limit of the interval 29–31 is 28.5, and we know that the total frequencies to this limit are 28. We need 12 more frequencies to reach the 40th pupil, or $N/2 - 28 = 12$. There are 14 cases in this interval ($f = 14$), and we assume that they are spread equally throughout the interval. We need 12 of them, so we will go 12/14 of the distance through this interval of 3 score units.

These steps can be shown briefly in formula form as follows:

$$\text{Mdn} = 28.5 + \frac{12}{14}(3)$$
$$\text{Mdn} = 28.5 + 2.57$$
$$\text{Mdn} = 31.07$$

Measures of central tendency, whether means or medians, are useful in two ways. (1) They provide a point in a frequency distribution which enables the teacher to tell whether the scores of given pupils are above or below the average performance of the class or other group involved. (2) They make comparisons between groups possible whenever two or more groups have taken the same test. Given the average scores of two successive classes, the teacher can compare the average of the first class with that of the second.

The choice of the mean or the median depends on whether the teacher desires to include or exclude the influence of the extreme or highly atypical scores which sometimes occur. If some pupils obtain perfect or zero scores on a test, they are not fairly measured, for the test is too easy or too difficult to reveal their true performance. Using the median excludes the influence of these atypical scores on the typical score of the group as a whole.

If we wish to compare communities as to average family income, the arithmetic mean will tell how they compare when extremely wealthy and extremely poor families are taken into account. This is useful for comparing community wealth for school tax purposes. The median is not influenced by the extremes of wealth and poverty; hence it yields better comparisons of the typical standards of living in the communities. In other situations, the mean is often more desirable, especially since it lends itself better to mathematical treatment in computing other statistical measures described in this chapter.

MEASURES OF VARIABILITY

In addition to describing a group by *one* measure most representative of it—the mean or the median—it is also necessary to have some indication of the amount of spread or scatter in the scores. In other words, we want to know how heterogeneous or homogeneous a group is. Two frequency distributions may have the same central tendency and yet be quite dissimilar in variability, as shown in the accompanying tabulation.

The mean (also the median, because these are symmetrical distributions; i.e., they have the same shape on both sides of the average) of the distributions for both Class I and Class II is 95; yet it is evident that the scores in Class I are scattered around the mean far more than those in Class II. The pupils in Class I differ among themselves far more than those in Class II. Obviously it is desirable to compute an index of variability rather than to rely merely on the impression gained from inspection of a frequency distribution.

Class Interval	Class I f	Class II f
123–127	1	. . . . .
118–122	2	. . . . .
113–117	4	. . . . .
108–112	7	. . . . .
103–107	10	15
98–102	12	18
93–97	15	21
88–92	12	18
83–87	10	15
78–82	7	. . . . .
73–77	4	. . . . .
68–72	2	. . . . .
63–67	1	. . . . .

The Range

Earlier we defined the range as 1 plus the difference between the highest and lowest scores. In the above illustration, the range for Class I is 1 plus $(125 - 65)$, or 60, and that for Class II is 1 plus $(105 - 85)$, or 20. The range, however, is unsatisfactory as a measure of variability because of its complete dependence on the extreme scores in a distribution. One atypical pupil in Class II could have greatly increased the range if his score had fallen in the highest or lowest class interval, but the scatter of the majority of pupils would not have been changed. Because of this, the range is not a dependable measure of variability.

The Quartile Deviation

Another measure of variability is the quartile deviation, or semi-interquartile range. It is defined by the following equation:

$$Q = \frac{\text{Upper quartile} - \text{Lower quartile}}{2} = \frac{Q_3 - Q_1}{2}$$

The upper quartile, or Q_3, is the point in a frequency distribution *below* which lie 75 percent of the cases. The lower quartile, or Q_1, is the point in the distribution *below* which lie 25 percent of the cases. Thus, the quartile deviation, or Q, provides a range of scores within which lie the middle 50 percent of the cases.

The calculation of Q_1 is similar to that of the median, except that this time we divide N by 4, or take 25 percent of N. To go back to the original illustration in Table 2, we divide N, 80, by 4 and obtain 20. Q_1 then is the point on the score scale that has 20 pupils below it. We can see that the interval 23–25 has a cumulative frequency of 20. Since these 20 pupils have scores below the upper real limit of the interval, Q_1 is 25.5.

We compute Q_3 by taking ¾ or 75 percent of N—in this case 60 pupils. The cumulative frequency column of Table 2 shows that the 60th pupil has a score in the interval 35–37. The lower limit of the interval is 34.5; there is a cumulative frequency of 48 below that point. Thus, we need $60 - 48$, or 12 pupils from the 35–37 interval to obtain the value of Q_3. Now:

$$Q_3 = 34.5 + \frac{12}{15} \, (3)$$
$$Q_3 = 34.5 + 2.4$$
$$Q_3 = 36.9$$

Then,
$$Q = \frac{Q_3 - Q_1}{2} = \frac{36.9 - 25.5}{2} = 5.7$$

The quartile deviation is probably the best measure of variability for the kind of purpose for which the median is the best measure of central tendency, that is, in situations where we wish to discount extremely high and low scores.

The Standard Deviation

The standard deviation, the most commonly used measure of variability, is the square root of the mean of the squared deviations of the scores from the arithmetic mean and is commonly referred to as sigma or the symbols s or σ. This definition is better comprehended in the following fundamental equation:

$$s = \sqrt{\frac{\Sigma x^2}{N}}$$

where Σ = the sum

$x = X - M$, or the deviation of each score from the arithmetic mean

N = the number of scores

Since the above formula requires the use of x, the deviation of each score from the arithmetic mean, the computation of the standard deviation can become quite laborious. A less laborious procedure for finding the standard deviation is the "deviation method" as described below. This procedure is also useful for computing the means of grouped measures.

The calculation of the *mean* by the short method (or deviation method) in a group distribution may be summarized as follows:

1. Make a group frequency distribution as described on pp. 39 and 40.
2. Select some arbitrary reference point (AR) as the midpoint of an interval as near the center of the distribution as possible. The interval with the greatest frequency is often the best one to pick.
3. Mark in the deviation (d) column the number of intervals each interval deviates from the interval whose midpoint has been selected for the arbitrary reference point. The value of the AR interval is marked zero in this column. Values above AR are marked plus and those below are marked minus.
4. Multiply each interval deviation (d) by its corresponding frequency (f) and write the product in the next column (fd).
5. Find the algebraic sum of the plus and minus fd's.
6. Divide the result of step 5 by the number of scores (N) in the total distribution. This gives the correction $\frac{\Sigma fd}{N}$ in *interval units* of the mean of the distribution from the arbitrary reference point.
7. Multiply the correction value obtained in step 6 by the number size of the intervals (i). This gives the correction in *score units* of the mean from the arbitrary reference point.
8. Add the result of step 7 algebraically to AR. The result is the *arithmetical mean* of the distribution of scores.

The formula corresponding to these steps is as follows:

$$\text{Mean } (M) = AR + i\left(\frac{\Sigma fd}{N}\right)$$

The calculation of the *standard deviation* by the short method may be summarized as:

1. Multiply each interval deviation (d) by the corresponding product of the frequencies and deviations (fd) and write the product in the next column (fd^2).
2. Find the algebraic sum of the fd^2's.
3. Divide the results of step 2 by the number of scores (N) in the total distribution.
4. Square the correction value found in step 6 in the computation of the *mean*. This gives $\left(\dfrac{\Sigma fd}{N}\right)^2$
5. Subtract the value obtained in step 4 from the value obtained in step 3.
6. Extract the square root of the result of step 5. (This may be done also with use of a table of "squares" and square roots; e.g., N. M. Downie and R. W. Heath, *Basic Statistical Methods*, Harper & Row, revised ed., 1965, pp. 290ff.)
7. Multiply the result of step 6 by the size of the intervals (i) to obtained the *standard deviation*.

The formula corresponding to these steps is as follows:

$$\text{Standard deviation } (s) = i \sqrt{\frac{\Sigma fd^2}{N} - \left(\frac{\Sigma fd}{N}\right)^2}$$

The above two methods, while appearing more involved than the methods discussed in the text, are much simpler to perform and yield the same results for practical purposes.

Illustrative Example

Using the scores obtained for 80 pupils in the fourth grade on a 50-word spelling test, as indicated in Tables 1 and 2 (pp. 39–40), it will be seen that the values necessary for finding the mean and standard deviation are obtained from the table below as follows:

$$N = 80 \qquad \Sigma fd = 20 \qquad \Sigma fd^2 = 658 \qquad i = 3$$

When these values are substituted into the formulas for the mean and standard deviation, the mean is found to be 30.75, and the standard deviation, 8.58.

X Scores	Midpoint	f	d	fd	fd²
47–49	48	1	6	6	36
44–46	45	4	5	20	100
41–43	42	3	4	12	48
38–40	39	9	3	27	81
35–37	36	15	2	30	60
32–34	33	6	1	6	6
29–31	30(AR)	14	0	0	0
26–28	27	8	−1	− 8	8
23–25	24	6	−2	−12	24
20–22	21	5	−3	−15	45
17–19	18	4	−4	−16	64
14 16	15	2	−5	−10	50
11–13	12	2	−6	−12	72
8–10	9	0	−7	0	0
5 7	6	1	−8	−8	64
		$\overline{80}$		$\overline{20}$	$\overline{658}$
		N		Σfd	Σfd²

$$M = AR + i\left(\frac{\Sigma fd}{N}\right) \qquad s = i\sqrt{\frac{\Sigma fd^2}{N} - \left(\frac{\Sigma fd}{N}\right)^2}$$

$$M = 30 + 3\left(\frac{20}{80}\right) \qquad s = 3\sqrt{\frac{658}{80} - \left(\frac{20}{80}\right)^2}$$

$$M = 30.75 \qquad s = 8.58$$

It is recommended that each student work through the processes using the above data to obtain a good understanding of each of the steps involved.

THE NORMAL CURVE

Interpreting the Standard Deviation

To interpret a standard deviation, the reader should have an introduction to the ideal, theoretical, mathematically defined frequency distribution known as the normal curve of error, the normal probability curve, or normal distribution. The normal curve is a mathematical ideal in the sense that it is a product of pure reason rather than of experimental results. Its importance in statistics is due to the fact that it describes the distribution of random sampling errors of many statistical measures and coincides closely with the actual distribution of certain types of data to be described below. Whenever a given phenomenon is the result of a large number of independently operating factors none of which has a disproportionately great influence, the shape of the distribution of the frequencies of various magnitudes of the phenomenon will tend to approach the normal curve.

An example of such a phenomenon is the frequency with which varying numbers of heads will be obtained if ten coins are tossed simultaneously many times. The range of the frequency distribution of the number of heads is from 0 to 10 and the theoretical mean is 5. The actual mean obtained from a large number of throws will be very close to 5. The frequencies with which different numbers of heads will be obtained will decrease as we proceed from 5 upward to 10 or downward to 0. The distribution will be bell-shaped, as shown in Fig. 6.

Human traits may or may not be distributed in a form similar

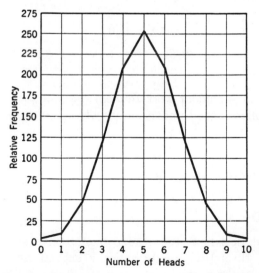

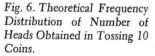

Fig. 6. Theoretical Frequency Distribution of Number of Heads Obtained in Tossing 10 Coins.

to the normal curve. The form of the frequency distribution of a human trait depends not only on the trait but also on the way it is measured and on the sample of persons included in the frequency distribution. Thus human skin or eye color is not distributed normally because people fall into fairly distinct groups on the basis of these traits. Human height is a more continuous trait, people being less distinctly grouped according to height.

Similarly, one test of mental ability for a given group of pupils may yield scores that fall into a bell-shaped distribution. But an easier test may yield scores that pile up toward the high end of the range of scores, or in a *negatively skewed* distribution, as shown in Fig. 7. A too difficult test may yield scores that fall into a *positively skewed* distribution.

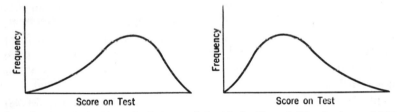

Fig. 7. *Negatively Skewed (Left) and Positively Skewed Distributions of Test Scores.*

The group included in a distribution of human heights might include half Japanese and half Scandinavians. The resulting frequency curve might have two peaks, i.e., be bimodal, with one peak at the average of Scandinavian height and the other at the average of Japanese height, as in Fig. 8. Thus it is evident that human traits

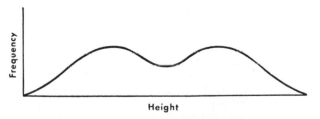

Fig. 8. *Bimodal Distribution.*

are not necessarily distributed according to any fixed law, such as the normal curve. Hence, the usefulness of the normal curve is *not* a result of its fitting the frequency distributions of traits or abilities of pupils.

But for another class of data the normal curve *is* descriptive of the form of distributions. This class includes the various statistical measures discussed in this chapter, such as arithmetic means, medians, proportions, standard deviations, semi-interquartile ranges, and differences between means. As shown below, if we know that a given set of measures, such as means, is distributed normally and if we know the standard deviation of the set of measures, we can infer the frequency with which measures of various magnitudes will occur.

Area Relationships

One property of the normal curve used in interpreting frequency distributions is the following: The *area* under the curve included between a vertical line (ordinate) erected at the arithmetic mean of the curve and a vertical line (ordinate) erected at a given distance from the arithmetic mean, where the distance is expressed as a multiple of the standard deviation, is always the same proportion of the total area under the curve. But why be concerned about this area? Because the area is equivalent to the number of cases in the distribution. The area included between the ordinates at the mean and one standard deviation from the mean will always include 34.13 percent of the total area under the normal curve. This is shown in Fig. 9.

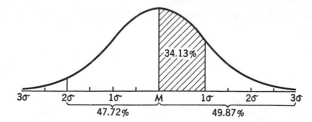

Fig. 9. Relationship Between Sigma Distances of Ordinates from Mean and Area Included Between Ordinates.

If the difference between the mean ordinate and another ordinate is equal to .6745 standard deviation, the area between the two ordinates will equal 25 percent of the total area under the normal curve. This distance, .6745 standard deviation, is known as the *probable error*. Thus, it is evident that 50 percent of the total area under the normal curve will be included between ordinates erected on both sides of the mean ordinate at a distance of one probable error from it. In a normal distribution, the quartile deviation equals the probable error. The proportions of cases included between ordinates erected at various other distances from the mean, when the distances are expressed as multiples of the standard deviation, are shown in Table 3. Practice using this table by verifying the figures for various values given in this chapter.

It is important to realize that the area included under any part of a curve is analogous to the number of cases in that area. Hence, the various proportions of the area signify proportions of the total number of cases in a frequency distribution. The importance of the standard deviation follows from this equivalence of area to number of cases.

Refer to Fig. 9 again. Notice that between plus and minus one standard deviation from the mean will be included approximately two-thirds (68.26 percent) of the total number of cases; within plus and minus one probable error from the mean will be included approximately 50 percent of the cases. Within plus and minus two standard deviations from the mean will be included roughly 95 percent of the cases, and between plus and minus three standard deviations from the mean will be included practically all, or 99.74 percent, of the cases. These interpretations of the standard deviation are valid, of course, only to the degree that the frequency distribution obtained approximates the normal curve. However, in determining the reliability of any test (see pp. 124ff.) and in the interpretation of test scores (see pp. 135ff.), the relationships of standard deviation distances from the mean to the area under the normal curve, as given in Table 3, become extremely important.

Table 3. Percentage of Total Area Under the Normal Curve Between Mean Ordinate and Ordinate at Any Given Sigma Distance from the Mean

$\frac{x}{\sigma}$	.00	.01	.02	.03	.04	.05	.06	.07	.08	.09
0.0	00.00	00.40	00.80	01.20	01.60	01.99	02.39	02.79	03.19	03.59
0.1	03.98	04.38	04.78	05.17	05.57	05.96	06.36	06.75	07.14	07.53
0.2	07.93	08.32	08.71	09.10	09.48	09.87	10.26	10.64	11.03	11.41
0.3	11.79	12.17	12.55	12.93	13.31	13.68	14.06	14.43	14.80	15.17
0.4	15.54	15.91	16.28	16.64	17.00	17.36	17.72	18.08	18.44	18.79
0.5	19.15	19.50	19.85	20.19	20.54	20.88	21.23	21.57	21.90	22.24
0.6	22.57	22.91	23.24	23.57	23.89	24.22	24.54	24.86	25.17	25.49
0.7	25.80	26.11	26.42	26.73	27.04	27.34	27.64	27.94	28.23	28.52
0.8	28.81	29.10	29.39	29.67	29.95	30.23	30.51	30.78	31.06	31.33
0.9	31.59	31.86	32.12	32.38	32.64	32.90	33.15	33.40	33.65	33.89
1.0	34.13	34.38	34.61	34.85	35.08	35.31	35.54	35.77	35.99	36.21
1.1	36.43	36.65	36.86	37.08	37.29	37.49	37.70	37.90	38.10	38.30
1.2	38.49	38.69	38.88	39.07	39.25	39.44	39.62	39.80	39.97	40.15
1.3	40.32	40.49	40.66	40.82	40.99	41.15	41.31	41.47	41.62	41.77
1.4	41.92	42.07	42.22	42.36	42.51	42.65	42.79	42.92	43.06	43.19
1.5	43.32	43.45	43.57	43.70	43.83	43.94	44.06	44.18	44.29	44.41
1.6	44.52	44.63	44.74	44.84	44.95	45.05	45.15	45.25	45.35	45.45
1.7	45.54	45.64	45.73	45.82	45.91	45.99	46.08	46.16	46.25	46.33
1.8	46.41	46.49	46.56	46.64	46.71	46.78	46.86	46.93	46.99	47.06
1.9	47.13	47.19	47.26	47.32	47.38	47.44	47.50	47.56	47.61	47.67
2.0	47.72	47.78	47.83	47.88	47.93	47.98	48.03	48.08	48.12	48.17
2.1	48.21	48.26	48.30	48.34	48.38	48.42	48.46	48.50	48.54	48.57
2.2	48.61	48.64	48.68	48.71	48.75	48.78	48.81	48.84	48.87	48.90
2.3	48.93	48.96	48.98	49.01	49.04	49.06	49.09	49.11	49.13	49.16
2.4	49.18	49.20	49.22	49.25	49.27	49.29	49.31	49.32	49.34	49.36
2.5	49.38	49.40	49.41	49.43	49.45	49.46	49.48	49.49	49.51	49.52
2.6	49.53	49.55	49.56	49.57	49.59	49.60	49.61	49.62	49.63	49.64
2.7	49.65	49.66	49.67	49.68	49.69	49.70	49.71	49.72	49.73	49.74
2.8	49.74	49.75	49.76	49.77	49.77	49.78	49.79	49.79	49.80	49.81
2.9	49.81	49.82	49.82	49.83	49.84	49.84	49.85	49.85	49.86	49.86
3.0	49.87									
3.5	49.98									
4.0	49.997									
5.0	49.99997									

MAKING TEST SCORES COMPARABLE

We have considered the meaninglessness of a single raw score. This applies not only to the raw scores on a single test but also to the relative standing of a single pupil on two or more tests. That is, raw scores from different tests are not directly comparable. Suppose that Ray Brown, a ninth-grade pupil, made the following scores at the end of the semester:

Algebra	52
Problems of democracy	116
Mechanics of written English	163
Attitude toward high school	8.4

These raw scores tell nothing more than the number of answers marked "correct" on each test. They are not a common scale. We need to know his *relative* standing, that is, his standing in comparison with a defined group, such as all ninth-grade pupils in his school or in the county, state, or nation. Also, we cannot tell from the raw scores alone whether Ray Brown was better in algebra than in prob lems of democracy, and so on. To compare his standing in the four different evaluations, we need to know the degree to which he was above or below average.

If on one of these tests, say algebra, the pupils' scores did not differ much from one another, their standard deviation would be small. To achieve a relatively high standing on the algebra test, Ray would not need to exceed the average of his class by as many raw score units as would be necessary if the standard deviation were large. Obviously, then, both central tendency and variability must be taken into account in finding the relative standing of any pupil within a group.

Of the many methods for making scores on different tests comparable in central tendency and variability, we shall discuss *standard scores, T-scores, percentiles,* and *stanines.*

Standard Scores

A standard score, or z-score, is defined as the deviation of a score from the arithmetic mean in standard deviation units. The formula for z-scores is found on the next page.

$$z = \frac{X - M}{s}$$

where z = standard score M = arithmetic mean of raw scores
X = any raw score s = standard deviation of raw scores

All raw scores below the arithmetic mean will thus become negative z-scores. The arithmetic mean will equal the z-score of zero. A score of one standard deviation above or below the arithmetic mean will equal a z-score of 1 or -1 respectively. In z-scores, the standard deviation becomes the unit distance of a frequency distribution whose mean is equal to zero.

The usefulness of these scores may be illustrated by comparing Ray Brown's relative standing on each of the four evaluation devices. By obtaining the required additional information, the arithmetic mean and the standard deviation of each test, and substituting in the formula above, we obtain the z-scores shown in the accompanying tabulation.

	X (score)	M	X − M	s	z
Algebra	52	47.92	+4.08	10.00	+0.41
Problems of democracy	116	120.26	−4.26	21.02	−0.20
Mechanics of written English	163	163.00	0.00	23.19	0.00
Attitude toward high school	8.4	7.20	+1.20	2.40	+0.50
Combined z-score (arithmetic mean)					0.18

It is clear from the tabulation that Ray is well above average in algebra and in attitude toward high school, slightly below average in problems of democracy, and exactly average in mechanics of written English. Every pupil's relative standing can thus be found.

T-Scores

T-scores serve the same purpose as z-scores and are based on the same principle. They have the advantage, however, of being always positive and expressed in larger units, thus removing the necessity of dealing with negative numbers and decimal fractions. We obtain the T-score by converting the mean of the distribution to 50 and the standard deviation to 10 with the following formulas:

$$T\text{-score} = T = 10z + 50$$

or

$$T = \frac{10(X - M)}{s} + 50$$

A *T*-score of 60 means a score of one standard deviation above the mean; a *T*-score of 70 is two standard deviations above the mean, and so on. *T*-scores of 40, 30, and 20 similarly indicate scores at one, two, and three standard deviations *below* the mean, respectively. The accompanying tabulation illustrates the changes from *z*-scores based on Ray Brown's *z*-scores given above.

	z-Score	*T*-Score
Algebra	+0.41	54
Problems of democracy	−0.20	48
Mechanics of written English	0.00	50
Attitude toward high school	+0.50	55

Any distribution of raw scores can be similarly transformed to any arbitrarily chosen mean and standard deviation. For example, in some testing programs the mean is transformed to 500 and the standard deviation to 100 for all tests, as in the Graduate Record Examination (GRE). The Army General Classification Test (AGCT) used a mean of 100 and a standard deviation of 20. Note the relationships among the various standard scores shown in Fig. 10.

Although the figure shows the relationships among scores that are normally distributed, *T*-scores, *z*-scores, and other standard scores are

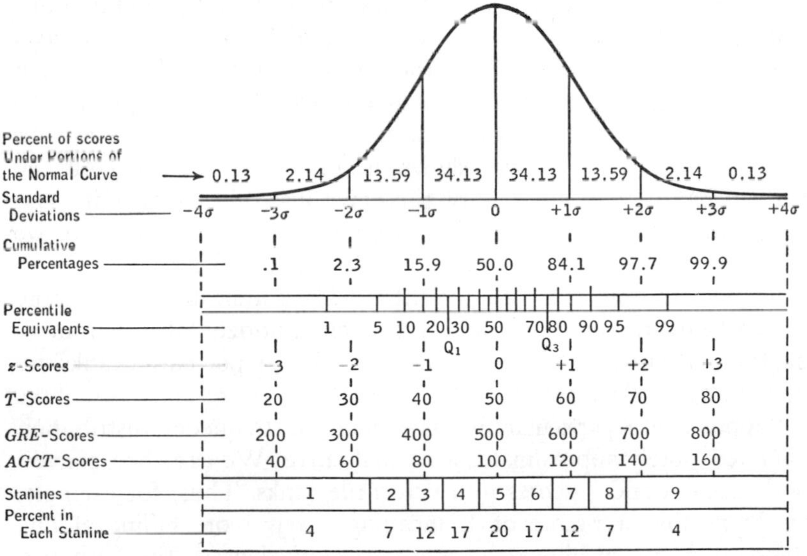

Fig. 10. *The Normal Curve with Corresponding Standard Scores.*

not always normally distributed. When raw scores are converted to
T's, or *z*'s, etc., the distribution of standard scores retains the same
shape as the original distribution of raw scores.

Percentiles

A third method of making test scores comparable is by computing
percentile rank. This indicates the percentage of all the scores in a
frequency distribution that equal or fall *below* a given raw score.
If a raw score is equivalent to a percentile of 50, it equals or exceeds
50 percent of the scores in a group. A raw score equivalent to a
99th percentile equals or exceeds 99 percent of all the scores in a
group; a raw score equivalent to the 1st percentile equals or exceeds
only 1 percent of the scores in a group. The 50th percentile thus
equals the median; the 75th percentile equals the upper quartile,
or Q_3; and the 25th percentile equals the lower quartile, or Q_1.

We compute percentile equivalents for each raw score by arranging
the raw scores in order of decreasing magnitude and finding for each
the number of scores equaling or lying below it. Each of these numbers we then divide by the total number of scores, and multiply the
quotient by 100. If we group the scores into a frequency distribution
and assume that all within a given class interval have the same value
(the interval midpoint), we can determine for each class interval
the total frequency of scores in the intervals in it and below it. For
such purposes a *cumulative frequency distribution* is frequently desirable. This procedure was illustrated in Table 2. The curve for this
distribution, the ogive, was shown in Fig. 5. By marking off the
vertical bar at the right side of the ogive into 100 equal units, and
numbering them from 1 to 100 from the bottom to the top, we
can read off the percentile ranks for any of the scores on the score
scale. For example, the 50th percentile will be indicated by the score
falling below the point on the curve where a horizontal line from 50
on the percentile scale crosses the curve. Other percentile ranks are
determined in like manner.

Suppose, in a particular instance, that the frequency distribution
obtained closely approximates a normal curve. We can then convert
both *z*-scores and *T*-scores into percentile ranks. Thus, for example,
we know that a *z*-score of 1, meaning a raw score falling at one
standard deviation above the mean, is equivalent to the 84th per-

centile, as is also a *T*-score of 60. We must emphasize that this holds only for *normal* distributions.

Stanines

Stanines are a type of standard score which divides the score distribution into nine groups. They are determined by using a standard score with a mean of 5 and a standard deviation of approximately 2. However, stanines represent bands of scores, not specific points on the score scale. Stanine 5, the middle stanine value, is a band including all scores falling within one-fourth of a standard deviation above and below the mean. Each stanine represents the band of scores included within one-half of a standard deviation unit. Thus, stanines 6, 7, and 8 represent one-half standard deviation units successively above stanine 5; and stanines 4, 3, and 2 are successively below stanine 5 in equal units of one-half a standard deviation. Stanine 9 includes all scores above stanine 8; and stanine 1 includes all below stanine 2. The distribution of stanines in a normal distribution is shown near the bottom of Fig. 10, with the corresponding percentage of cases included in each stanine below it.

DERIVED SCORES

The major function of the statistical techniques thus far described is in interpreting scores obtained by pupils on educational and psychological tests. Of these techniques the measures of central tendency and of variability are most important in setting up norms. A *derived score* is a raw score expressed in terms of norms. Norms are the levels of performance on a test attained by defined groups of pupils. They differ from standards in that they describe *what is* rather than *what should be*.

Among the various types of norms are (1) age norms, (2) grade norms, (3) percentile ranks, (4) standard scores, and (5) quotient norms. We shall briefly describe each of these, together with its various advantages and limitations.

Age Norms

To obtain age norms, we give a test to representative groups of pupils at various age levels and compute measures of central tendency of the distribution of the scores obtained in each age group. Thus we can say that a given raw score indicates a level of performance typical of a certain chronological age. For mental ability tests the raw score is interpreted as a *mental age*, for reading tests as a *reading age*, and so on. If the average score of all ten-year-old pupils on a test is 46, any pupil who scores 46 on that test will receive a derived score of ten years on it, regardless of his chronological age. By assuming that there is a regular increase in test score from one age level to the next, some authors of standard tests provide norms for intermediate age levels, say ten years and three months. The test score obtained by adding one-fourth of the difference between the eleventh- and tenth-year mean raw scores to the latter is a raw score equivalent to ten years and three months.

Age norms are easy to understand. This is especially true for measures highly correlated with age, such as mental ability, reading ability, and various skills taught in the elementary grades. Age norms are not so useful for other aspects of pupils. Achievement of instructional objectives of secondary schools and higher levels cannot be stated well in age norms. Also, very high or very low scores are difficult to interpret with age norms, for these norms usually do not go beyond fairly intermediate raw score levels. Beyond these levels, it becomes necessary to "extrapolate," and hence get involved with dubious assumptions.

A third disadvantage of age norms is their dependence on administrative policies concerning age at school entrance, promotion, retardation, and acceleration. If the sample used to establish norms for the ten-year level consists of pupils who have made regular progress through school, the norms will differ from those based on ten-year-olds whose progress has been retarded. The proportions of retarded, normal, and accelerated pupils at a given chronological age must be well defined; otherwise, the age norms based on them will be ambiguous.

Grade Norms

Grade norms characterize a pupil's raw score as equivalent to that achieved by typical pupils at a given grade level. We obtain these norms by giving a test to representative groups of pupils at various grade levels and computing measures of central tendency for the pupils in each grade. We can then use the average score of the group in a given grade in interpreting raw scores as equivalent to the test performance of that level. As with age norms, grade norms depend greatly on the selection of the schools and pupils used in deriving them. Schools in representative systems whose promotion and retardation policies are known must be used; otherwise grade norms will not be meaningful.

Norms for intermediate grade levels, say for the fifth month of the fifth grade, are usually obtained by an interpolation similar to that for age norms.

Grade norms in elementary schools depend on the relative emphases given to various subjects at different grade levels. Suppose a subject is emphasized in one grade and neglected in another; the expected rate of increase in raw scores on a test in that subject in successive grade levels may be considerably affected. This effect will be especially active in determining the applicability in one school system of norms established in other school systems.

Furthermore, grade norms are particularly open to the danger of becoming standards for all pupils, regardless of individual differences. A further disadvantage is that grade norms are hard to apply to extreme scores obtained by pupils in the lowest and the highest grade for which norms are provided. Raw scores beyond the means obtained in these extreme grades can usually be interpreted only vaguely.

In the secondary school, grade norms are often supplanted by semesters-of-study norms, a given raw score being interpreted as the average for pupils who have studied a subject for a certain number of semesters.

Percentile Ranks

Percentile rank norms are easy to interpret. Like age and grade norms, they require that the group of pupils be described and understood in all aspects related to performance on the test. These aspects include at least chronological age, mental age, grade placement, semesters of study, and socioeconomic status. Rural or urban residence, sex, and education of parents are often also relevant aspects of pupils; hence different sets of norms may be required on the basis of these groupings.

Percentile ranks provide very unequal units along the scale of performance on a test. The difference in performance between scores, say, at the 50th and 55th percentile levels is much less than that between scores at the 90th and 95th levels in all bell-shaped distributions of raw scores, even though the differences in percentile rank are equal. These unequal units are undesirable for two reasons. First, a false impression is given the unwary teacher. Second, percentile ranks should not be arithmetically manipulated as in computing means and standard deviations. The percentile rank of two averaged raw scores is not equal to the average of their separate percentile scores. Despite these disadvantages, percentile ranks are so easy to understand that they are used as norms for many standard tests.

Standard Scores

Standard scores are based on the principle of the z-score and T-score already discussed. They avoid the disadvantage of the unequal units of percentile norms. Standard score norms change the distribution of raw scores into a new distribution with a specified central tendency and variability, without changing the shape of the distribution.

Although not so readily understood by most teachers, parents, and students, standard scores have the advantages (1) of probably providing more equal units along all parts of the scale of performance on a test, and (2) of being based on the most reliable statistical measures obtainable from a frequency distribution, namely, the arithmetic mean and standard deviation. Like all norms, they require knowledge of what kinds of pupils they are based on. Interpreting standard scores in terms of percentile ranks involves the assumption that the raw scores are distributed according to the normal curve.

Quotient Norms

Quotients are frequently used with age norms to obtain a measure of the relative status of a pupil's performance. The best known of the quotients, the intelligence quotient or IQ, is the pupil's mental age divided by his chronological age multiplied by 100. That is, $IQ = 100 \times \dfrac{MA}{CA}$. By definition, the average child's mental age equals his chronological age. Hence IQ's over 100 indicate above-average mental ability and those below 100 indicate below-average mental ability. The IQ's obtained with many group tests of mental ability have been equated to those obtained with the Stanford-Binet individual intelligence test.

Test makers have tried to arrange quotient norms so that the IQ remains constant for a given pupil as he grows older. This goal has been only partially realized. One problem has been that the standard deviation of the distribution of mental ages tends to be larger in older groups of pupils. This results in a tendency toward increasing IQ's for pupils with IQ's greater than 100 and decreasing IQ's for pupils with IQ's less than 100.

Furthermore, the mental age concept is actually inapplicable for chronological age levels above about fifteen years. Mental age does not increase with chronological age throughout an individual's lifetime; with currently used tests, the curve of average mental growth levels out somewhat during early adulthood. Consequently, mental age cannot keep pace with chronological age. So the IQ will decrease as a person grows older unless some limit is placed on chronological age. For the Stanford-Binet intelligence test, and similarly for most group intelligence tests, chronological age is held constant after an individual reaches the age of about 16. Hence IQ's have questionable meaning for older pupils and adults.

The educational quotient, EQ, can be found whenever an educational age or subject-matter age is known. The EQ equals educational age divided by chronological age multiplied by 100. It has the same advantages and limitations as the IQ, especially as far as the limitations of age norms discussed above are concerned.

The accomplishment quotient, AQ represents a fallacious attempt to obtain a measure of whether a pupil is achieving instructional objectives to the limits of his mental ability. It is equal to educational age divided by mental age multiplied by 100. If the tests used to determine educational age and mental age were not administered at the same time, the EQ and IQ may be substituted; the AQ then equals $\frac{EQ}{IQ} \times 100$.

There are several reasons why the AQ should not be used. (1) Not only must it inevitably be based on imperfectly reliable tests, but it accentuates the unreliability of the tests on which it is based. (2) The age norms for the two tests used in determining the AQ are seldom derived from the same group of pupils and hence the norms are seldom strictly comparable. (See the discussion of comparable norms in Chapter 6.) (3) So far as the correlation between a single mental ability test and a single achievement test is less than perfect (typically it is between .40 and .80), a mathematical necessity—the so-called "regression effect"—insures that pupils above the average on the mental test will tend to be relatively lower (nearer the average) on the achievement test. Conversely, pupils below average on the mental test will tend to be relatively higher (nearer the average) on the achievement test. Hence brighter-than-average pupils will typically have AQ's of less than 100, and below-average pupils will typically have AQ's of more than 100.

The teacher who is unaware of this fallacy of the AQ often puts pressure on the brighter students to achieve "up to their capacity." This pressure may have unfortunate effects on pupil adjustment; moreover, in any case it is usually ineffective. Sometimes the achievement of the pupil who is above-average in mental ability is significantly below the average of the above-average-mental-ability group with which he is being compared. In such cases the teacher *may* conclude with some justification that the pupil "is not achieving up to his capacity." Comparison of a student's achievement with that of his own ability group is justified, whereas the use of the AQ is not.

The uses and interpretations of these various types of norms will be discussed more fully in the section on test interpretation in Chapter 6.

MEASURES OF RELATIONSHIP–CORRELATION

Scattered throughout this book are references to various relationships. Some of these are relationships between various aspects of pupils; others, relationships between various methods of evaluating these aspects; still others, relationships of successive applications of the same evaluation device to each other. These relationships have various names according to the kind of measurement involved. Under *reliability* (see Chapter 5) we shall consider the relationship between two applications of the same device, obtained by splitting the device into equivalent halves, by retesting with the same device, or by applying two equivalent forms of the same device. Under *validity* (see Chapter 5) we shall discuss relationships between measurements obtained with an evaluation device and some criterion or external standard of the same aspect of pupils, or the degree to which scores obtained on the test agree with elsewhere-obtained ideas about that aspect of a pupil.

The classroom teacher often wants to know the relationships between measured aspects of pupils. This knowledge helps in understanding the nature of pupils, their learning processes, and reactions to teaching procedures. In the present section we consider the correlation techniques by which the teacher can discover such relationships. An understanding of these techniques will prove useful in working with data locally obtained and in reading the literature of experimental education and standardized tests.

Closeness and Direction of Relationships

Relationships vary in closeness and in direction. The *closeness* of a relationship is the degree to which one variable changes as the other changes. For example, as the length of one of its sides increases, the area of a square also increases in a completely fixed, perfectly "close" relationship. Or as the temperature increases, the height of the mercury in a thermometer also increases, following the temperature very closely. On the other hand, the body weight and height of a group of people are not as closely related; that is, although height tends to increase with weight, there are many exceptions to its doing so. Similarly, an intermediate degree of closeness is illustrated by the relationship usually found between a pupil's scores on mathematical and on verbal ability tests; whereas some pupils excel in both tests and others do poorly on both, many differ greatly in their standing on the two. There is hardly any closeness at all in the relationship between height and verbal ability for persons of a given age.

The *direction* of a relationship refers to whether one variable increases as the other increases. In a *positive* relationship, an increase in the value of one variable accompanies an increase in the value of the other. As the temperature rises, the column of mercury in a thermometer also rises. As the scores on a verbal ability test for a class change from low to high, the corresponding scores for the same pupils on a reading test usually tend to run from low to high. In a *negative* relationship, an increase in the value of one variable accompanies a corresponding decrease in the value of the other. The relationship between pupils' scores on a test of mental ability and the number of their failures in school subjects is negative. Similarly, as the outside temperature goes down, the amount of fuel used to heat homes goes up.

With some variables the direction of relationship may differ at different stages or levels of one of the variables. Such combinations of both positive and negative relationships are called *curvilinear*. Physical strength tends to increase with chronological age up to early adulthood and then decreases with the approach of old age. The length of a shadow decreases as the day grows older during the first half of the day and increases during the latter half.

Data Required for Determining Relationship

How can we find the closeness and direction of the relationship? The first requirement is that we obtain and pair the measurements. Usually we pair on the basis of individual persons, as when we measure each person in a group by two tests. The net result should be three columns of data, the first denoting the pupil, the second his score on one variable, and the third his score on the other variable. This requirement is illustrated in the different methods of determining relationships which follow.

Rank Correlation (ρ)

There are several methods of finding the closeness and direction of the relationship between two series of measures. If the data are in the form of ranks rather than raw scores or derived scores, we can apply the *Spearman rank-difference coefficient of correlation.* This coefficient of correlation is usually referred to simply as the *rank-order coefficient* and is indicated by the lower-case Greek letter rho (ρ). The formula for this coefficient is

$$\text{rho} = \rho = 1 - \frac{6\Sigma D^2}{N(N^2 - 1)}$$

where D = difference between a pair of ranks
N = number of pairs of ranks

We illustrate the use of this formula by applying it to the ranks of twelve pupils on two different tests. Table 4 shows these data and the necessary computations. Note that in some instances in these distributions two individuals have the same raw scores. Whenever two or more pupils receive the same score in the original distributions, we average the ranks their scores would occupy and then

Table 4. Method of Computing ρ

Pupils	Raw Scores X	Y	Ranks X	Y	Difference in Ranks D	Differences Squared D²
A	30	12	1	2	1.0	1.00
B	28	13	2	1	1.0	1.00
C	26	11	3	3.5	.5	.25
D	24	11	4	3.5	.5	.25
E	22	10	5	5	.0	.00
F	20	9	6.5	6.5	.0	.00
G	20	8	6.5	8	1.5	2.25
H	18	9	8	6.5	1.5	2.25
I	16	7	9	9.5	.5	.25
J	14	7	10	9.5	.5	.25
K	12	6	11	11	.0	.00
L	10	5	12	12	.0	.00

$$\Sigma D^2 = 7.50$$

$$\rho = 1 - \frac{6\,\Sigma D^2}{N(N^2-1)} = 1 - \frac{6(7.5)}{12(144-1)} = 1 - \frac{45}{1716}$$
$$\rho = 1 - .026 = .974$$

assign the mean rank value to each. For example, Pupils C and D, each of whom has a score of 11 on distribution Y, occupy ranks 3 and 4. Since one pupil should not have a higher rank than the other, the two ranks are averaged arithmetically and the rank of 3.5 is assigned to each. We treat other tie scores in the same manner.

The coefficient of correlation is so worked out that when there is complete agreement (closeness of relationship) it has a value of 1.00, indicated as 1.00 if the relationship is positive, and −1.00 if the relationship is negative. *The sign of the coefficient has no meaning other than to indicate the direction of the relationship.* If there is no relationship between two sets of data, the value of the coefficient is zero. This means that there is no systematic increase or decrease of scores on one set of data corresponding to scores on the other set of data. Thus, the range of numerical values of the coefficient of correlation is defined as extending from a perfect negative relationship (−1.00), to a zero relationship (.00), to a perfect positive relationship (1.00). Zero and perfect relationships are rarely if ever obtained in actual situations. Usually correlations fall somewhere between the two extremes.

Scatter Diagrams

If the paired variables are in the form of scores instead of ranks, the direction of the relationship between the variables can be found by plotting each pair of scores on a two-way table. To illustrate, let us look at Table 5, which shows the paired scores for 25 students on Forms A and B of the Purdue Reading Test. Fig. 11 shows the scatter diagram for these paired scores. We point off the vertical axis in regular steps for as many class intervals as are used in the frequency distribution of one of the variables, and point off the horizontal axis similarly for the other.

We then plot each pair of scores by entering the vertical axis at the proper point for the size of the score of one of the variables and then moving across horizontally until we reach the proper point for the score on the other variable. At this intersection we make a mark for this pair of scores. We repeat the process until we have plotted all the pairs. You may wish to plot the 25 pairs of scores from

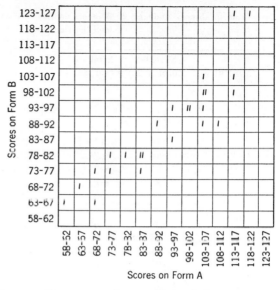

Fig. 11. Scatter Diagram for 25 Paired Scores on Forms A and B of Purdue Reading Test.

Table 5 on Fig. 11 and thus verify your understanding of the procedure.

Most two-way tables are arranged so that the horizontal axis indicates increasing scores to the right, the vertical axis from bottom to top. For a positive relationship the scores tend to fall in a diagonal band from the lower left to the upper right corner of the table. For a negative relationship they tend to fall in a diagonal from the upper left to the lower right corner. Absence of relationship is indicated by the degree that the tabulated scores tend to fall on neither of these diagonals, but rather along a horizontal or vertical line or in a circle. These various relationships are shown in Fig. 12.

Sometimes the pairs of scores tend to fall along a curved line or in a curved band. These represent a *curvilinear relationship*. Paired scores that tend to fall along a straight diagonal line or band show a *linear relationship*. Research workers are on the lookout for curvilinear relationships, because special statistical methods are necessary to determine the closeness of such relationships. Methods for determining the degree of curvilinear relationship are beyond the scope of this book.

Table 5. Scores Made by 25 Students on Forms A and B of the Purdue Reading Test, and the Computation of r

Student	Score on Form A(X)	Score on Form B(Y)	X^2	Y^2	XY
1	62	65	3,844	4,225	4,030
2	115	106	13,225	11,236	12,190
3	117	98	13,689	9,604	11,466
4	120	125	14,400	15,625	15,000
5	84	73	7,056	5,329	6,132
6	87	78	7,569	6,084	6,786
7	80	82	6,400	6,724	6,560
8	110	90	12,100	8,100	9,900
9	93	95	8,649	9,025	8,835
10	100	96	10,000	9,216	9,600
11	89	91	7,921	8,281	8,099
12	101	97	10,201	9,409	9,797
13	103	100	10,609	10,000	10,300
14	63	71	3,969	5,041	4,473
15	104	94	10,816	8,836	9,776
16	74	74	5,476	5,476	5,476
17	76	81	5,776	6,561	6,156
18	115	125	13,225	15,625	14,375
19	104	103	10,816	10,609	10,712
20	71	74	5,041	5,476	5,254
21	68	66	4,624	4,356	4,488
22	95	85	9,025	7,225	8,075
23	104	92	10,816	8,464	9,568
24	86	78	7,396	6,084	6,708
25	105	98	11,025	9,604	10,290
Σ	2,326	2,237	223,668	206,215	214,046
$\dfrac{\Sigma}{N}$	93.04	89.48			

$$r = \frac{\Sigma XY - NM_xM_y}{\sqrt{\Sigma X^2 - NM_x^2}\sqrt{\Sigma Y^2 - NM_y^2}}$$

$$r = \frac{214,046 - 25(93.04)(89.48)}{\sqrt{223,668 - 25(8658.44)}\sqrt{206,215 - 25(8006.67)}}$$

$$r = \frac{5915.5200}{6623.5968} = .893$$

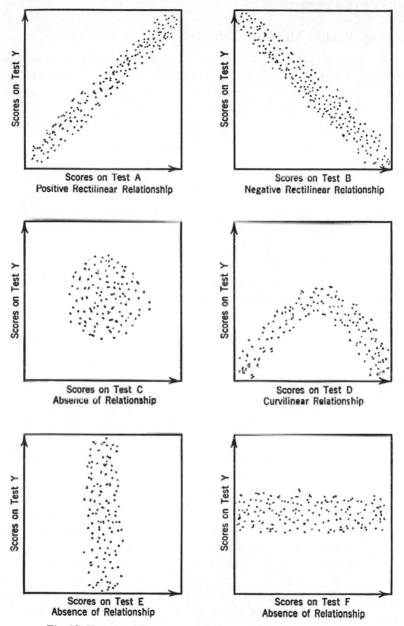

Fig. 12. Types and Degrees of Relationship Between Two Tests.

Pearson Product-Moment Coefficient of Correlation (r)

A scatter diagram is a visual aid in discovering whether using the formula for the Pearson Product-Moment coefficient of correlation (r) is justified. If inspection reveals no marked tendency toward curvilinearity, the formula applies. This coefficient (r) is defined as the mean of the products of the paired z-scores for two distributions. It may be calculated by using the following formula:

$$r = \frac{\Sigma z_x z_y}{N}$$

where $r =$ Pearson Product-Moment coefficient of correlation
z_x and $z_y =$ paired z-scores on each of the variables (for definition of z-score see pp. 59–60)
$N =$ number of pairs of scores

The calculation is simplified, however, by using only the deviations of the scores from the mean, instead of the z-scores, with the following formula:

$$r = \frac{\Sigma xy}{\sqrt{\Sigma x^2 \cdot \Sigma y^2}}$$

where $x =$ deviation of scores from the mean of X, $(X - M_x)$
$y =$ deviation of scores from the mean of Y, $(Y - M_y)$
$\Sigma x^2 =$ the sum of the squares of the deviation scores in one distribution
$\Sigma y^2 =$ the sum of the squares of the deviation scores in the other distribution

The second formula does not require computation of the standard deviations of the two distributions. Table 6 shows the form for arranging the scores for twelve pupils on Test X and Test Y to carry out the computational procedures.

Whenever more than about 20 pairs of scores are to be correlated, the preceding method is very laborious. Many more convenient formulas yield the same results. Algebraically it can be shown that the coefficient defined by the above formulas can also be obtained

Table 6. Deviation Method of Computing r

Pupils	Raw Scores		Deviation Scores[a]				
	X	Y	x	y	x^2	y^2	xy
A	30	12	10	3	100	9	30
B	28	13	8	4	64	16	32
C	26	11	6	2	36	4	12
D	24	11	4	2	16	4	8
E	22	10	2	1	4	1	2
F	20	9	0	0	0	0	0
G	20	8	0	−1	0	1	0
H	18	9	−2	0	4	0	0
I	16	7	−4	−2	16	4	8
J	14	7	−6	−2	36	4	12
K	12	6	−8	−3	64	9	24
L	10	5	−10	−4	100	16	40
Sums:	240	108	0	0	440	68	168
$N = 12$	$M_X = 20$		$M_Y = 9$		$\sigma_x = 6.055$		$\sigma_x = 2.380$

$$r_{yx} = \frac{\Sigma xy}{\sqrt{\Sigma x^2 \Sigma y^2}} = \frac{168}{\sqrt{(440)(68)}} = \frac{168}{\sqrt{29920}} = \frac{168}{172.974} = .971$$

[a] $x = X - M_X, \ y = Y - M_Y$

by means of the following formula, which is much easier to apply, especially if an adding machine or calculator is available:

$$r = \frac{\Sigma XY - NM_x M_y}{\sqrt{\Sigma X^2 - NM_x^2} \sqrt{\Sigma Y^2 - NM_y^2}}$$

where X and Y = raw scores on each variable

M_x and M_y = arithmetic means of the two distributions

The application of this formula is illustrated for the 25 pairs of measures in Table 5. You should follow through the computations in this table for an understanding of the procedure.

LABORATORY EXERCISES AND DISCUSSION QUESTIONS

1. Obtain a list of scores on tests in reading, language, and arithmetic for students in Grades 4, 5, 6, 7, and 8 of a school. Make relative frequency polygons on the same sheet of graph paper for the several

grades for each subject area. In which subject area is there the greatest overlapping of scores from grade to grade? In which is there the least overlapping? How do you explain the differences in the amount of overlapping from grade to grade?

2. For what general purposes do the characteristics of the mean make it a specially useful measure? The median? Which would be the more appropriate measure in the following situations? Give reasons for your answer.
   a. Reporting the taxable value of real estate in a city.
   b. Describing the ages of pupils in the sixth grade.
   c. Appraising the board feet of timber per acre on a 500-acre tree farm.
   d. Reporting the salaries of university faculty members according to their academic rank—instructor, assistant professor, etc.

3. What practical value do you see in changing standard test scores into grade placement scores? Into percentile ranks? What are the relative advantages and limitations of each procedure?

4. Give two illustrations of each of the following:
   a. High positive correlation.
   b. Low positive correlation.
   c. High negative correlation.
   d. Low negative correlation.
   e. Approximately zero correlation.
   f. Curvilinear correlation.

5. Indicate, by using the letters used in the preceding exercise for the types of correlation, the kind of correlation you would expect to find in each of the following comparisons:
   a. IQ and marks in algebra.
   b. Age and IQ in an entire school of 12 grades.
   c. Age and IQ in a single grade.
   d. Speed and accuracy in multiplication.
   e. Reading achievement and arithmetic achievement.
   f. Reading achievement and achievement in the social studies.

SUGGESTED REFERENCES

Downie, N. M., *Fundamentals of Measurement*, New York: Oxford, 1958.

In Chapters 3 and 4, the author presents the basic essentials of statistical procedures for measurement, the various types of scores used in measurement, the problem of changing test scores to grades, and the types and uses of norms.

——— and R. W. Heath, *Basic Statistical Methods*, New York: Harper & Row, 2nd ed., 1965.

A straightforward approach to elementary statistics—both descriptive and sampling—in which mathematical derivations are kept to a minimum. Includes material on test psychology.

Edwards, A. L., *Statistical Analysis*, New York: Holt, Rinehart and Winston, 1958.

A basic book on statistical methodology for the nonmathematically trained student.

Gerberich, J. R., H. H. Greene, and A. N. Jorgenson, *Measurement and Evaluation in the Modern School*, New York: McKay, 1962.

Chapters 13 and 14 present procedures for summarizing the results of measurement and simple statistical procedures for interpreting and determining relationships among them.

Green, John A., *Teacher-Made Tests*, New York: Harper & Row, 1963.

Chapter 9 introduces only those statistical techniques necessary for summarizing data in graphs, locating the central tendency of group scores, finding the variability of a group, and converting test scores to standard scores.

Guilford, J. P., *Fundamental Statistics in Psychology and Education*, New York: McGraw-Hill, 1956.

A general textbook on statistical methodology.

Lindquist, E. F., *A First Course in Statistics*, Boston: Houghton Mifflin, 1942.

This text presents statistical concepts and procedures in an exceptionally meaningful manner for students who have not had an extensive mathematical background.

Manuel, Herschel T., *Elementary Statistics for Teachers*, New York: American Book, 1962.

An introductory book on the statistics of educational measurement for students just beginning their study of statistics or who feel the need of only basic concepts or skills.

Nelson, M. J., E. C. Denney, and A. P. Coladarci, *Statistics for Teachers*, New York: Holt, Rinehart and Winston, 1956.

A presentation of statistical techniques designed primarily for elementary- and secondary-school teachers interested in the interpretation of test results.

Thorndike, R. L., and Elizabeth Hagen, *Measurement and Evaluation in Psychology and Education*, New York: Wiley, 2nd ed., 1961.

Chapter 5 points out to the novice some basic types of questions that the statistician tries to answer, and introduces him to the simplest tools used to answer them.

Walker, Helen, and J. Lev, *Elementary Statistical Methods*, New York: Holt, Rinehart and Winston, rev. ed., 1958.

A general text for an introduction to statistical methods. Highly respected by professional statisticians, but not difficult.

PART TWO
The School Testing Program

CHAPTER 4

Development and administration of the evaluation program

Beginning-of-Year vs. End-of-Year Testing

General Areas of the Testing Program
  Measuring General Mental Ability
  Evaluating Achievement of Instructional Objectives
  Appraising Interests and Special Abilities
  Appraising Emotional and Social Adjustment
  Appraising Other Aspects of Pupils

Minimum and Optimum School Testing Programs

  Sample Minimum Programs
  The Optimum School Testing Program

Training Personnel for an Effective Program

In Chapter 2 we called attention to the broad problem of measurement and evaluation in the school system. That brief survey pointed out the major steps in the school evaluation program and the areas and instruments often used. In the present chapter we shall concern ourselves in some detail with the problems involved in the organization, development, and administration of a school evaluation program.

FACTORS AFFECTING PROGRAM SUCCESS

Because of insufficient and inadequately trained personnel to direct and carry out the necessary phases, testing programs sometimes lack effectiveness. Another obstacle is lack of testing materials of the type necessary for a particular school situation. Furthermore, many schools lack funds for necessary materials. Many other factors may affect the success of the school testing program. All teachers and supervisors, especially those most directly responsible for the development and evaluation of the program, should consider these factors in the form of a check list. The check list in Table 7 provides a frame of reference for the discussion of the school testing program in this and the next two chapters.

STEPS IN PLANNING A TESTING PROGRAM

The following activities can contribute to effectiveness in planning a new testing program or revising a program already in operation:

1. Secure cooperation from the entire staff.
2. Determine the purposes of the program so it will fit the various needs of the specific school.

Table 7. A Check List of Factors Affecting the Success of a Testing Program

	Check
1. Purposes of the program	
Clearly defined	————
Understood by parties involved	————
2. Choice of tests	
Valid	————
Reliable	————
Appropriate difficulty level	————
Adequate norms	————
Easy to administer and score	————
Economical ,,......................................	————
Best available for purpose	————
3. Administration and scoring	
Administrators well trained	————
All necessary information provided	————
Scorers adequately instructed	————
Scoring carefully checked	————
4. Physical conditions	
Sufficient space ,,,,,,,,,,,,,,,,,,...................	————
Sufficient time	————
Conveniently scheduled	————
5. Utilization of test results	
Definite plans for use of results	————
Provision for giving teachers all necessary help in using scores .	————
Provision for systematic follow-up on use of results	————
6. System of records	
Necessary for purpose	————
Sufficient for purpose	————
Convenient form for use	————
7. Personnel	
Adequately trained for the purpose	————
8. Affiliated research	
Full advantage taken of results	————
Provision for special studies, analyses, etc.	————

Source. Roger T. Lennon, *Planning a Testing Program*, Test Service Bulletin No. 55, New York: Harcourt, Brace & World.

3. Find out about available instruments.
4. Decide what kind of instruments will best fulfill your purposes

and either select them from available tests or develop them within the school.

5. Make plans for administering the testing program and set up a tentative schedule for the year.
6. Train the personnel necessary for the administration, scoring, and analysis of test results.
7. Put the program into operation and use the results to achieve your purposes.

The administrative aspect of these steps is the primary focus of attention in this chapter. Chapter 5 discusses the details of test selection. Chapter 6 presents procedures for giving, scoring, and interpreting the tests.

A COOPERATIVE PROGRAM

Since test data are of direct concern to all teachers, counselors and guidance workers, supervisors, administrators, and pupils, the testing program should be jointly planned. Thus, decisions on the extensiveness of the program, the selection of tests, the time of year for which they are scheduled, their administration and scoring, and use of the test results should be made jointly by members of the school staff. Only such cooperation assures that staff members will have common understanding of the purpose of the program and a realization of its possible benefits.

The role of the administrator, principal, or supervisor includes (1) leadership in planning for teachers' meetings and in-service programs on measurement and evaluation, (2) guidance of committee work of teachers in selecting and administering standardized tests and constructing classroom tests, and (3) provision for both an adequate measurement library containing reference books, catalogues, and handbooks on tests and related statistics, and a comprehensive file of specimen sets of standardized tests.

The classroom teacher plays an important part in the program. The use and interpretation of test results become his ultimate responsibility if he is to base instruction on the needs and abilities of pupils. He may also work with other teachers as a member of a group concerned with construction, criticism, and revision of teacher-made tests in addition to those he uses in his own classroom.

A faculty committee should be set up to develop the testing program. This committee should be representative of the staff as a whole at all grade levels and include key personnel who are interested and have abilities in developing a comprehensive evaluation program. The testing committee should keep the entire staff informed of its progress in planning. If any member of the committee has specialized training and previous experience in testing, he should perhaps be put in direct charge of administrative details. His primary duties include working with the teachers who are going to examine pupils and jointly studying or developing the materials to be used.

A cooperative program may also include pupils and their parents. To insure adequate motivation without unnecessary tenseness, pupils should understand the purposes for which tests are given. They should be assured that test results will be explained to them, and that the tests are used especially for their benefit. They should be told as much about their performance on the tests as they can understand correctly.

It is also desirable to enlist the cooperation of parents by discussions of the testing program at parent-teacher meetings and by various reports mailed to them. Parents should understand the kinds of information being accumulated about their children, the types of programs on which the testing program can throw some light, and the use of the results in the instructional and guidance program. Obviously, parents and the community at large have a vested interest in the school program; appropriations and school budgets are community affairs. Often the community needs to be educated about the importance of the testing program and its relative cost. The cost of educating a child today is typically close to $500 per year. But as one writer has stated, ". . . Only about 7 cents per pupil per year is being used for standardized tests. This is far below a recommended minimum allotment of 30 to 35 cents per child, and very low considering the importance of a sound testing program. In contrast, a business may spend 3 percent of annual sales receipts to determine whether its practices are effectual."[1] Once parents, school board members, and the community at large find out what the test-

[1] Audrey K. Boag, Standardized tests: How, when, why? *Instructor*, 1955, 65:24.

ing program is like and what it can accomplish, the school should have little difficulty in obtaining the funds needed to carry on an adequate program.

PURPOSES OF THE PROGRAM

Through the school testing program educators at all levels appraise the progress that individuals, classes, and the school as a whole are making toward established objectives. The program may include teacher-made tests, both written and oral, observation check lists of many aspects of behavior and skill, and the more expertly prepared standardized tests. Standardized tests indicate how achievement of pupils in the local schools compares with that of pupils elsewhere; they serve as a yardstick that is less likely to reflect the special biases of teachers in covering a specific course or the idiosyncrasies of a particular school.

Since the objectives of schools are so extensive and diverse, every school system must establish its own specific objectives and its purposes in testing. Table 8 lists some possible purposes of a testing program. These have been grouped into categories on the basis of the classroom teacher, the guidance counselor, and the school administrator. This list is not exhaustive but it can guide a testing committee in establishing the specific purposes of its school.

Classroom Purposes

One widely accepted premise of teaching is: "You must know your pupils before you can teach them." Hence the testing program should provide a teacher with data that will improve his understanding of his pupils. It should give as comprehensive a view of pupil characteristics as group-testing facilities permit.

Tests can guide teaching when they furnish a diagnosis of specific strengths and weaknesses in the pupil's achievements or capacities. The teacher may then seek either to eliminate the weaknesses by using special teaching methods and emphases, or to circumvent them by directing learning toward areas where the pupil's efforts will be more fruitful. The causes of weakness in a specific subject

Table 8. Illustrative Purposes for a Testing Program and Appropriate Types of Tests to Use

(The type of test that is sometimes more effective for a specific purpose is indicated by a double asterisk: **)

	Standardized Test	Teacher-Made Objective	Essay
Classroom Purposes			
Grouping pupils for instruction within a class	**	*	
Guiding activities for specific pupils	*	*	*
Determining reasonable levels of classroom achievement for each pupil	*	*	*
Identifying pupils who need special diagnostic study and remedial instruction	**	*	*
Measuring class progress for any given period	*	*	*
Appraising ability to organize ideas and write effectively	*	*	**
Appraising relative achievement within a class	*	**	
Assigning course grades	*	*	*
Guidance Purposes			
Building realistic self-pictures on the part of pupils	*	*	*
Helping pupils to set educational and vocational goals	**	*	*
Improving counselor, teacher, and parent understanding of problem cases	**	*	*
Preparing evidence to guide discussions with parents about their children	**	*	*
Selecting suitable courses of study	**		
Choosing an occupation	**		
Planning for further education	**	*	*
Determining interests in types of occupations not previously considered or not known by the pupil	**		
Predicting success in future educational work	**		
Administrative Purposes			
Determining emphasis to be given different areas of instruction	**		
Measuring progress of school from year to year	**		
Identifying changing character of student body	**		
Determining appropriateness of the school curriculum for students of different levels of ability	**		
Determining how well students are attaining worth-while educational goals	**		
Evaluating curricular experimentation	**		
Evaluating the school as a unit	**		
Providing evidence for improvement of public relations	**	*	
Providing information for outside agencies	**	*	*
Forming classroom groups and in student placement	**	*	*
Providing basis for pupil promotion or retardation	*	*	*

he can trace, by means of tests, to any one of the various possible pupil inadequacies underlying it. Weakness in the study of history or geography, for example, may be due to lack of comprehension power or speed in reading, as revealed by a test of reading ability. Or it may be due to lack of general intelligence, or to lack of presupposed background material, a lack which tests designed to measure achievement at a lower level of the subject could reveal. A pupil's difficulties in arithmetic may stem from a specific inadequacy, such as inability to deal with certain combinations of digits, or lack of a correct technique for carrying, or the use of a cumbersome method of short division.

Diagnostic testing may thus reveal the precise sources of a pupil's shortcomings and guide the teacher to the best way of overcoming them. He can study inadequately equipped pupils and give them special attention aimed at the basic roots of the "failure." He can show them in what parts of a subject or in what desired outcomes of the course they are weak. The teacher can find out what parts of a topic or unit need to be retaught or taught differently. He can discover pupils capable of doing exceptional work and guide them toward special tasks and references.

Guidance Purposes

Measurement and evaluation often become central to the guidance process because teachers and counselors are obligated to provide information of vital significance to the pupil and society. When the pupil makes plans that he might radically modify if he were aware of certain facts about his tested abilities or interests, is it not the teacher's responsibility to give him that information? If a pupil and his parents are embarked on a program of education leading toward a medical degree, for example, whereas test data of the most valid kind indicate that his abilities and interests are distinctly unsuited for this profession, is it not the school's responsibility to bring this evidence to bear in the process of vocational guidance? Conversely, a pupil's abilities and interests may indicate exceedingly high promise for success in pursuits for which society has an urgent need, such as research in social science. But the pupil and his parents may be proceeding as if not aware of this rare talent and its prime importance to society. Must not the school in its guidance function use the most valid evidence, including measurements and evaluations of the kind described in this book, so that it can make appropriate changes in his educational and vocational plans for the benefit of both the pupil and the society of which he is a part? This book assumes affirmative answers to these questions.

Guidance requires the evaluation of pupils so that their specific abilities, both strengths and weaknesses, may be determined. As pupils move up the educational ladder in elementary school, with its general curriculum providing the skills (reading, writing, arithmetic, etc.) that everyone in our civilization must acquire, they must be evaluated as to their aptitudes, abilities, achievements, interests, and other attributes. During this elementary schooling pupils set off on diverging paths, with differing interests and goals. By the time they reach secondary school they already differ widely in their educational needs and capacities.

At this point the teacher's knowledge of the pupil should guide the decision of the pupil and his parents regarding the type of secondary education to choose. This knowledge must be the result of *continuous* evaluation throughout the six or eight years of the elementary educational process. And the evaluation must have been *comprehensive* throughout these years, involving as many important aspects of the pupil's personality as it is possible for a teacher to perceive. Similarly, guidance and evaluation should be carried on during and at the end of the secondary schooling.

The *continuity* of the evaluation process implies that it should go on during all the time that the teacher can observe the pupil, not merely on the special occasions when he gives tests or determines report-card grades. Every behavior of a pupil that the teacher can observe may provide evidence for evaluation and improved understanding of that pupil.

The *comprehensiveness* of evaluation refers to its extension over the whole personality of the pupil, rather than merely to his intellectual achievement. Evaluation of a pupil's knowledge is, of course, extremely important in guiding him. But also important for his happiness and for fitting him into the world of work is evidence concerning his aptitudes and interests, his temperament, his attitudes, his social adaptability, his habits of work and play, his physical characteristics. Each of these aspects must be understood in relation both to other aspects or dimensions of the pupil and to similar aspects of the population at large.

With such continuous and comprehensive evaluative evidence concerning its pupils, a school can properly undertake its guidance function. This guidance should operate not solely at the pupil's entrance into and departure from a particular level of schooling or vocation, although these are occasions for its most striking occurrence. Rather, guidance should operate within the entire school period. For example, evaluations should assist in solving such guidance problems as the choice of elective subjects. Should a pupil take a twelfth-year English course or a course in typewriting? Which laboratory science should a pupil elect, physics, biology, or chemistry? Why is a certain pupil becoming a disciplinary problem? Answers to such questions, of which these are only a few illustrations, all come under the heading of guidance. And the answers should be based on valid evaluative data for the pupil.

Administrative Purposes

The school administrator has the responsibility of insuring an adequate educational program in his school, and the testing program can provide an important basis for judging how well the pupils are attaining worth-while educational goals. In addition to the administrative purposes listed in Table 8, a good testing program may well provide information for experimental purposes. The use of tests in appraising educational instrumentalities—such as teachers, teaching methods, and textbooks—is easily understood but not easily practiced. The prudent administrator will not use test results to evaluate the efficiency of individual teachers, for he realizes that many factors other than the teacher influence pupil achievement over a period of years. Hence, the unusually good or poor performance of a class at a particular time cannot be attributed solely to the efforts of any *one* teacher. On the other hand, the administrator will be be able to assess the general effectiveness of the school program, in which teachers play major roles, from one year to another or over a period of years.

The basic principle underlying the administrative use of evaluation is that whatever produces the greatest realization of the educational objectives is the best teacher, teaching method, textbook, or other tool of the educational process. And since most educational objectives can be stated as desired behaviors in pupils, evaluations of pupils indicate the degree of attainment of the objectives and the effectiveness of the means used. The difficulty in using educational evaluations for these purposes is that no worthwhile reliable results can be obtained unless the appraisal becomes a controlled investigation, with relevant variables held constant and with statistical tests of significance applied to the results.

Some of the factors pointed out as having to be held constant to justify an effect being ascribed to any "treatment," such as teaching method, are the pupil's intelligence, educational background, study habits, home environment, the teacher's skill, and school conditions. Subtleties of experimental design are involved in the valid use of educational evaluations for appraisal research. Hence, tests should not be used for this purpose except by qualified research workers. Principals, superintendents, and others who wish to make such appraisals must therefore either master these scientific methods themselves or turn the problem over to experts.

QUESTIONS FREQUENTLY RAISED IN PROGRAM PLANNING

In planning the school testing program, the testing committee has several questions to consider. The following are some of the types of questions often asked of specialists when they are invited to assist in developing a school testing program:

What are the advantages and limitations of standardized tests as compared with teacher-made tests?

Should we use a general achievement battery or select specific tests in subject-matter content areas?

How often should we give intelligence tests?

How often should we give other tests?

At what grade levels should we give tests?

What are the best instruments for identifying and encouraging exceptional talent?

What should we use to identify retarded pupils?

Is it better to use group or individual tests?

What tests are good for measuring clerical aptitude? For predicting success in college?

At what time of the year is it best to administer the testing program?

What will a testing program cost? What constitutes a minimum testing program?

How should we use tests for best results?

The testing committee in any school will undoubtedly have to answer some of these questions, and probably many others, before agreement is reached and a school testing program can be set up. The remaining sections of this chapter provide a background helpful in considering questions such as these.

ADVANTAGES AND LIMITATIONS OF STANDARDIZED TESTS

One of the first questions we should consider is the relative merit of standardized tests. Standardized tests (1) have norms based on a systematic sample of pupils obtained under prescribed conditions, and (2) are administered and scored by definite rules. Usually the items on these tests have been evaluated experimentally and evidence of their validity and reliability has been obtained. As a rule, they are developed commercially. Chapter 5 discusses the characteristics of such tests.

Fitting Instructional Objectives

Standardized achievement tests usually are designed so that their content will be common to a great many schools. So far as this effort is successful, standardized tests provide comprehensive measures of the basic knowledges, skills, and abilities widely recognized as important. Conversely, they may not fit closely the specific instructional objectives of a particular classroom, school, or school system. This shortcoming varies, of course, with the variation in classroom objectives. In tool subjects such as reading, writing, and arithmetic, the differences among classrooms, teachers, and school systems may not be as great as they are in the social studies and the natural sciences. In any case, users of standardized tests must be sure that the test content is in agreement with instructional objectives or be prepared to face the charge of "testing what hasn't been taught." In short, the proper use of standardized achievement tests depends upon selecting tests that fit the instructional objectives of a particular school.

Refinement of Construction

Under this heading we consider the selection and expression of test content, the procedure for administering the test, and the tools for scoring and interpreting responses. Subject-matter experts usually select the content of standard achievement tests, referring to the most respected textbooks and courses of study, statements of objectives, teaching methods, and expressions of the "philosophy" underlying the teaching of a subject. Generally they subject each item of content to the criticism of many other experts and try them out on pupils. From these preliminary tryouts they compute statistical measures of the difficulty and validity[2] of the item.

On the basis of these statistical measures the test makers weed out or revise the poor items. They usually arrange the remaining items in order of difficulty and divide them into two or more groups to comprise equivalent forms of the test.

Standardization of administrative procedure means that definite directions have been formulated, with provisions for practice exercises, time limits, and oral instructions to pupils, all designed to provide the best possible testing conditions held uniform from one classroom to the next. Standardization of scoring means that scoring directions, question weightings, and corrections for guessing, if any, have been definitely worked out.

Classroom teachers can standardize their own tests in all these respects by applying the statistical methods required. But it is extremely unlikely that most teachers will have the resources for extensive preliminary tryouts of tests and for the statistical treatment

[2] Item validity may be roughly defined here as the success with which an item discriminates between good and poor pupils in terms of their achievement of instructional objectives.

of the results. The technical and time-consuming nature of the standardization process prevents most teachers from producing evaluation devices as refined as the better standardized tests.

Interpretations Possible with Each Type of Test

Norms supplied with standard tests enable comparisons with other groups of pupils. Thus a teacher can compare the achievement of his class with that of pupils throughout the nation. The pupils used for standardization may have been grouped according to age, sex, or grade, and made representative either of the nation at large or of urban groups, rural groups, etc. The validity of comparisons of classroom or individual pupil achievement depends almost entirely on how well the sample used in the standardization process represents the specific group it claims to represent. That is, if a set of norms for fifth-grade arithmetic achievement is based on a small group of pupils or on a group not representative with respect to certain factors affecting arithmetic achievement (intelligence, socioeconomic status, sex, etc.), the comparisons will be misleading and the teacher will not be justified in interpreting a given pupil's achievement as above or below that of the average fifth-grader.

Furthermore, the group used in standardizing an arithmetic test, for example, may be different from that used in standardizing a geography test; so that even though both tests may have sets of norms for fifth-graders, there is an unknown degree of uncertainty in comparing a pupil's relative achievement in the two subjects. The teacher cannot say that a pupil who has the same standing on the norms in these two tests really has the same standing in the two subjects. Only tests of the same quality and form, with norms established at the same time and under the same conditions on the same groups of pupils and schools, make possible such comparisons between subjects or from year to year. Only then can teachers interpret test scores as indicators of differences in individual pupils from subject to subject and from year to year.

Comparisons between pupils and between groups, moreover, are valuable only so far as the nature of the "normative" group is known and understood. Tests constructed independently by different classroom teachers probably do not meet these requirements for comparability. Hence standardized tests are clearly superior in the types of interpretations they make possible. Not all standardized tests, however, can meet these requirements. Tests that are independently constructed and standardized on different groups under different conditions are *not* comparable. The Stanford Achievement Test is typical of tests which have been standardized to meet requirements for comparability from one subject to another, e.g., from arithmetic reasoning to reading comprehension.

TEACHER–MADE VS. STANDARDIZED TESTS

Different objectives require different evaluation devices. Frequently, not all the objectives of instruction can be covered by a given device. Hence a school needs to determine which aspects of its total evalua tion program can make use of standardized tests and which can be handled more effectively by means of teacher-made tests. Since standardized tests may not be applicable or valid for measuring a teacher's objectives in a specific course because of the variation in course content from teacher to teacher, teacher-made tests are often preferable. The reader should refer to Table 8, which indicates the effectiveness of teacher-made and standardized tests for various purposes, and to Chapters 7–9, which deal with the construction and use of teacher-made tests.

The school testing program should supplement the ordinary informal evaluations of achievement made by classroom teachers. It should yield measures that the usual school records and classroom procedures do not provide; that is, it should give a meaningful and comprehensive picture of the general educational status of the individual pupil at a given time and his relative growth from year to year in major aspects of educational development. The standardized testing program provides an additional frame of reference for evaluating the performance of a pupil, class, or school.

INTELLIGENCE VS. ACHIEVEMENT TESTS

The definitions of intelligence are many and varied. Illustrative are the following: "The ability to think in abstract terms." "The capacity to judge well, to reason well, and to comprehend well."

"The aggregate or global capacity of the individual to act purposefully, to think rationally, and to deal effectively with his environment." "The ability to undertake activities that are characterized by difficulty, complexity, abstractness, economy, adaptiveness to a goal, social value, emergence of originals, and to maintain such activities under conditions that demand a concentration of energy and a resistance to emotional forces." "The degree of availability of one's experiences for the solution of immediate problems and the anticipation of future ones." "The power or act of understanding." "The power of meeting any situation, especially a novel situation, successfully by proper behavior adjustments." "The ability to apprehend the interrelationships of presented facts in such a way as to guide action towards a desired goal."

In view of these many possible definitions, some writers have held that the most meaningful definition of intelligence for practical purposes is achieved when we perform operations or construct tests to measure it. According to this position, intelligence may be defined as "what intelligence tests measure." Such a definition begs the question, but it turns attention to the more illuminating *practices* of psychologists and away from their inadequate abstract definition.

Purposes of Intelligence Tests

The first successful intelligence tester, Alfred Binet, shortly before the turn of the century was seeking a technique by which to separate the school children of Paris on the basis of whether they were mentally fit or unfit to be taught in the regular public schools. After great effort in many different directions, such as head measurements, physiognomy, graphology, palmistry, and sensory discrimination, Binet finally achieved a somewhat successful approach in terms of "higher mental processes." Note that his criterion for the validity of his test was ability to succeed in school work. He derived the content of his measuring instruments not by an a priori, armchair reasoning process, but by an almost random process of trial and error toward a practical goal.

This criterion, "success in school," has pervaded many subsequent operational definitions of intelligence. Whatever the fate of various general definitions or theories about the organization or determiners of intelligence, ability to succeed in school must always remain a major part of the conception of intelligence, at least in the present civilization. Ever since Binet, teachers' judgments of pupil intelligence and teachers' marks, all based on judgments of the pupil's success in dealing with school subjects, have been important criteria for the validity of measurements of intelligence.

The question may be asked, "If school success and teachers' judgments of intelligence are such important criteria of intelligence test validity, why do we need special instruments?" The answer traditionally given is that teachers' unaided judgments are not sufficiently reliable, valid, or in many practical situations administrable. Binet investigated the ways in which teachers judge the intelligence of their pupils, both by using a questionnaire and by asking three teachers to come to his laboratory to judge the intelligence of children they had never seen before. He found that teachers "do not have a very definite idea of what constitutes intelligence, . . . tend to confuse it variously with capacity for memorizing, facility in reading, ability to master arithmetic, . . . fail to appreciate the one-sidedness of the school's demands upon intelligence, . . . are too easily deceived by a sprightly attitude, a sympathetic expression, a glance of the eye, or a chance 'bump' on the head, . . . show rather undue confidence in the accuracy of their judgments."[3] His observations of the teachers' actual procedures indicated that each one attempted to construct on the spot a little intelligence test which was poorly thought-out, unstandardized, and errorful and resulted in little agreement among their estimates. The intelligence test method of evaluating mental ability thus emerges as merely a refinement, organization, and standardization of the teacher's or layman's "common-sense" but error-ridden approach.

Criteria for Content of Intelligence Tests

Let us now examine the criteria used by Binet and subsequent intelligence test builders in selecting and arranging their test content. Every builder must select his content according to some conception of intelligence, explicit or implicit. Binet's conception stressed such

[3] L. M. Terman, *The Measurement of Intelligence*, Boston: Houghton Mifflin, 1916, pp. 28–35.

characteristics of thinking as its power to continue along purposeful lines, to criticize itself, and to adapt itself to a specific goal. This conception took many varied forms in test content: tests of time orientation, several kinds of memory, language comprehension, knowledge about common objects, free association, number mastery, constructive imagination, and ability to compare concepts, to see contradictions, to bind fragments into a unitary whole, to comprehend abstract terms, and to meet novel situations.

In addition to its agreement with some conception of intelligence, test content has a second criterion—equal opportunity for human beings within a given culture to have experience with that content. In setting up this requirement, intelligence test builders wanted to hold constant the factor of environment or learning so that the differences between individuals that are revealed by the testing will be attributable to innate factors. To a large extent this attempt is justifiable, especially so far as it excludes test content explicitly taught in the schools. It would be folly to use shorthand writing ability to measure high-school students' intelligence, since learning opportunity or environmental influence varies so greatly from pupil to pupil with respect to this test content. On the other hand, test builders and users must realize that this requirement—equal opportunity to learn test content—is seldom fully met. The unwarranted assumption that intelligence tests require only what everybody in a given group has had an equal opportunity to learn explains much of the confusion in the nature-nurture controversy and much unwarranted fatalism in the interpretation of test results.

To rule out differences in the previous experiences or training of pupils, intelligence test builders try to use equally familiar (or unfamiliar) material. Equally familiar material is illustrated by such tests as asking a child to point to his nose, to draw a picture of a man, or to complete a picture in which one of the shadows is missing. Equally unfamiliar material is illustrated by tests in which the individual is required to learn and apply an artificial language composed of nonsense syllables, or by maze tests.

Test material in which environmental factors play a major role is illustrated by vocabulary tests, arithmetic computation tests, and any other test involving words or mathematical symbols. This kind of material is obviously influenced to a large extent by learning opportunities and by the type of activity in which the individual is constrained to engage by the culture in which he lives. Yet such material constitutes a major proportion of the content of many intelligence tests. It also varies in amount in different tests. Although this fact may invalidate the tests as measures of "innate ability," it does not necessarily detract from their usefulness in guidance. Regardless of the unknown extent to which differences in genes or environment determine differences in pupils' scores, the ability reflected in such scores must still be taken into account in making vocational plans or understanding school success or failure.

Relationship Between Intelligence and Achievement Tests

High correlations are generally obtained between a test of general intelligence and a battery of general achievement tests. T. L. Kelley, among others, has shown that this is the case.[4] He obtained correlation coefficients of about .90 after correcting for the unreliability of the tests. This enabled him to estimate the community of function between intelligence and achievement tests. He concluded that the community of function among different intelligence tests is about 95 percent; between intelligence tests and achievement batteries, about 90 percent; between intelligence tests and reading tests, about 92 percent; between intelligence tests and arithmetic tests, about 88 percent. Although these figures are based on grade-school pupils, such similarities between achievement and intelligence test scores would probably be obtained at any other age. Kelley derived from these data his point of view that the distinction between intelligence and achievement tests is largely spurious and due to the "jangle" fallacy—the belief that two separate names for the same thing necessarily denote a real distinction.

If intelligence and general achievement tests are such good measures of each other, why do we need intelligence tests? The answer is, because of practical usability and convenience. We usually cannot measure general scholastic achievement in as brief a time and with as short a test as we can intelligence. The test by which we measure

[4] T. L. Kelley, *Interpretation of Educational Measurements*, New York: Harcourt, Brace & World, 1927.

achievement in a single subject is generally as long as the average intelligence test; to obtain a measure of general achievement would require several of these achievement tests. Furthermore, when pupils have varying educational backgrounds—come from different school systems, for example—it is difficult to select an achievement test that is not prejudicial to some of them.

Ruch and Segel[5] state that group intelligence tests are of most value when (1) they are used with achievement tests for pupils whose school attendance has been irregular, (2) transfers from other schools must be given tentative class assignments without delay even though adequate cumulative records are not available, (3) financial resources permit extensive testing programs including both achievement intelligence tests, and (4) the intelligence tests provide diagnosis of differential mental abilities.

Another possible advantage sometimes claimed for intelligence tests over general achievement test batteries is their use as measures of scholastic aptitude. The novelty of the intelligence test and its apparent unrelatedness to ordinary school subject matter may create greater interest and better testing morale on the part of students who have antipathies toward one or more school subjects. A child may show low achievement because of emotional maladjustment, boredom, or poor teaching. The intelligence test may be able to reveal abilities that have escaped the influence of such debilitating factors. If so, in these respects the individual intelligence test tends to be more appropriate than the group paper-and-pencil type.

Many "intelligence" tests have been developed primarily to predict school success. Accordingly, it is often more appropriate to use the term "scholastic aptitude" or "educational aptitude" for such tests. Also, in recognition of the great similarity in practice between intelligence, aptitude, and achievement, many of the newer tests provide derived scores that yield a measure of a person's "age" in many different academic areas (such as reading age, arithmetic age, language age, etc.) These "ages" are convertible into quotients for the respective areas.

[5] G. M. Ruch and D. Segel, *Minimum Essentials of the Individual Inventory in Guidance*, Washington: U.S. Dept. of the Interior, Office of Education, Vocational Division Bulletin No. 202, p. 24.

BEGINNING–OF–YEAR VS. END–OF–YEAR TESTING

The time of year for giving tests in the school testing program varies considerably in practice, with logical reasons for the differences. The decision on timing should accord with the purposes of the program in the individual school or system. Regardless of the time selected, there is an advantage to testing at about the same time year after year. A regular time makes it easier to determine growth in the various aspects of the school's instructional program. Some schools administer their tests early in the year for diagnostic purposes and for grouping and grade placement of pupils. Others administer them late in the year primarily for marking and promotion purposes. When all factors are taken into consideration, the beginning-of-the-year testing appears to have greater benefits.

A teacher should have available at the beginning of the year the information about his pupils that he will need to adapt instruction most effectively to their ability and achievement. He cannot reasonably assume that all his pupils are equally ready for the work done by his class. He must recognize that a typical class has a wide range of individual differences, both in general mental ability and in the specific knowledges, skills, and aptitudes needed for achievement of curricular objectives. If there is a record of test results for the class, based on tests given late the previous year, he will have a good basis for instruction at this time. He often finds, however, that the records are incomplete for some students because of their irregular progress, their transfer from another school system, or other reasons. The fall testing program provides a record for the class as currently organized and also indicates where pupils stand on measures that have increased validity because they are as recent as possible.

A better incentive for a teacher to administer tests early in the school year is the fact that he can obtain a better picture of the pupils with whom he has to work and will have more time to use the test results. In addition, the teacher appears to have less feeling that he is being evaluated by the tests than when they are administered at the end of the year.

Students tend to be motivated by tests, and this motivation can be used better when the tests are given at the beginning of the year. A pupil can be helped to identify his learning problems in objective terms, and with this knowledge he may be more likely to apply himself than if he has only a vague idea of his problems. Tests can give the pupil a basis for determining his gains during the year, and if his gains can be demonstrated to him in objective terms his desire to improve can be strengthened.

GENERAL AREAS OF THE TESTING PROGRAM

The general areas usually included in a school testing program include general mental ability, achievement of instructional objectives, interests and special abilities, and social-emotional adjustment. How often the school should evaluate the various aspects of pupils depends both on the nature of the aspects and the facilities available to the school. It can carry on the more informal observations and diagnostic testing in the classroom with teacher-made tests quite frequently. The general school testing program will be adequate if all the pupils are tested only once a year. To measure their progress it is desirable to test them every year. The annual testing program provides a continuous record of growth for all students and enables a more accurate interpretation of the development of those whose progress varies from year to year in different areas.

Measuring General Mental Ability

Since the primary purpose of "general mental ability," "intelligence," or "scholastic aptitude" tests is to predict school success, or the ability to learn, such tests may appear to be valuable. Many studies indicate substantial relationships between scores on "intelligence" tests and overall success in school work. However, research has not yet established that the results of aptitude tests in specific subjects, areas, or fields have significantly greater relationship to success in those areas than do the results of general academic achievement tests. All in all, aptitude tests for specific aspects of school work may play a useful role in evaluation, but it is a less important role than that of general achievement tests.

If a school can afford *only a minimum program of evaluation*, its program should at least be able to identify individuals who are pretty much alike with respect to mental ability and those who are somewhat above and below the "average." If the testing program must be confined to a *single brief measure*, a test of general mental ability is undoubtedly the answer. However, this is only a beginning; the educator must supplement this measure by other information in planning an adequate program of evaluation. Testing in additional areas—achievement, interests, and adjustment—is essential in an adequate educational program.

The general mental ability of pupils needs to be evaluated less frequently than every semester but more often than once in the school career. In general, two considerations determine the grades in which intelligence tests should be given. First, intellectual level as indicated by general mental ability tests does not have perfect constancy. Hence, the scores or standings of pupils on these tests should be "refreshed" at intervals during their school career. This retesting reveals any fluctuations resulting either from real changes in rate of intellectual growth or from errors of measurement due to imperfections in the tests. Second, the need to measure mental ability and other characteristics is greater at some stages in a pupil's school career than at others.

To give a group test of mental ability to every pupil in the school every third or fourth year is probably sufficient. The best times for this testing probably are when pupils begin a new kind of experience or must make a choice among various curricula: (1) entrance in the first grade, when there is lack of preliminary data on a pupil that will help a teacher become acquainted with him in the shortest possible time; (2) the beginning of the elementary level at the fourth- or fifth-grade, since it is known that the predictive value of test scores decreases appreciably over a period of two or three years; (3) entry into junior high school in the seventh grade, when the pupil may have to choose among various subjects; (4) entry into high school in the ninth or tenth grade, when he often chooses among various curricula; and (5) during the last year of secondary education before he goes to work or enters college. Here, however, a battery of achievement tests may serve even better as a basis for vocational guidance.

Evaluating Achievement of Instructional Objectives

The major purposes of achievement testing are at least twofold. First, this testing enables teachers, administrators, and counselors to keep themselves more intimately and reliably acquainted with the educational development of each pupil. The information from such a program provides bases upon which to adapt instruction and guidance to each pupil's unique and changing needs. Second, achievement testing provides more dependable and objective bases for evaluating the total educational offering. Since teachers should have a comprehensive acquaintance with each pupil, it is obvious that instruments yielding only an estimate of general mental ability are not adequate for a satisfactory program of evaluation. General educational development tests usually produce information of greater practical value in school situations than any of the available tests of intelligence.

General educational development tests should provide a basis for directing curriculum emphasis, for giving pupils educational guidance, for stimulating learning activities, and for directing and motivating administrative and supervisory efforts. The directing of curriculum emphasis may be implemented by focusing attention on as many important ultimate objectives of education as possible, by clarifying specific educational objectives for teachers and pupils, and by determining the elements of strength and weakness in the school's instructional program. These tests also provide a basis for predicting and guiding individual pupil achievement in each major learning area, for initially grouping pupils in these areas, for discovering special aptitudes and disabilities, for determining the difficulty of material a pupil can read with understanding, and for determining the problem-solving ability of pupils in various major areas. The stimulation of learning activities is furthered by these tests, in part at least, because they enable pupils to think of their achievements in objective terms, give them satisfaction for the progress they make, and permit them to compete with their own past performance records. In directing and motivating administrative and supervisory efforts these tests help teachers discover the areas in which they need supervisory aid, and they afford an overall measure of the effectiveness of the prevailing organizational, administrative, and supervisory policies.

Obviously, then, some type of general educational development test is necessary in the school's program of evaluation. Since the content of available tests ranges from tests that measure one or two general areas to comprehensive batteries, it is possible for a school to select a test which fits its particular situation with respect to such practical considerations as cost, administrative time, curriculum, and personnel. The ideal program of evaluation includes the most comprehensive battery of such tests obtainable.

Appraising Interests and Special Abilities

Interest inventories and tests of special ability provide worthwhile information for guidance purposes. The school should use such instruments whenever information is necessary for counseling the pupil, as when he is to make choices of curricula and vocations or his failures or success in school work require explanation. Such devices, except in art and music, will probably be used mainly in the last two years of high school. A test of mechanical aptitude at the beginning of high school may throw light on the desirability of a technical curriculum for a given pupil.

So far as interests, special abilities, and attitudes are assigned a role in educational outcomes, the school may evaluate them as often as the achievement of other instructional objectives. Thus, it may measure them before and after certain educational experiences, at the beginning and end of a school year. When attitudes and interests are considered mainly as factors affecting pupils' choices among curricula and vocations, the school usually evaluates them at the beginning of high school and toward the end of high school or in college by means of interest blanks. Every pupil should fill out these blanks, not merely those who express a need for educational or vocational guidance.

Appraising Emotional and Social Adjustment

The school must not overlook the importance of appraising adjustment during the school career. Basic knowledge in this field, however, is relatively inadequate at present. There are few valid instruments for appraising the few dimensions that have been even tentatively established. With respect to the school's program of evaluation, *formal testing* of adjustment should not receive attention until an adequate program has been established in the areas of intelligence, achievement, interests, and special abilities. However, the emotional and social adjustment of pupils should be *informally* evaluated frequently. It may be desirable at intervals for pupils to fill out a problem check list or inventory or undergo sociometric procedures and other techniques.

Appraising Other Aspects of Pupils

This chapter so far has covered briefly, and in no respect completely, various aspects of the testing program with regard to intelligence, achievement, special abilities, interests, and adjustment. Many other sources of information are necessary for a complete evaluation program. These include methods for appraising an individual's environment and background and his physical condition. Physical condition may be appraised by methods commonly known to teachers or those taught in other courses in the teacher education program; hence physical aspects of pupils are mentioned only slightly in this text.

Biographical histories and information about a pupil's environment and background may be compiled in various ways—socioeconomic score cards, for example, and the many types of records for reporting family background, parental occupation, size of family, income, home ownership, and other relevant items. When a pupil changes teachers, the next teacher should receive the results of these evaluations in the form of a cumulative record.

Evaluations of the physical aspects of pupils also vary in frequency and extensiveness. The teacher should observe his pupils every day and seek to discover any who are ill and in need of medical care. In the lower grades this may be a formal, organized classroom inspection of cleanliness, clothing, and general health. In the upper grades, a more casual and informal approach is probably adequate.

In no case should pupils complete their school careers without being thoroughly examined by a physician. However cursory this examination may be under the most limited circumstances, it is probably better than none at all. The frequency of periodic health examinations by physicians recommended by the American Medical Association is as follows:

From 2 to 5 years of age, semiannually
From 5 to 15 years of age, every two to three years
From 15 to 35 years of age, every two years

These frequencies are minimal, of course; physical examinations should be more frequent whenever a teacher or nurse notices abnormal changes in the appearance or behavior of a pupil.

MINIMUM AND OPTIMUM SCHOOL TESTING PROGRAMS

Every school, regardless of size, should have at least a minimum testing program for all pupils every year. No specific program, however, can fit every situation. In every case, the purposes of the program should be the dominating factor in determining its nature and extent. In general, the minimum program in the elementary or junior high school should probably include one measure of intelligence at some time and a regular schedule of achievement testing every year. To obtain full benefit from this program the school should also provide for the recording of test data on a cumulative basis, the records to be made available to all the school's professional staff.

Sample Minimum Programs

The following programs are merely illustrative of various types in existence today. A school should consider adopting a program like one of these only if it fits the school's established purposes. In particular, the specific tests or batteries named are merely illustrative.

Program A

Grades Kg. to 3: To assist in appraising abilities, aptitudes, and readiness for a reading program.

Tests: (1) Metropolitan Readiness Test or SRA Primary Mental Abilities Tests and (2) Alice and Jerry Readiness Tests (Harper & Row).

110 THE SCHOOL TESTING PROGRAM

Grades 4 and 5: To assist in appraising the academic achievements and needs of pupils at the beginning of the intermediate grades.

One of the following test batteries to be administered as early as possible in the school year:

Tests: (1) SRA Achievement Series, (2) Stanford Achievement Tests, (3) California Achievement Tests, (4) Metropolitan Achievement Test.

Grades 6 to 8: To assist in diagnosing the needs of pupils beginning junior high school and to follow up with an evaluation of their development. At this time it is important to note particularly the ability to read with understanding, to use numbers, and to work effectively.

Tests: The advanced form of the *same* tests used in Grades 4 to 5.

Grades 9 to 12: To assemble materials for use in placement and guidance; in adapting instruction to individual needs of pupils; and in providing a comprehensive, dependable survey of students' understanding of what is learned rather than mere knowledge of facts.

One of the following batteries of tests should be administered early in the school year.

Tests: (1) Iowa Tests of Educational Development (ITED), (2) Sequential Tests of Educational Progress (STEP), (3) California Achievement Tests, (4) Essential High School Content Battery, (5) Metropolitan Achievement Tests (limited to Grades 9–10), (6) Stanford Achievement Tests (limited to Grades 9–10).

In addition, a measure of interests may be administered at any time during these years, and it may be desirable to administer it more than once. Kuder Preference Record: Personal and Vocational.

Program B

Grades Kg. to 1: California Test of Mental Maturity
Grade 3: Stanford Achievement Tests
Grade 6: Stanford Achievement Tests
Grade 9: Iowa Tests of Educational Development
Grade 12: Iowa Tests of Educational Development

Program C

Grade 1: SRA Primary Mental Abilities Tests
Grade 4: Stanford Achievement Tests
Grade 5: Stanford Achievement Tests
Grade 7: Stanford Achievements Tests and California Test of Mental Maturity
Grade 9: Iowa Tests of Educational Development
Grade 11: Iowa Tests of Educational Development

The Optimum School Testing Program

An optimum program, as opposed to the three minimal programs just illustrated, is one which uses tests whenever they are needed to obtain information concerning pupils. In an optimum program, annual achievement testing in all grades is standard practice; and measures of readiness, intelligence, aptitudes, interests, and adjustment are used nearly as frequently as achievement tests. The optimum program also includes the administration of special types of tests—analytical tests of reading, study skills, or critical thinking, and specialized tests designed to determine the status of students with exceptional abilities or handicaps. The optimum program is simply the minimum program supplemented by tests at other times and at other grade levels for more extensive purposes.

TRAINING PERSONNEL FOR AN EFFECTIVE PROGRAM

If the evaluation program is to be effective, the school staff must understand its purposes and the techniques for carrying it out. There are many measurement problems and areas of evaluation in which the typical school staff does not consider itself competent. The more frequently indicated are (1) formulation of the minimum school program, (2) evaluation and diagnosis in reading, (3) follow-up and use of test results, (4) analysis of school failures, (5) development and use of cumulative records, and (6) construction of local tests.

In planning for training the staff, one should be aware of some of the many misconceptions about measurement which have their roots in ordinary misinformation. Dyer lists eleven such misconceptions:

1. That an objective test is objective in the sense of being wholly independent of human judgment,
2. That educational measurement is synonymous with objective tests,
3. That a norm is something you try to be better than,
4. That grade scores really mean something,
5. That aptitude tests measure something that is not achievement,
6. That achievement tests measure something that is not aptitude,
7. That achievement tests by definition measure only factual information,
8. That a test score profile provides readily usable information about a pupil's relative performance in several fields,
9. That statistics are for the birds,
10. That objective test scores can tell you nothing worth knowing,
11. That objective test scores can tell you everything you need to know.[6]

Cook reported on what teachers should know about measurement. The following ten items from his report have been selected as being especially pertinent to this discussion. Teachers should:

1. Be able to analyze a standard test in the subject and at the grade level he teaches with reference to skills, subject matter and mental processes tested, ease of administration and scoring, and the nature and adequacy of norms and scores provided.
2. Know the proper procedures and ethics of test administering, reporting of results, and using teacher-made and standardized tests.
3. Know how to compute percentile ranks, grade placement scores, and various standard scores and interpret them with reference to equal units on the base line of a normal frequency curve, and how to convert raw scores to various standard scores by either the linear or area method. Simple methods of statistics are involved in these processes.
4. Know how to compute and interpret coefficients of reliability and validity with an understanding of the factors inherent in the test, the factors inherent in students, and of the factors inherent in the situation which influences each.

[6] Henry S. Dyer, What point of view should teachers have concerning the role of measurement in education? *15th Yearb. Natl. Council on Measurements Used in Educ.*, 1958, p. 13.

5. Know how to interpret a test score with reference to the standard error of measurement.
6. Know how to construct individual and class educational profiles to show development over a period of years, and to evaluate the adequacy of test batteries, testing programs, norms, scores, and reporting.
7. Know how to prepare for and conduct an interview with a parent, analyzing the achievement and behavior characteristics of a pupil.
8. Know the relative value of so-called intelligence tests, different types of school marks, achievement tests, and prognostic tests in predicting pupil achievement in a given field.
9. Understand that the proper use of measurement makes possible the child development approach to education as opposed to the subject-matter-to-be-covered approach, and the ways of relating this to the school marking system.
10. Understand that the purpose of measurement is to adjust instruction and teaching to the learning abilities of students, that the use of test scores for grouping, grading, and passing is always secondary to the adjustment of instruction to the needs of the pupil.[7]

Staff personnel may be trained by in-service training meetings with the assistance of outside consultants. Many state departments of education and state universities offer consulting services at a moderate cost. Private institutions and agencies are being established in many parts of the country. The in-service training may include short courses, workshops on dismissed school time, or regularly scheduled staff and faculty meetings.

An effective in-service training meeting should avoid the short lectures that teachers are required to attend outside of their regular working time, and especially lectures filled with platitudes or mysticism about measurement. Consultants should be directed to assist with the problems teachers have indicated as most pressing and to be quite specific in their instruction. Hastings suggests the following method in such meetings:

Arrange to work with fairly small groups of teachers—four to ten—who know some pupils in common. Start with discussions of inference, prediction, and decision making. Introduce testing only after the general everyday process is fairly clear. Have the group suggest material for a "case staffing" procedure—that is, write down test results and other sam-

[7] Walter W. Cook, What teachers should know about measurement, 15th Yearb. Natl. Council on Measurements Used in Educ., 1958, pp. 16–19.

ples of behavior which various members of the group can recall concerning one student. Get them to come forth with their inferences and predictions. As soon as a mass of such data is before the group, direct attention to those samples of behavior which support the same inferences and those inferences which tend to support the same predictions. At the same time direct attention to the discrepancies among the data with the question of what kinds of samples of behavior are needed to obtain convergence instead of divergence of the predictions. Finally, encourage individuals to attend to the process in the regular classroom activity and encourage the group to carry on the "case staffing" procedure in your absence.[8]

The school administrator may also secure considerable assistance in planning for in-service meetings from Chapters 1, 5, 9, and 10 of *In-Service Education*[9] published by the N.S.S.E.

LABORATORY EXERCISES AND DISCUSSION QUESTIONS

1. Distinguish between achievement of instructional objectives and such aspects of pupils as high mental ability, cultured family background, and preference for artistic rather than scientific activities.
2. On what type of objective has most evaluational emphasis been placed in the past? For what reasons? With what desirable or undesirable results?
3. Formulate your own definition of intelligence and defend it against possible criticism.
4. Discuss the values and dangers of a state-wide testing program.
5. What are the major types of pupil problems that a counselor is likely to encounter in the high-school grades? In the upper elementary grades? In the intermediate grades? In the primary grades?
6. In what areas should instruments and devices be available for both group and individual measurement? Identify specific instruments in these areas. What are the purposes and specific uses of each?
7. Identify several factors, other than the cost of the tests, that affect the cost of a measurement program.

[8] J. Thomas Hastings, How can in-service training in measurement techniques be provided most effectively? *15th Yearb. Natl. Council on Measurements Used in Educ.*, 1958, pp. 28–32.
[9] Nelson B. Henry (ed.), In-service education, *56th Yearb. Natl. Socy. Stud. Educ.*, 1957, Part 1.

SUGGESTED REFERENCES

Ahmann, J. S., and M. D. Glock, *Evaluating Pupil Growth*, Boston: Allyn and Bacon, 1959.

A school-wide program of evaluation is described in Chapter 15.

Durost, W. N., *What Constitutes a Minimal Testing Program for Elementary and Junior High School*, Test Service Notebook No. 1, New York: Harcourt, Brace & World, rev., 1956.

Standardized tests of achievement and aptitude, how to choose and schedule them, and a check list of steps in setting up a school testing program.

Ebel, R. L., and Dora Damrin, Tests and examinations, in C. W. Harris (ed.), *Encyclopedia of Educational Research*, New York: Macmillan, 3rd ed., 1960.

An excellent presentation of the uses and limitations of achievement tests, concepts used in evaluation, and problems involved in test construction. Has a useful bibliography.

Educational Testing Service, *Essential Characteristics of a Testing Program*, Evaluation and Advisory Service Series, No. 2, Princeton: Educational Testing Service, 1956.

Identifying purposes and assuring understanding by everyone concerned in a continuous program of evaluation.

Lindvall, C. M., *Testing and Evaluation· An Introduction*, New York: Harcourt, Brace & World, 1961.

Chapter 13 is concerned with some of the points that must be considered in planning and evaluating testing programs.

Nunnally, J. C., *Educational Measurement and Evaluation*, New York: McGraw-Hill, 1964.

Chapter 17 discusses some guideposts for applying psychological measurement methods in establishing testing programs.

Stanley, J. C., *Measurement in Today's Schools*, Englewood Cliffs: Prentice-Hall, 4th ed., 1964.

Chapter 10 deals with the steps in the testing program.

Thorndike, R. L., and Elizabeth Hagen, *Measurement and Evaluation in Psychology and Education*, New York: Wiley, 2nd ed., 1961.

Chapter 16 answers the questions: What standardized tests should be used, and when? What is a sound testing program? Appendix III summarizes the more commonly used testing instruments in various areas of evaluation.

Selection of measurement instruments

Administrability

Interpretability

A Test Evaluation Outline

When standardized tests are to be purchased, the testing committee of a school may evaluate many possible choices before deciding on the specific tests. Test selection should not be limited only to those that various committee members already know about, but other tests which may provide even more comprehensive and valid information should be considered.

SOURCES OF INFORMATION CONCERNING TESTS

This book mentions only a small number of published tests. It describes only the general nature and content of any particular area of educational and psychological measurement. The reasons for limiting the discussion in this fashion are twofold. (1) Lack of space precludes any attempt to provide detailed information, evaluations, and recommendations concerning the large numbers of tests available in each of the fields discussed. (2) Other publications satisfy, far more thoroughly than is possible here, the need for an exhaustive listing and evaluation of available tests. We refer here specifically to Buros' *Mental Measurements Yearbooks* and *Tests in Print*.[1] Not only are they specifically designed for the functions which this book does not discuss, but they also have the advantage of being recurrent. Several have already been published.

A further source of information concerning the ongoing development of evaluation devices is the *Review of Educational Research*.[2] The issues entitled "Psychological Tests and Their Uses," "Educational Tests and Their Uses," "Methods of Research and Appraisal

[1] O. K. Buros (ed.), *Mental Measurements Yearbooks*, Highland Park, New Jersey: Gryphon, 1938, 1940, 1949, 1953, 1959. *Tests in Print*, Highland Park, New Jersey: Gryphon, 1961.

[2] Published by the American Educational Research Association.

in Education," and "Counseling and Guidance" are especially rich in references to new tests and to research findings with old tests. These reviews appear every three years and critically evaluate the literature of the preceding three years in a given field.

Various journals, such as *Educational and Psychological Measurement, Journal of Educational Psychology, Journal of Applied Psychology, Journal of Educational Research,* and *Journal of Experimental Education* carry reports of research with tests of the kind considered in this book. *Psychological Abstracts* has abstracts of the world's psychological literature, including notices of new tests and abstracts of articles reporting research on specific tests. The *Journal of Consulting Psychology* contains brief reviews of new tests, especially those of interest to counselors and psychotherapists.

The Encyclopedia of Educational Research[3] provides information useful in judging and selecting tests. It is valuable for the professional library of any school.

The catalogues of test publishers are a further source of information as to available tests. Schools can readily keep up-to-date collections of such catalogues. These catalogues tell how to obtain specimen sets of tests (consisting generally of test booklet, manual, answer sheet, scoring key, norms, etc.). Obviously, test publishers' catalogues and manuals present their tests as favorably as possible. But the intelligent user can make wise decisions by inspecting the specimen set, applying the concepts and principles set forth in this chapter and elsewhere in this volume, and consulting the critical and research literature on the test. Appendix A lists the names and addresses of the major test publishers from whom catalogues can be obtained.

Every classroom teacher and school administrator should have access to these sources when selecting evaluation devices. When this is impossible, they should write to the educational research bureaus of universities for specific information concerning tests available in a particular field. These bureaus answer inquiries most helpfully when the inquiries specify the purposes, time limits, financial resources, and other factors that affect the proposed testing program.

[3] C. W. Harris (ed.), *The Encyclopedia of Educational Research,* New York: Macmillan, 3rd ed., 1960.

DESIRABLE CHARACTERISTICS OF TESTS

Certain considerations in selecting a standardized test apply to all evaluation devices, including teacher-made tests. Consequently, the present discussion lays the general foundation for understanding how all evaluation devices should be judged.

In general, we should use standardized tests when the instructional objectives whose achievement is to be evaluated are objectives for which such tests have been designed. The objectives are usually common to a great many classrooms, teachers, and school systems. The objectives of instruction in reading, arithmetic, writing, and other tool subjects vary little from one classroom to another and from one school system to another. Thus, standardized tests designed for wide use can usually be selected to fit a particular situation. In other subjects such as American history and general science, there is still enough in common between the objectives of different teachers and school systems that useful standardized achievement tests can be made. Granted the communality of instructional objectives in various classrooms, the problem becomes one of selecting the proper standardized test. The basic characteristics to look for in making a selection are (1) validity, (2) reliability, (3) administrability, and (4) interpretability.

VALIDITY

The validity of an evaluation device is the degree to which it measures what it is intended to measure. Tests are used for several types of judgment, and each type of judgment requires a somewhat different type of validating evidence. Although many textbooks discuss validity in different ways, we present here the definitions of four types of validity that have been accepted by the American Psychological Association, the American Educational Research Association, and the National Council on Measurements Used in Education.[4] These four are called *content* validity, *concurrent* validity, *predictive* validity, and *construct* validity.

[4] *Technical Recommendations for Psychological Tests and Diagnostic Techniques*, Suppl. to *Psychol. Bull.*, 1954, *51*, No. 2, Pt. 2; Committee on Test Standards, AERA, and Committee on Test Standards, NCMUE, *Technical Recommendations for Achievement Tests*, Washington: Nat. Educ. Assn., 1955.

Content Validity

Content validity is evaluated by showing how well the content of the test samples the class of situations or subject matter about which conclusions are to be drawn. It is especially important in the case of achievement and proficiency measures. It is also known as "face validity" and "logical validity" and is described by the relevance of a test to different types of criteria, such as analyses of courses of study and jobs, statements of instructional objectives, analyses of textbooks, analyses of teachers' final-examination questions, pooled judgments of competent persons, concepts of social utility, and logical or psychological analyses of mental processes, motor performances, or other behaviors.

Concurrent Validity

Concurrent validity is evaluated by showing how well test scores correspond to already accepted measures of performance or status made at the same time. For example, we may give a social studies class a test on knowledge of basic concepts in social studies and at the same time obtain from its teacher a report on these abilities as far as pupils in the class are concerned. If the relationship between the test scores and the teacher's report of abilities is high, the test will have high concurrent validity.

Predictive Validity

Predictive validity is evaluated by showing how well predictions made from the test are confirmed by evidence gathered at some subsequent time. It is quite similar to concurrent validity, except that the evidence on the criterion measures used is collected later. This type is especially important, for example, when the tester wants to estimate how well a student may be able to do in college courses on the basis of how well he has done on tests he took in secondary school. It is also applicable in long-range prediction of such factors as vocational success or reaction to therapy. Because of the time lag between giving the test and obtaining the criterion measures, as in predicting success in college from tests in high school, predictive validity is not as useful with achievement tests as are content and concurrent validity.

Construct Validity

Construct validity is evaluated by investigating what psychological qualities a test measures, or in other words, by demonstrating that certain explanatory constructs account for performance on the test. It is ordinarily used when the tester has no definitive criterion measure. By its very nature, construct validity is inferential rather than conclusive; it is used primarily when the other three types of validity are insufficient to indicate the degree to which the test measures what it is intended to measure. However, the other three types may be considered specialized aspects of construct validity when other criteria are available. Construct validity may be illustrated by the relationship of the items in a test to a description of the universe of items from which the selection was made. This type of validity is usually involved in such tests as those of study habits, appreciations, understandings, and interpretations of data.

For instructional uses of tests—diagnosis of achievement, planning of remedial work, within-subject determination of instruction materials—content validity is most important. For various administrative uses—pupil classification, prediction of success, comparison of curricula—concurrent, predictive, and construct validity are important.

Obviously, validity must eventually be thought of as relevance to the interacting needs of individuals and society. Fig. 13 illustrates the chain of criteria from test item to "welfare of humanity" that may be implicitly involved in validating a single test item. Each criterion may be validated against a "more ultimate" criterion.

On this ground, many school evaluation programs can immediately be declared at least partly irrelevant because of their lack of comprehensiveness, since they relate to only a few relatively minor educational objectives. It is of course the aim of the present book to increase the comprehensiveness of evaluation by outlining techniques for the evaluation not only of information and verbal and numerical skills, but of ways of thinking, attitudes, and the like. Evaluation will become more relevant as it becomes more comprehensive in terms of these aspects of pupils.

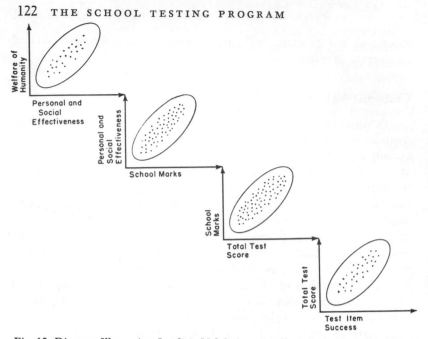

Fig. 13. Diagram Illustrating Implicit Validation of a Test Item Against a Series of Criteria Increasingly Remote from the Test Item.

Identifying Types of Validity

How can the test user discover what type and degree of validity a standardized test possesses? This information should be found in the test manual. Test manuals should contain information concerning the method of choosing test items, the characteristics and composition of the sample of students upon whom the test was standardized, the criteria used in validating the test, and the degree of validity of the test against these criteria. The absence of such information should incline the test user to consider the test of doubtful value. Of the thousands of standardized tests published, only a few have manuals that give sufficient information to make possible an accurate judgment of validity. To supplement the information in these manuals, or as a substitute if there is no manual, the user may consult various educational and psychological journals which report experimental studies and reviews of tests (see pp. 117–110).

Extremely valuable for this purpose are the *Mental Measurements Yearbooks* previously mentioned. These volumes present critical evaluations of standardized achievement tests in most of the subject-matter fields, and also tests of other aspects of pupils. The reviews cover not only newly published tests but older, widely used ones. Competent individuals representing a variety of points of view among curriculum specialists and test technicians review each test. If those responsible for the selection of tests will read these *Yearbooks* before making their decision, they will secure much data on which to base an intelligent judgment.

Time may not permit teachers to obtain specimen copies of tests from the test publishers or to look over the available tests in a given field. However, they may make such an appraisal after they have given the test and it may considerably modify the interpretation of the results obtained with it. If on inspection a test has important shortcomings with respect to validity, reliability, etc., or neglects or overemphasizes certain instructional objectives, the interpretation of scores should be modified accordingly. There is no substitute for familiarity with whatever evaluation devices are used. And, of course, *one of the best ways to acquire this familiarity is to take the test before giving it.*

Some Factors Affecting Test Validity

Test users should recognize factors that tend to make tests invalid for their purposes. Among them are (1) cultural influences, particularly in so-called intelligence and aptitude tests, (2) response sets, (3) increased reliability at the expense of validity, and (4) difficulty or lack of clarity in directions to pupils.

Cultural Influences. Research has shown the effect of *culture—*socioeconomic status, social class structure, differential sex roles, etc. —on general mental ability as measured by tests. Among Hopi Indians,[5] for example, the average boys' IQ on the Goodenough Draw-a-Man test was 123; the average girls', 102. Navaho boys and girls, on the other hand, did not differ significantly—107 and 110

[5] R. J. Havighurst, M. K. Gunther, and I. E. Pratt, Environment and the Draw-a-man Test: the performance of Indian children, *J. Abnorm. Soc. Psychol.*, 1946, 41:50–63.

respectively. Cultural anthropologists explain these differences in terms of the opportunities for learning to draw as determined by the different ways of bringing up boys and girls in the different tribes. Navaho boys and girls have similar experiences and opportunities to learn art. But Hopi Indian girls are restricted to routine household tasks, whereas the boys are stimulated to observe and work with their world.

Such cultural effects have often been underestimated or not recognized at all. In a brief vocabulary test a national sample of high-school students, divided on the basis of religious preference, showed widely different degrees of understanding. Of the Catholic students, 32 percent defined the word "absolve" correctly, as contrasted with 14 percent of Protestant and 18 percent of Jewish students. Of the Jewish students, on the other hand, 56 percent knew the meaning of "incite," as against 41 percent of the Protestant and 44 percent of the Catholics.[6] "Subcultures" in our total culture thus complicate the problems of validity enormously. There is much evidence, as Anastasi[7] points out, that "cultural differentials" are present not only in the more complex forms of behavior, but even in motor and discriminative or perceptual responses.

Response Sets. Response sets are test-taking habits which affect persons' scores, usually in ways irrelevant to the purpose of the test. Cronbach has summarized the phenomenon as follows:

. . . Response sets have been identified in tests of ability, personality, attitude and interest, and in rating scales. Among the most widely found sets are acquiescence (tendency to say "True," "Yes," "Agree," etc.), evasiveness (tendency to say "?," "Indifferent," "Uncertain," etc.), and similar biases in favor of a particular response when certain fixed alternatives are offered. Other sets include the tendency to work for speed rather than accuracy, the tendency to guess when uncertain, the tendency to check many items in a checklist, etc. Response sets become most influential as items become difficult or ambiguous. Individual differences in response sets are consistent throughout a given test. . . . Response sets dilute a test with factors not intended to form part of the test content and so reduce its logical validity. These sets may also reduce the

[6] H. H. Remmers and A. J. Drucker, High school youth re-ponder some national problems and issues, *Purdue Opinion Panel*, 1950, 9, No. 3.

[7] Anne Anastasi, Some implications of cultural factors in test construction. *Proc. 1949 Invitational Conf. on Testing Problems*, 1950.

test's empirical validity. Response sets tend to reduce the range of individual differences in score.[8]

Increased Reliability at the Expense of Validity. Suppose a teacher of mathematics finds that a test he constructed to measure ability to solve verbal problems is not adequately reliable. He knows (as is explained below) that increasing the number of test items generally increases the reliability of the test. He must also administer the test during a class period. Hence he decides to add a considerable number of items calling for the less complex skills required in solving verbal problems—such skills as removing parentheses in algebra, factoring, and the like. It is quite possible that a student who has learned many of these skills in a rote memory fashion will receive a higher score than a student who has greater ability to solve verbal problems but has "memorized" fewer of the less complex skills. The test now has a higher reliability coefficient, but its validity may actually have been reduced.

Difficulty or Lack of Clarity of Directions to Pupils. Poor directions may for some pupils render the test a measure of something different than the test author intended. For example, if the directions for a sixth-grade geography test include vocabulary of tenth-grade difficulty, the test becomes to a great extent one of ability to understand directions rather than one of ability in geography.

RELIABILITY

Reliability is the consistency with which a test yields the same results in measuring whatever it does measure. What a test measures may not be what it is being used to measure; i.e., a test may be invalid. But if it yields consistent results, it is reliable. If height is used as a measure of intelligence it will be reliable—because height measured with a yardstick is very consistent—but will not be valid for that purpose. Although less reliable—because less consistent from teacher to teacher—ratings of intelligence by teachers will be far more valid for this purpose. A somewhat unreliable measuring instru-

[8] L. J. Cronbach, Further evidence on response sets and test design, *Educ. Psychol. Meas.*, 1950, 10:3-4.

ment used for an appropriate purpose may be more valid than a reliable instrument used for a purpose for which it is invalid. Reliability pertains to a *class* of test characteristics. Members of this class are stability, equivalence, and internal consistency. Different techniques are used to estimate each of these kinds of reliability. These techniques, and the different meanings of the three kinds of coefficients obtained with them, are now described.

Methods of Estimating Reliability

The methods of estimating reliability all involve some way of obtaining at least two measures with the same instrument or with different forms of the same instrument and determining the agreement between them. For example, if a foot rule is used to measure the length of a table ten times, the disagreement among the ten measurements will indicate the unreliability of the foot rule and its use. If the ten measurements of length agree perfectly with one another, the foot rule is perfectly reliable. If the length is first 50.1 inches, then 49.9 inches, then 51.0 inches, then 50.2 inches, then 50.0 inches, and so forth, the unreliability can be stated as the amount of variability among the different measures of length. Similarly with evaluation devices in education—the closer the agreement between different applications of the device, the greater its reliability.

Test-Retest Method. The test-retest method of estimating reliability requires that the same evaluation device be used twice with the same group of pupils. The agreement between the scores from the two applications of the same test is determined by means of a correlation coefficient which, for this method, is sometimes called the *coefficient of stability.*

This method, however, has certain disadvantages. Repeating the test at too short an interval introduces the memory factor and tends to make the self-correlations of the test too high, unless, of course, the memory factor is what one wants to measure. On the other hand, repeating the test after a longer time interval permits such factors as growth, intervening learning, and unlearning to come into play so as to make the self-correlation lower than it should be.

Equivalent-Forms Methods. The equivalent-forms method of estimating reliability makes it possible to avoid the disadvantages of too short or too long a time interval between successive administrations of the evaluating device. Two equivalent forms of the test must be constructed so they are as similar as possible (but not identical) in the kind of content, mental processes required, number of items, difficulty, and all other respects. The pupils take one form of the test and then, as soon as possible, the other form. The agreement between the two is again determined by means of a correlation coefficient which for this method is sometimes called a *coefficient of equivalence*. If the agreement is high, we can say that each form does an accurate job of measurement.

The reader may question how two forms can be equivalent while differing in specific content or test items. The notion of equivalence may become clearer when it is compared with the process of sampling from any large population. When a medical technician examines a droplet of blood for the number of red corpuscles it contains, he may determine the reliability of his count by examining another droplet from the same person. The two droplets are equivalent and yet distinct, in that no corpuscle of one is contained in the other. Similarly, we may consider a test to be a sampling of test items from a large "population" of possible test items. Each sample of test items, or "form" of the test, can be equivalent to the other, although not a single test item is common to both forms. If we give the two forms or samples to a group of pupils, the scores on the two will correlate or agree in proportion to the equivalence of the two samples of test items.

Split-Halves Method. The split-halves method of estimating reliability also yields what is sometimes referred to as a *coefficient of equivalence*. This method divides the items of a single test into halves, usually by pooling the odd-numbered items for one score and the even-numbered items for another score. This usually makes the two scores obtained from a single testing reasonably equivalent in such respects as practice, fatigue, distractions, boredom, mental set, item difficulty, and content. After the test has been given to a group of pupils, two scores are obtained for each pupil, one on the odd-numbered and the other on the even-numbered items. The agreement between these two scores on the same test, as determined by a correlation coefficient, reflects the reliability of half the test.

Since this reliability holds only for half of the whole test, the reliability of the whole test must still be obtained. This is so because the reliability of tests increases with the number of functioning items they contain; hence the reliability of a half test is lower than that of the whole test. But a technique is available for estimating the reliability of a whole test from that of its halves. This technique, the Spearman-Brown prophecy formula, requires merely the substitution of the calculated reliability of the half test in the following equation in order to estimate the reliability of the whole test:

$$\text{Reliability of lengthened test} = \frac{nr}{1 + (n-1)r}$$

where n = number of times test is lengthened
r = original reliability coefficient

When the r is between scores on two *half* tests, this formula becomes:

$$\text{Reliability of whole test} = \frac{2(\text{reliability of half test})}{1 + (\text{reliability of half test})}$$

The applicability of the Spearman-Brown formula depends on how well the test meets certain assumptions. The two halves of the test must be as equivalent as possible in average score, variability of scores, and type of items. The formula has been found experimentally to give results in close agreement with the actual reliabilities of whole tests; that is, predicted and obtained whole-test reliabilities have been found to be approximately the same.

Two other split-test methods of estimating reliability involve no assumptions that are contradictory to the data. Moreover, these methods do not require computing the correlation coefficient or correcting by the Spearman-Brown formula. As shown in the following formula, the first method[9] requires only the standard deviations of each half test and of the total test:

$$r = 2\left(1 - \frac{s_o^2 + s_e^2}{s_t^2}\right)$$

where s_o = standard deviation of odd half
s_e = standard deviation of even half
s_t = standard deviation of total test

[9] L. Guttman, A basis for analyzing test-retest reliability, *Psychometrika*, 1945, 10:255–282.

The second formula[10] yields the same results and requires only the standard deviation of the *differences*, s_d, between half-test scores and standard deviation of the total test.

$$r = 1 - \frac{s_d{}^2}{s_t{}^2}$$

Kuder-Richardson Method. Methods of estimating the internal consistency, or homogeneity, of a test have been presented by Kuder and Richardson.[11] These methods do not require splitting the test into halves and rescoring and calculating a correlation coefficient. The only data required for this simpler method are the number of items in the test, the standard deviation of the test, and the arithmetic mean of the total scores on the test. Assuming that all the items in the test measure essentially a single ability, that the correlations between items are all equal, and that all items are of the same difficulty, Kuder and Richardson arrived at the following formula:

$$r = \frac{n}{n-1} \cdot \frac{s_t{}^2 - n\bar{p}\bar{q}}{s_t{}^2}$$

where n = number of items in the test

s_t = standard deviation of the total test scores

$$\bar{p} = \frac{\text{arithmetic mean of test scores}}{n} = \frac{M_t}{n}$$

$$\bar{q} = 1 - \bar{p}$$

This formula underestimates the internal consistency of a test if there is variation in difficulty among the items. In any case, it yields a figure that is usually lower than that obtained by the split-halves method. If the test items do not vary greatly in difficulty and if we are interested in how homogeneous the test is, the quick estimate made possible by this formula will probably be good enough for all practical purposes.

Another Kuder-Richardson formula for estimating internal consistency has been shown to yield a coefficient equal to the *mean of all*

[10] P. J. Rulon, A simplified procedure for determining the reliability of a test by split-halves, *Harvard Educ. Rev.*, 1939, 9:99–103.

[11] G. F. Kuder and M. W. Richardson, The theory of the estimation of test reliability, *Psychometrika*, 1937, 2:151–160.

the possible split-half coefficients of the test. This formula, called Kuder-Richardson's "20," is:

$$r = \frac{n}{n-1} \cdot \frac{s_t^2 - \Sigma pq}{s_t^2}$$

where n = number of items in the test

s_t = standard deviation of the total test scores

p = proportion of persons passing each item

$q = 1 - p$

The formula requires counting the number of persons passing each item, dividing this by the number of persons taking the test, subtracting the resulting proportion p from 1 to obtain q, getting pq from a table, and adding the pq's for all items to get Σpq. Since p is often valuable as part of the item analysis of a test in computing the difficulty of each item, the labor required in determining p for each item serves more than one purpose.

This coefficient provides some indication of how internally consistent, or homogeneous, a test is for the sample to which it is administered. If the test is not intended to be homogeneous, the coefficient is irrelevant. That is, if an achievement test is designed to measure different kinds of achievement, not necessarily homogeneous, a low coefficient obtained with the Kuder-Richardson formula does not mean that the test is unreliable. For achievement tests it is usually better to estimate reliability with one of the split-half coefficients given above, than with the Kuder-Richardson formula. The latter, however, is relevant for tests intended to be homogeneous, such as an unspeeded vocabulary test of a single kind of knowledge or an attitude scale designed to measure only one attitude dimension.

Factors Affecting Reliability

The reliability coefficient may be affected by the length of the test, the range of talent among pupils, and the conditions under which the test is administered.

Length of Test. In discussing the Spearman-Brown formula, we mentioned that the length of a test may affect the reliability coefficient. Other things being equal, the reliability of a test is a function of its length. Longer tests tend to be more reliable than shorter tests. Logically, the more samples we take of a given area of knowledge, skill, behavior, and the like, the more reliable will be our appraisal of that area. However, the Spearman-Brown formula shows that after we have reached a high degree of reliability additional items do not improve the reliability enough to justify the extra time and effort required for building items or for testing pupils. For example, using the formula (p. 128) $r_{nn} = \dfrac{nr}{1 + (n-1)r}$ for a test of 50 items with a reliability coefficient of .80, we could double the length of the test to 100 items and get a whole-test reliability coefficient of .888, triple it for a coefficient of .923, or quadruple it for a coefficient of .941. From 50 to 100 items the reliability improved considerably, but from 150 to 200 items there was very little increase in the reliability coefficient. Fig. 14 shows how the curve of increase in reliability flattens out with continued lengthening of a test.

Range of Talent. The range of talent, achievement, or ability of the pupils on whom the reliability is based has a direct effect on the

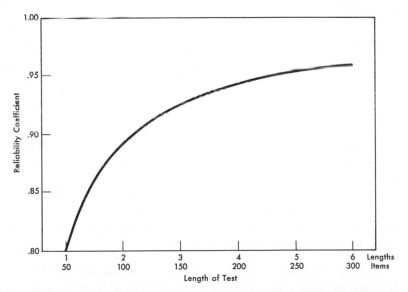

Fig. 14. Relationship Between Reliability and Length of Test. (Reliability of original test of 50 items is .80.)

reliability coefficient. The greater the variability in the group of pupils, the higher the reliability coefficient. Consequently, the reliability coefficient of a test given to several grades is higher than that of the same test given to a single grade because the range of achievement is larger in the first case. Fig. 15 shows this fact graphi-

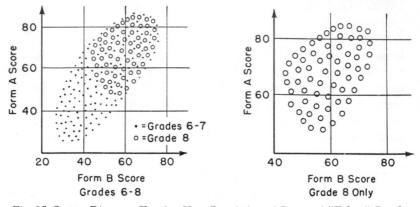

Fig. 15. *Scatter Diagrams Showing How Restriction of Range of "Talent" Results in Lower Reliability Coefficients.*

cally. The reliability coefficient should therefore always be determined on a group of pupils whose range of achievement is similar to that of the group who are to be discriminated from one another by the test. The reliability of a test designed to reveal differences in achievement in a single classroom should be determined on a group of pupils within a similarly restricted range of achievement. Reliability determined on pupils in several classrooms or in different geographic areas or who differ in certain other factors that affect achievement, will give a false picture of the reliability of the test when used in a single classroom. In selecting standardized tests for use at a single grade level, it is advisable to consider reliability determined on a single grade (sometimes referred to as "within-grade" reliability) rather than on several grades.

Testing Conditions. The conditions of administering and scoring the test may raise or lower the reliability of a given test. The mental set of pupils for accuracy or speed of work and the level of their motivation and emotional stability affect the reliability of their scores. Distractions and accidents, like breaking a pencil or finding a defective test blank, lower reliability. Cheating by pupils and scoring inaccuracy due to clerical errors also affect reliability adversely.

How High Should Reliability Be?

Obviously evaluation devices are never perfectly reliable. How unreliable a test may be and still be useful depends mainly on the fineness of discrimination desired from the test scores. In general, most standardized tests published for school use (achievement, primarily) have reliability coefficients of at least .80 in the population for which they are designed. For research purposes tests may be useful if their reliability coefficients fall as low as .50, especially if group performance only is at issue.

It is sufficient, perhaps, to say that the teacher should seek a standardized test whose reliability is as high as possible. But he must interpret this reliability coefficient in light of the groups of pupils on which it is based, the variability of this group, and the method of estimating reliability. Coefficients of stability tell how similar the scores may be expected to be over a specified time interval. Coefficients of equivalence tell how similar the scores on each of two forms of a test are. Coefficients of internal consistency tell how much all the items, combined to yield a single score, may be considered to measure a single homogeneous characteristic of the persons tested.

The variability of the obtained score in relation to the individual's "true score" is one of the most important determiners of how high a reliability coefficient should be for various purposes. If we gave the same test to a pupil many times and could assume that he had not learned anything or forgotten anything between testings, we would expect him to obtain slightly different scores on the test. We would also expect that his "true score" would lie somewhere within the range of the scores he actually made. But this kind of testing is impossible; hence we give him only one test for our purposes. We expect that his obtained score will fall somewhere near his true score. We can estimate the standard error of his score, and this figure will tell the range within which scores on the same test would be expected to fall approximately two-thirds[12] of the time if a very large number of the tests, equivalent in all respects, were given to the pupil. The *standard error of a score* is computed as follows:

$$S.E._{(Meas)} = s_t\sqrt{1 - r_{tt}}$$

where s_t = standard deviation of the scores on the test
r_{tt} = reliability coefficient of the test

Note in the example below how the standard error of an obtained score increases with decreasing reliability coefficients for a group having the same standard deviation of scores. Let us assume that the standard deviation of the scores on a test is 10. Let us further assume that the different forms of the test have reliability coefficients of .91, .84, .64, and .36, respectively. Using the formula, we have the following standard errors:

$$\text{For } r = .91, \quad S.E. = 10\sqrt{1 - .91} = 3$$
$$= .84, \qquad = 10\sqrt{1 - .84} = 4$$
$$= .64, \qquad = 10\sqrt{1 - .64} = 6$$
$$= .36, \qquad = 10\sqrt{1 - .36} = 8$$

Thus as the reliability coefficient decreases from .91 to .36, we can expect an individual's obtained score to fall, about two-thirds of the time, within a range of 3 to 8 score units above and below his true score on the test.

STANDARD ERROR OF A SCORE

Since all measurement contains error, it is important for the teacher to appreciate the size of the error of test scores. The error of an obtained score can be conceptualized by defining it as its probable deviation from the "true score," a score that would be obtained by an ideal, infallibly accurate measurement. Diederich has prepared a very useful aid for the do-it-yourself teacher in estimating the standard error of a score for tests which permit all students to respond to

[12] From Table 3 on p. 58, we saw that 68.26 percent, or approximately two-thirds of the scores would be expected to fall one standard deviation below the mean and one standard deviation above the mean.

all items, i.e., are unspeeded, "power" tests and in which the items have been scored 1 or 0. It must be realized that these are rough approximations. Nevertheless, they make the teacher aware of the large errors in test scores. There is some comfort in an observation once made by Bertrand Russell: "All science," he said, "is dominated by the idea of *approximation*. When a man tells you that he knows the exact truth about anything, you are safe in inferring that he is an *inexact* man."

The following tabulation gives approximate standard errors rounded to nearest whole numbers:

Approximate Standard Errors of Test Scores
(rounded to nearest whole number)

S.E. = 0   when score is zero or perfect

1   (a) when score is 1 or 2
    (b) within 2 points of perfect score

2   (a) on tests of less than 24 items
    (b) when score is 3–6 (and 7 with less than 45 items)
    (c) within 3–7 points of perfect score

3   (a) on tests of 24–27 items
    (b) when score is 8–15 (and 7 with 45 items or more)
    (c) within 8–15 points of perfect score

4   on tests of 48–89 items
5   on tests of 90–109 items
6   on tests of 110–129 items
7   on tests of 130–150 items

Except at extremes as noted above. Some high scores on these tests have been disregarded.

SOURCE. Paul B. Diederich, *Short-cut Statistics for Teacher-made Tests*, Princeton: Educational Testing Service, 1960.

The procedure used is explained and defended by Frederic M. Lord in "Do Tests of the Same Length Have the Same Standard Error of Measurement?"[13] It applies only to tests in which items are scored either 1 or 0, and does not apply to speeded tests. The formula may be written:

$$\text{S.E.} = \sqrt{\frac{\text{Number right} \times \text{number not right}}{1 \text{ less than number of items}}}$$

Except at extreme scores (as noted above), the chief determinant of

[13] *Research Bulletin* 56–7, Princeton: Educational Testing Service, 1956.

the standard error of a test score is the number of items in the test. For most classroom purposes, a test of less than 24 items has a standard error of 2; of 24–27 items, a standard error of 3; of 48–89 items, a standard error of 4, and so on. The most common exception will be "mastery tests" in which most of the scores are close to a perfect score. Then the figures for nearness to a perfect score determine the standard error.

Obtained scores fall within one standard error of true scores in two-thirds of the cases and within two standard errors in 95 percent of the cases. Differences of less than two standard errors between scores should not be regarded as significant. Obtained scores may vary to this extent by pure chance in random selection of items from a large pool of actual or potential items of the same sort. Intentional or unintentional differences between tests in abilities tested or difficulty level, stupid errors in test construction and scoring, and external circumstances that affect test performance are not included in the standard error.

A graphic illustration of the distribution of errors will help clarify the concept. Suppose that a teacher has given a test of 100 items and that the test conforms reasonably well to the Diederich specifications. Student John Doe has obtained a score of X. The theoretical distribution of error (S.E. = 5) for any student would look like Fig. 16.

Now, since the teacher cannot know where any student's score is

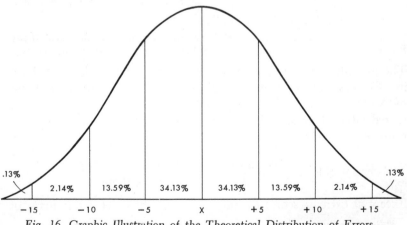

Fig. 16. Graphic Illustration of the Theoretical Distribution of Errors.

in this distribution, all he can do is make probability statements such as: "Any student's true score has approximately a two to one chance of being within plus or minus five score points of his obtained score."

$$34.13 + 34.13 \text{ vs. } 2(13.59) + 2(2.14) + 2(0.13)$$

The chances are about 99.7 out of 100 that any student's "true" score is the score that he achieved plus or minus 15.

$$2(34.13) + 2(13.59) + 2(2.14) \text{ vs. } 2(0.13)$$

ADMINISTRABILITY

The administrability of evaluation devices refers to the ease and accuracy with which the directions to pupils and evaluator can be followed. Requirements of good directions are noted in Chapter 8. Here we wish to point out the need for concern with administrability. An example of a highly valid and reliable test that is difficult to administer is the Stanford-Binet Intelligence Test. This test can be given to only one individual at a time and requires approximately one hour for the individual and about an hour and a half for the examiner. The directions for the examiner are very detailed and complex. Indeed, learning how to give and score this test usually requires a full one-semester university course.

In many tests the administration time is divided among several subtests with specific time limits. In such cases the examiner must be provided with an accurate timepiece with a second hand so that he will make no serious errors in administration. In speed tests especially, slight errors in timing can make the norms and interpretations worthless.

Other tests require little supervision by the examiner. These "self-administering" tests require merely passing out test papers, giving the starting and stopping signals, and collecting the papers. These tests are obviously desirable when tests are to be given in widely separated classrooms by examiners who differ greatly in testing ability. A further aid is to separate the directions to the pupils from the directions to the examiner so that the pupils will not be confused or distracted by material they do not need. For maximum administrability in schools, the time required for a test should preferably fit into the normal classroom period. Tests requiring more time than this may be more reliable and valid as a result of their additional length, but only at some sacrifice of administrability. Many test publishers have had to shorten their tests to meet this need. Obviously, these shortened tests must be more highly refined to reduce the sacrifice of validity and reliability to a minimum. The mechanical features of the test, such as the paper on which it is printed, the typography, and the spaces for pupils' responses, are further considerations.

The price of standardized tests also affects their administrability. Other things being equal, the best test is the cheapest test. But cost should always be figured in relation to test validity.

Administrability may often be increased—at least after the primary grades—by using separate answer sheets for pupils' responses. These answer sheets are easier to handle during scoring and they make it possible to use the test booklets more than once. Analysis of the time required to score a single test, the complexity of the operation, the provision of schemes for checking the scoring and summation of responses, throw light on the test's administrability. Evaluation devices whose cost of scoring is high may be severely limited in usefulness for many schools.

INTERPRETABILITY

The interpretability of an evaluation device refers to how readily scores may be derived and understood. The first step in interpreting a test is obviously applying the scoring key to obtain "raw" scores. Some of the considerations in maximizing scorability are discussed in Chapter 6. Obviously scoring is easiest when it requires merely the counting of simple marks or numbers. It takes more effort when weights and correction formulas must be applied. For a large-scale testing program the problem of scoring may assume considerable proportions. Numerous mechanical scoring devices have been invented to lessen this labor.

After the "raw" score has been obtained, it must be given meaning. Tables of norms are usually provided for this purpose. These norms and the groups on whom they are based must be considered in relation to the kinds of interpretation required. Some norms enable comparisons of pupils of the same and different ages, or grades, or other types of groupings. Norms may be provided for each part of a test so that separate scores may be interpreted. Here again we are concerned only with the need for considering interpretability in selecting evaluation devices. A fuller discussion of the interpretation of evaluation devices is presented in Chapter 6. Various kinds of norms were discussed in Chapter 3.

A TEST EVALUATION OUTLINE

Table 9 presents an outline for use in describing and evaluating any standardized test. The major headings follow those in this chapter. The reader will understand the ideas in this chapter better if he follows this outline with one or two tests. For some tests the information under various headings may be lacking or scanty; this outline will at least make the test user aware of what he does not know about a particular test.

Table 9. An Outline for Describing and Evaluating Tests

A. *Identifying Data*

1. Title:

2. Authors:

3. General purpose:

4. Group to which applicable:

5. Year of publication:

6. Cost, booklet:
   answer sheet:

7. Time required:

9. Publisher's name and address:

8. Forms available:

B. *Validity*

10. *Content:* Names of scores as given by authors, mental or behavioral function represented by each score as seen by present analyst of the test (response sets, speed), basis for selecting items, basis for scoring items (correction formulas, empirical weighting, etc.)

11. *Empirical* (concurrent, predictive, construct): Criteria, size and na-

B. Validity (continued)

ture of samples, correlation coefficients obtained; correlations with other tests, specifying subjects used, etc.

C. Reliability

12. Method of estimating (stability, equivalence, internal consistency), size and nature of sample, types and values of coefficients obtained.

D. Administrability

13. Rapport, special problems or methods in establishing:

14. Directions to test taker: Adequacy, clarity, etc.

15. Special problems: Timing, effect of practice or previous experience with test, mental sets to be sought, etc.

E. Interpretability

16. Provisions for scoring: Hand scoring keys, machine scorability, self-scorability, scoring costs, etc.

17. Norms: Type of derived score, size and nature of sample on which based.

18. Special interpretations: Cutting scores, meaning of various patterns of scores, need for local norms, etc.

F. Summary Evaluation

19. Comments of reviewers in Buros' *Yearbooks, Review of Educational Research,* research journals, etc.

20. Advantages and disadvantages in the local situation.

LABORATORY EXERCISES AND DISCUSSION QUESTIONS

1. How can a teacher determine the content and construct validity of his own tests?
2. Why are test manuals issued by the publishers often not an adequate source of information concerning tests?
3. According to the first Kuder-Richardson method, given on p. 129

what is the reliability of a test of 100 items on which the mean score is 50 and the standard deviation is 10? What is the reliability of a total test when the correlation between its halves is .60? Interpret these two coefficients.

4. Examine a copy of the California Achievement Test and a copy of the California Test of Mental Maturity for the same grade level. In what respects are they alike and different? Are the differences between them sufficiently important to teachers to justify administering both tests to all pupils?

5. Select several group intelligence tests intended for the same grade levels, for detailed comparisons with one another. What are their comparative merits?

6. Compare readiness tests with intelligence tests for primary-school pupils. What are the similarities and differences between them?

7. Using the test evaluation form on p. 139, and using only the information available from several catalogues of test publishers, evaluate five tests for your specific area of instruction. How much information does each catalogue give you concerning the criteria discussed in the text?

8. Repeat Exercise 7, using information available from specimen sets of the five tests. Examine the test manuals for information concerning the criteria discussed in the text. In what respects are the manuals adequate and inadequate?

9. Read the reviews in the *Mental Measurements Yearbook* for the tests selected for Exercises 7 and 8. On the basis of these three exercises write a thorough summary review of one of the tests.

10. Examine a so-called "diagnostic" test in your area of interest. How does it differ from a general achievement test? What makes the test diagnostic? Are there sufficient items in each subsection to provide reliable interpretation for diagnostic purposes?

SUGGESTED REFERENCES

Downie, N. M., *Fundamentals of Measurement*, New York: Oxford, 1958.

The concepts of reliability and validity and the statistical procedures for their determination are presented in Chapter 4. Chapters 12 and 13 offer constructive assistance in the selection of mental tests and tests for the evaluation of special abilities.

Educational Testing Service (Martin R. Katz), *Selecting an Achievement Test, Principles and Procedures,* Evaluation and Advisory Series, No. 3, Princeton: Educational Testing Service, 1958.

A broad survey at an intermediate level of technicality, especially in later sections on equality of score units, estimating true gain, and the like.

Lindquist, E. F. (ed.), *Educational Measurement,* Washington: American Council on Education, 1951.

Robert L. Thorndike, in Chapter 15, and Edward E. Cureton, in Chapter 16, discuss the theory of measurement as it applies to reliability and validity of tests. These discussions cover not only the basic considerations but the more advanced technical aspects as well.

Stanley, Julian C., *Measurement in Today's Schools,* Englewood Cliffs: Prentice-Hall, 4th ed., 1964.

Chapters 5 and 6 discuss characteristics of a satisfactory measuring instrument and general principles of test construction.

Technical Recommendations for Achievement Tests, Washington: National Education Association, 1955.

This bulletin, prepared jointly by the Committee on Test Standards of the American Educational Research Association and the Committee on Test Standards of the National Council on Measurements Used in Education, presents standards of professional practice in achievement testing for the guidance of both test producers and test users.

Technical Recommendations for Psychological Tests and Diagnostic Techniques, Suppl. to Psychol. Bull., 1954, 51, No. 2, Pt. 2.

This bulletin, prepared jointly by committees of the American Psychological Association, American Educational Research Association, and the National Council on Measurements Used in Education, presents standards of professional practice for those who wish to apply high standards of professional judgment in selecting and interpreting tests and for those who are constructing tests.

Thorndike, R. L., and Elizabeth Hagen, *Measurement and Evaluation in Psychology and Education,* New York: Wiley, 2nd ed., 1961.

Chapter 8 provides guides to sources of available tests and guides for evaluating them.

CHAPTER 6

Administration, scoring, and interpretation of tests

Rapport
Securing Rapport
Motivating Pupils

Obtaining Testing Materials

Preparation of Examiners

Steps in Administering Tests to Pupils
Avoiding Distractions
Distributing Tests to Examiners
Adhering to Directions
Timing
Supervision
Ending the Test
Making Notations
Security of Examinations

Scoring Evaluation Devices
Order of Scoring
Rescoring
Hand-Scoring Devices
Strip Keys. Window Stencils. Carbon or Pinprick. Machine-Scoring Stencil

Scoring Evaluation Devices (continued)
Machine Scoring Devices
Teacher vs. Commercial Agency Scoring

Recording Test Results

Using Test Results
Profiles

Precautions in Test Interpretation

The administration of a testing program has several distinct phases: (1) the establishment of rapport between teachers and pupils and the motivation of pupils; (2) obtaining testing materials and the preparation of examiners; (3) administration of tests to pupils; (4) the scoring of tests; (5) and use of the test results. The sections of this chapter take up these phases in turn.

RAPPORT

Rapport is an unconstrained relationship between pupil and teacher such that they are comfortable with and have confidence in each other. Rapport is necessary, in varying degrees, for the administration of all kinds of evaluation devices. Its absence means "nervousness" and inefficiency on the part of the pupil. He will not be able to do justice to his achievement. He may become so tense that he looks for absurd subtleties in the directions for the test. His ability to recall or recognize things he knows well may be "blocked."

Physicians have found that inadequate rapport between them and their patients results in increased pulse rate and blood pressure. Pupils taking physical examinations may attempt to deceive teachers concerning their posture, their health habits, or their general state of physical well-being. General and special mental ability may not be expressed fully if examiners do not establish rapport before giving ability tests. The importance of rapport in administering a self-inventory, a vocational interest questionnaire, or an attitude scale cannot be overemphasized. Rapport is needed throughout the evaluation program.

Securing Rapport

How can rapport be established and maintained? We can give no specific rules, because procedures vary with pupils, situations, and teachers. But the following discussion may help in the kinds of conditions frequently present in school testing.

For the pupil who is too highly motivated, so eager to perform well on a test that he becomes tense and inefficient, the teacher should deemphasize the testing situation and put it in its proper perspective. The lackadaisical pupil who does not take the testing situation seriously and will not exert his best efforts should be told about the importance of doing well. The discouraged pupil who has little hope of doing creditably on a test should be given encouragement in as subtle and friendly a way as possible; perhaps, to increase his confidence, he should be given a goal lower than the teacher knows he can achieve. The overconfident pupil who exerts less than his full effort may need to compare himself with higher standards. The pupil who is fearful or ashamed of the truth about himself may need to be reassured that the information will be considered confidential. For example, the teacher can tell him how frequently the same facts hold true of other pupils.

The teacher may need to point out the value of self-understanding as a basis for more adequate adjustment. He should adopt a completely noncritical, "nonmoral" attitude when appraising emotional and social adjustment.

In general, the teacher should give moderate encouragement and praise when evaluating intellectual or cognitive performance. Receptiveness and sympathetic understanding should keynote his role in evaluating physical aspects, emotional and social adjustment, attitudes, interests, environment, and background. The pupil should not be given the impression that in a certain respect he is good or bad, sinful or virtuous, desirable or undesirable. If such judgments are withheld, his hesitancy to talk about what is "on his mind" may be overcome and the basis laid for guidance in accordance with valid evidence.

The teacher's personality will determine how these general policies and procedures are expressed in any situation. Sincerity and honesty along with a "light touch" are necessary in all relationships with pupils. Encouragement and praise must always be natural and friendly, yet dignified. The teacher should be sensitive to the pupils' reactions to his approach and flexible in adapting to these reactions. In establishing and maintaining rapport there is no substitute for the teacher's "social intelligence."

When announcing that tests are to be given, the teacher should attempt to prevent them from assuming undue importance and creating crises. Teachers and pupils should take examinations "in their stride" rather than permit them to become the major focus of the educative process. The teacher should emphasize continuous, regular study habits as preferable to "cramming." He should explain that the purpose of evaluation is to find out how well pupils are achieving educational objectives so that schools can give them better help.

When testing fairly large groups, the examiner's preliminary remarks should place the test in its proper perspective. The uses of the results and their value to the pupil should all be explained. Preliminary instructions, to be read by the examiner, usually accompany standardized group tests. These concern the importance or unimportance of speed, the pupil's handling of items that are too difficult for him, the desirability of answering to the best of his knowledge items about which he is not certain, and similar points designed to establish the mental set most conducive to valid results. When tests do not provide such instructions, as in the case of teacher-made tests, they should be prepared in advance.

Motivating Pupils

Examinations can crystallize the social and self-criticism that the learning process needs. Through such criticism the form of the test can have crucial effects on the learning process. What the pupil expects the measure of his learning to be largely determines what he will seek to learn. If past experience leads him to expect that his learning will be evaluated by how much rote memorization he has done, then rote memorizing will be his method of study. If, on the other hand, he expects the test to measure ability to apply principles, interpret data, show broad "acculturation" in the lore of a subject, or demonstate technical skills, then he will direct his learning toward these ends. Thus evaluation affects not only the amount but also the *kinds* of learning.

Hence we can see both the dangers and the benefits latent in how tests motivate learning. Evaluation of insignificant, temporary outcomes of education leads to undesirable study habits. Evaluation of outcomes that are meaningful, long lasting, and congenial to a pupil's interests and capacities leads to desirable study habits. And since what is measured affects what will be learned, the decisions on what is to be measured are a vital part of the educational process.

OBTAINING TESTING MATERIALS

Standardized, externally made, and commercially available tests should be ordered well in advance of the date on which they are to be given, for it is desirable to plan the testing program several weeks in advance and have all the necessary materials on hand several days before giving the tests.

Orders for tests from a commercial publisher should include a complete description of the materials desired—the specific title of the test, as well as the date of publication, the form desired, the quantity needed, and the type of answer sheet. Instructions given in test publishers' catalogues for ordering test materials should be followed exactly, because the number of available tests is large, and there are several forms for many of the tests and often different types of accompanying answer sheets. Some publishers fill orders for any desired quantities, whereas others sell only packages of 25 or so. Since various publishers have different procedures, we give no specific illustrations here, but the reader is urged to study the catalogues for specific instructions.

PREPARATION OF EXAMINERS

When tests are administered to more than one classroom, as when a general achievement test is given on one day to all the pupils in a school, one person should have the responsibility for planning and executing the details of the testing program, making thorough preparations for every detail, and supervising each of the various steps in the test administration. If the whole school is to be tested at once or if several tests are to be given over a period of time, a schedule of hours and rooms in which specific tests will be given should be distributed to every teacher concerned in the testing program.

Each test administrator should receive a test manual and a sample copy of the test several days in advance and be urged to study the details of its administration. Every examiner should take the test himself, for this will make him better acquainted with the oral and written directions and with how the responses should be made.

Proctors should assist examiners when any testing room has more than 50 pupils. One proctor should be assigned for every 50 pupils to assist the examiner in handing out and collecting test materials and making sure that the pupils are following directions.

Before giving the test, each examiner should have a check list of his duties covering in proper order such procedures as (1) seating pupils, (2) announcing the nature and method of the test, (3) distributing writing materials, (4) distributing answer sheets, (5) distributing test booklets, (6) giving instructions for filling in names and other personal data, (7) reading aloud the general directions for the whole test, (8) giving the time limit for each subtest, (9) collecting the test booklets, answer sheets, and writing materials, and (10) packaging and forwarding the collected materials.

STEPS IN ADMINISTERING TESTS TO PUPILS

Administering a test or a battery of tests involves the following steps. We state them as they would apply to a comprehensive large-scale program for an entire school or school system. For smaller testing programs, as when one teacher gives his own students a test, many of these steps will be unnecessary or be modified in obvious ways.

Avoiding Distractions

Distractions during tests should, of course, be avoided as much as possible. A sign should be put on the door of the room warning visitors to keep out because testing is going on. Noises from the street or from other classrooms should be reduced if possible to the point where they no longer distract. Pupils should be informed if they are to disregard school bells and continue working past the regular school period.

Distributing Tests to Examiners

If more than one classroom is being tested at a time, the tests should not be distributed before the day of the examination. Packages for each classroom should be made up with the proper number of tests, answer sheets, special pencils, and other materials well in advance of the day set for testing.

Adhering to Directions

Strict adherence to the test manual regarding answering pupils' questions after a test has begun or assisting pupils with test items, unfamiliar words, or misunderstood directions is absolutely necessary with standardized tests if the scores are to be interpreted in the light of the norms provided. If the directions in the manual are violated, it may be impossible to tell whether the norms still apply.

Timing

Any time limits for the test should be followed carefully, using a watch or clock with a second hand, or a stop watch. Timepieces should be checked for accuracy. If possible, one of the proctors should also check the time throughout the test with his own timepiece. In timing tests the examiner should write down the exact hour, minute, and second at which the signal to start is given. He should also compute and write down the time for giving the signal to stop.

Supervision

While the pupils are working on the test, examiners and proctors should move about the room unobtrusively to make sure that everyone is recording his answers in the proper way and is working on the right part of the test. Watching a pupil over his shoulder or moving quickly about the room may distract pupils from their work.

Ending the Test

The examiner should make sure that all pupils stop work immediately when the time is up. The answer sheets, or test booklets if answers are recorded in them, should be collected first. Then all other testing materials should be collected.

Making Notations

After the testing materials have been collected, the examiner should make any necessary notations of abnormalities in the testing— whether anyone had to leave the room or showed marked anxiety, or whether there were such disruptions as a fire drill. Such notes are taken into account in interpreting the scores. In the case of standardized tests, the examiner should be especially careful to note any discrepancies between the conditions, directions, or time limits under which the test was administered and those stipulated in the test manual.

Security of Examinations

Whenever standardized tests are used, provisions should be made for their security. Many test publishers include instructions such as the following on the packages of tests, which are sealed when they are shipped:

To the Examiner: Keep these tests locked up and out of sight of examinees both before the examination and after. Remember that you may wish to give the same test again, or some other teacher may wish to give it, and the result of the later testings may be invalidated if stray copies of the test have fallen into the hands of students. [Instructions accompanying packages of the Stanford Achievement Tests.]

Tests are merely samplings of many learnings and the test maker did not intend that pupils be exposed to the learnings in a particular test until the test is administered. A number of practices should be followed in this respect. (1) Pupils should know some days in advance that they are to take a standardized test over a given *area* of work, and they should be informed of the purposes and general form of the test, but no reference should be made to its specific content. (2) It is also desirable, by means of practice exercises, to familiarize pupils with the mechanics of a standardized test before the actual test begins. This applies, however, only to the various *types* of objective test questions and the procedures for marking the answer sheets. (3) It is sometimes helpful to pass around a sample well-marked answer sheet before a test begins and to point out the possibility that pupils will lower their test scores if they do not mark the answer sheet properly.

Following an examination it is entirely proper and desirable to redistribute the corrected answer sheets and test booklets to a class for use in class discussion of the items and interpretation of the results. This practice calls the attention of the class to any group weaknesses in learning and may suggest a need for reteaching and relearning.

SCORING EVALUATION DEVICES

Despite the objectivity of scoring short-answer tests, certain procedures are indispensable if scoring is to be done with maximum accuracy and efficiency. The necessity for extreme care in scoring has been indicated by several studies showing that scoring errors occur with appalling frequency. Enough "constant" errors due to failure to understand scoring directions, with resultant scores which were consistently too low or too high, and "variable" errors due to carelessness in marking, adding, computing, or transcribing scores were found to warrant (1) the careful training and instruction of scorers and (2) the rescoring of at least a sample of any group of test booklets or answer sheets.

Order of Scoring

With essay tests it may be desirable to have one person score all tests on the first question, then all on the second, and so on. If for objective tests the answers are to be written directly into the test booklets instead of on separate answer sheets, the scorer may score a given page in all booklets first, then the next page, and so on, rather than scoring all of one booklet before going on to the next. If so many booklets must be scored that several scorers are needed, each person may specialize on a given page or group of pages of the booklet but should score only one page in all booklets at a time.

Rescoring

With a large number of booklets to be scored and sufficient help available, it is always worth while to rescore them so as to eliminate errors that otherwise are almost inevitable in a clerical task like this. If complete rescoring is not feasible, every fifth or tenth booklet should be rescored to get a rough idea of the frequency and magnitude of scoring errors. Rescoring a sample sometimes uncovers such inaccuracy as to make it desirable to rescore the remainder.

Hand-Scoring Devices

Before scoring can begin, scoring keys or stencils are needed. Standardized tests have scoring keys, stencils, or other devices which enable rapid and accurate scoring. These keys are of the following four major types.

Strip Keys. Strip keys are used with tests in which the answer spaces are aligned along one side of the page in the test booklet. They contain the correct responses in a vertical column on a narrow strip of paper and are used in scoring by placing them adjacent to the column of responses in the test booklet, as shown in Fig. 17.

Window Stencils. Window stencils are used when the answer spaces are scattered over the page of the test booklet rather than placed in a single column. The stencils usually consist of heavy paper or plastic in which holes are cut. When the stencil is placed over the page of the test booklet, the correct answer spaces show through the holes (Fig. 18). The scorer counts the number of pupil responses which agree with the correct answers on the stencil, thus obtaining the pupil's score for that page of the test. Frequently,

100. **avarice** [1] virtue [2] prominence

    [3] greed [4] honor _____ 100   100. 3

101. **eradicate** [1] destroy [2] vacate

    [3] use [4] solve _____ 101   101. 1

102. **impeachment** [1] prayer [2] burial

    [3] resignation [4] accusation _____ 102   102. 4

103. **discordant** [1] clashing [2] sad

    [3] unsteady [4] distinctive _____ 103   103. 1

104. **titanic** [1] reddish [2] acid

    [3] large [4] ancient _____ 104   104. 3

Fig. 17. Strip Key Device for Scoring a Test. (Reproduced by permission of the California Test Bureau.)

heavy black lines on the stencil connect the holes to guide the scorer's eye movements.

Carbon or Pinprick. Another set of scoring devices consists of test or answer sheets whose reverse side has been prepared in such a way that correct answers fall within circles or squares printed on that side. In the Clapp-Young Self-Marking Tests[1] answer sheets are attached to each page of the tests. The multiple-choice items are answered by placing an X in one of a row of small squares. The X is transferred by means of a thin coating of carbon on the reverse side of the answer sheet onto another sheet which contains only the squares for the correct answers. If the pupil writes his X in the correct square, it will show in the square on the second sheet. The teacher scores the tests simply by counting the number of X's in the

[1] Boston: Houghton Mifflin.

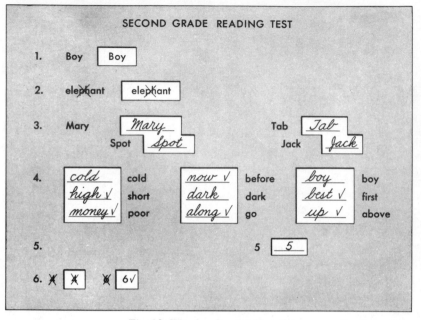

Fig. 18. Window-Scoring Stencil.

small squares on the second sheet. Under the name *Scoreze* (Fig. 19),[2] this technique is also used by the California Test Bureau for many of their tests.

In another scoring method, quite similar to the above, the pupil punches holes in the answer sheet, using a large-headed pin or a stylus. The teacher scores his answers by counting the number of holes which appear within the squares on the reverse side of the answer sheet. This method is used in one form of the Kuder Preference Record.

Machine-Scoring Stencil. On tests with a separate answer sheet, a machine-scoring stencil is used over the answer sheets in much the same manner as described above for the window stencils. This procedure is far more economical in both time and money than the carbon method. Scoring the carbon-type answer sheets requires counting the marks *inside* circles or squares on the back of the an-

[2] Monterey, California: California Test Bureau.

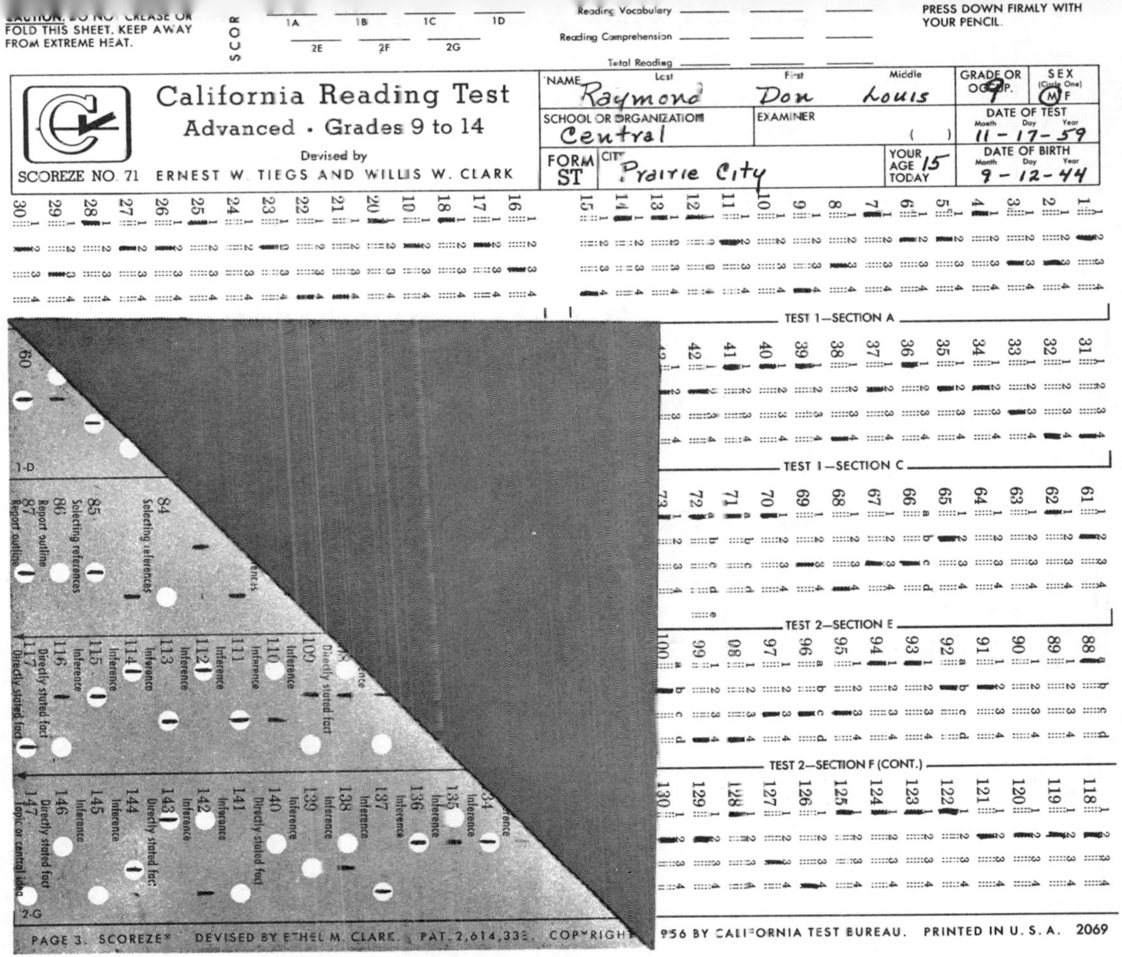

Fig. 19. Scoreze Answer Sheet. (Reproduced by permission of the California Test Bureau.)

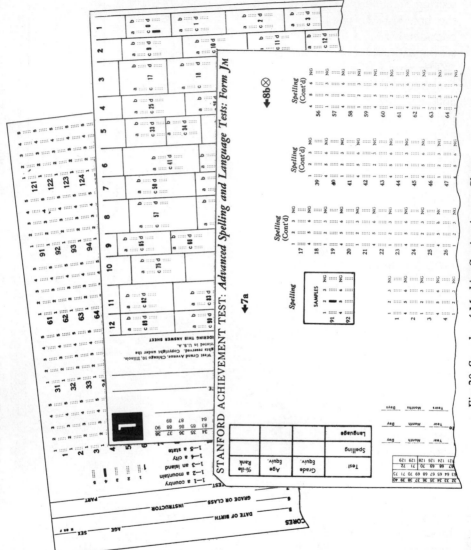

Fig. 20. Samples of Machine-Scoring Answer Sheets.

swer sheet and disregarding the other marks. Using the machine-scoring stencil requires only counting the marks showing through the holes in the stencils. The carbon-type answer sheets also cost considerably more than do the regular answer sheets used for machine scoring. Fig. 20 shows three machine-scoring answer sheets.

The answer sheet partially shown at the top is a standard IBM (International Business Machines) answer sheet especially adaptable to teacher-made tests. It provides for responses on 150 five-response items on a sheet approximately 9 by 11 inches in size. IBM also makes many other forms adaptable to specific purposes. The partial sheet shown in the center is an IBM answer sheet for Test 1 of the Iowa Tests of Educational Development. Note the conversion table along the top for immediate conversion of raw scores (the number of items answered correctly) to standard scores ranging from 1 to 38. The lower IBM answer sheet is used with the Advanced Spelling and Language Tests of the Stanford Achievement Test. Here the conversion table along the top is used to transform raw scores into grade-placement scores.

Machine-Scoring Devices

Several devices for machine-scoring answer sheets are now in use. Probably the best known at present is the International Test Scoring Machine[3] shown in Fig. 21. For tests to be scored by this machine the pupils' responses must be recorded with a special soft pencil whose marks will conduct electricity, and the answer sheet must be specially cut and printed. The answer sheet is scored by inserting it in the machine, pressing a lever to bring the sheet against contact units inside the machine, and reading the score registered by a needle on a meter. The machine can be set to distinguish between right and wrong answers by means of a window stencil prepared and inserted in it beforehand. Many different varieties of scoring formulas, part scores, and weighted scores can be obtained by setting various switches on the machine. International Test Scoring Machines are now available at many testing centers and university bureaus. For large-scale testing programs such machines often provide

[3] Manufactured by International Business Machines Corp., New York.

Fig. 21. The International Test Scoring Machine. (Reproduced by permission of IBM Corporation.)

the most accurate and least troublesome means of scoring objective tests.

The Digitek Corporation[4] has recently developed another type of scoring machine, the Digitek 100 Optical Reader, which feeds test or questionnaire answer sheets similar to the International Score Sheet at 2500 per hour, optically reads ordinary pencil mark responses and prints a formula computed score on the margin in one of ten available locations. (Other models are available which can handle 300 and 1750 answer sheets per hour.) The score key, which is a regular answer sheet premarked with the correct responses, can be inserted or removed in less than a minute and is easily filed for future use. Optional equipment is available for item analysis, punch-

[4] Digitek Corporation, Fairless Hills, Pennsylvania.

card or tape recording. With the optional equipment the Digitek Reader can be hooked up to an electronic computer for complete processing and printing of score reports. Scoring is much more rapid than by the older Test Scoring Machine, and the process of scoring, tabulating, and reporting scores is completely mechanical. This equipment can handle multiple test batteries for fairly large-scale testing programs and many types of research analyses. Fig. 22 illustrates a general type of answer sheet adaptable to a variety of different tests.

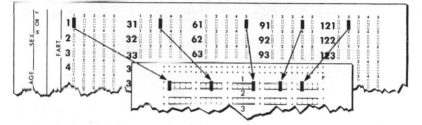

The standard 8½" x 11" answer sheet may be used. The number of choices for each question on the line is indicated by pencil marks on the key. However, special answer sheets and corresponding keys can be designed, provided the three lines per inch vertical spacing is maintained. Horizontally, response positions may be as close as .200 inch, providing 38 positions on the line.
All or any portion of any line may be used for response positions or left open for examples. The key is prepared with ordinary pencil and may be filed for future use. Several part scores of two digits maximum may be printed in a single pass on one side of the sheet. A blank line is left between parts.

Fig. 22. Digitek Optical Readers: Key and Answer Sheets with Printed Score. (Reproduced by permission of the Digitek Corporation.)

The Measurement Research Center in Iowa City uses the Iowa Electronic test processing equipment (Fig. 23) which performs, automatically and at high speed, practically all the clerical and statistical work involved in scoring and processing multiple test batteries for large-scale testing programs, test development, and measurement research in general. This equipment processes answer sheets at a basic rate of 6000 sheets per hour per scoring machine. The answer sheet design requirements are very flexible and can be readily adapted to nearly all tests now published. An answer sheet

Fig. 23. A Unit of the Electronic Test Processing Equipment at Measurement Research Center, Inc. (Reproduced by permission of Measurement Research Center, Inc.)

8½ by 11 inches can provide for a battery containing as many as 13 subtests with a total of over 800 five-response items (Fig. 24).

Teachers vs. Commercial Agency Scoring

There has been some controversy over whether teachers in the local school system should score the tests in a large standardized testing program or whether the answer sheets should be sent to a commercial agency for scoring and reporting scores. As an aid in further instruction, teachers usually want to know what questions each pupil misses. But when a number of standardized tests are used in the school testing program, the teachers as a rule do not feel close enough to the program to want to make a detailed analysis of how specific pupils answer specific questions on specific tests. Furthermore, when they are asked to score large numbers of answer sheets after regular school hours, they often feel that the task is an imposition. Although better arrangements of test items and the use of separate answer sheets with scoring stencils have greatly

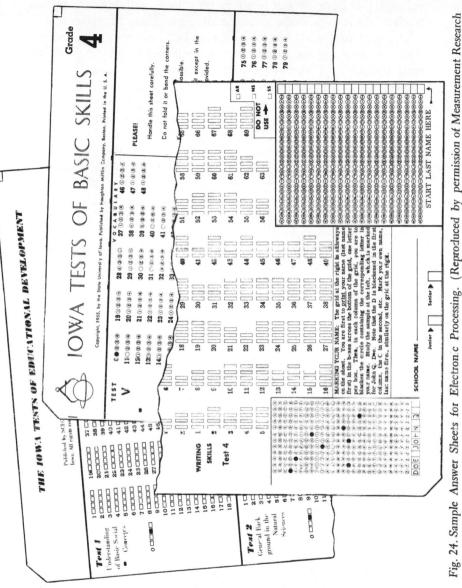

Fig. 24. Sample Answer Sheets for Electronic Processing. (Reproduced by permission of Measurement Research Center, Inc.)

reduced the labor of test scoring, the job is still tedious. Having teachers do it is perhaps a misuse of professional manpower.

The cost of having the tests scored by a commercial agency is relatively low—approximately 3 to 5 cents per pupil per score for most standardized tests. When the testing program is initiated, arrangements should be made so that funds will be available for the scoring process. If teachers were paid 3 to 5 cents per pupil per score, the typical teacher would probably be able to earn no more than $1.50 to $2.00 per hour. This is considerably less than he is being paid for his professional work as a teacher. Even if the school made some adjustment in the regular duties of teachers to give them time for scoring tests during regular school hours, the school would be paying a higher cost per pupil score than if the work were done by a commercial agency, although the payment would be in terms of teacher time rather than dollars and cents.

Scoring is usually more accurate and efficient when done by a commercial agency than by teachers. Great variation in accuracy is usual among teachers; some make relatively few errors in scoring, whereas others fail to be accurate in scoring at any time.

RECORDING TEST RESULTS

As soon as possible after the tests have been administered, they should be scored and checked, and the scores should be recorded on the permanent records of the school. Each teacher should be given copies of the score reports for the pupils in his classes. Usually schools have some type of permanent record for each pupil which provides space for recording standardized test results.

The form in which test results are recorded is often meaningless to anyone except the persons recording them. Sometimes permanent records for a pupil contain such information as the following:

| IQ | 104 | Mathematics | 97 |
| Reading | 68 | Science | 93 |

What do these scores mean? What test of intelligence was used? What was its standard deviation? Are the reading, mathematics, and science scores the raw scores, percentile ranks, grade placement scores, or some other type of standard or derived score? Unless the cumulative record contains complete information about the test and the type of score, the effort involved in carrying on a testing program, scoring the tests, and reporting the scores is practically wasted. If the records are to have value, the following must be indicated: test title, form of the test, date when the test was given, the raw score or standard score, and a grade placement or percentile rank under properly identifying captions. When percentile ranks are reported, the group on which the norms were based should be identified—for example, a national, state, district, local, or other group—and the nature of the group should be specified. Fig. 25 shows a cumulative record card

43. EDUCATIONAL TEST DATA—SENIOR HIGH

PL.	*DATE	GRADE	*TEST NAME & FORM	*SCORE	C.A.	%ILE	GR. PL.
	11/59	9	Reading	Incomplete			68
			Math				97
			Science				93
	11/59	9	Stanford Ach-Adv. Bat.-J				
Complete			Para. Mean	27	15-4	20	70
			Word. Mean	22	"	10	67
			Total Reading				68
			Arith. Reas.	34	15-4	55	95
			Arith. Comp.	35	"	60	100
			Total Math				97
			Science	56	15-4	50	93

44. SCHOLASTIC CAP. TEST DATA (INTELLIGENCE TEST)

*DATE	GRADE	*TEST NAME & FORM	C. A.	M. A.	INDEX
11/59	9	California			104
11/59	9	CTMM-Sec. '57 S-Form			
		Language	184	166	90
		Non-language	184	217	118
		Total	184	191	104

45. PERSONALITY OR SPECIAL INTEREST TESTS

DATE	GRADE	TEST	RESULT

Fig. 25. Section of a Cumulative Record Card Showing Completely and Incompletely Recorded Test Data.

with the above test results recorded both completely and incompletely. Many test-scoring agencies now provide "press-on" labels for each student on which his name and test scores with all the necessary identification data are printed. These may be ordered in sets so that copies are available for sticking on the cumulative record, on score interpretation reports to parents and pupils, and on other records for teachers and counselors. By using "press-on" labels many errors in transcribing score reports are avoided and the process of record keeping is considerably simplified.

When standardized tests are used, the teacher should receive a list report of the scores of each pupil in his class so that he may better understand and work with his pupils. Unless teachers use the information provided by the school testing program, the program is of little use. Whatever the record-keeping system, the records should be easily accessible to teachers, guidance and counseling personnel, supervisors, and administrators.

USING TEST RESULTS

We discuss here the use of standardized test results to help students understand themselves better, to explain pupil growth and development to parents, and to assist the teacher in planning instruction.

When students take standardized tests they are usually seriously interested in knowing how well they did. Their interest is highest immediately after the test. Thus, if teachers wish to use test results with optimum effectiveness, the sooner they report the scores to students the greater is the likelihood that students will use them to advantage. It is better to discuss test results in personal conferences with students, but this is a time-consuming process that most teachers find difficult. In most cases, the teacher can discuss results effectively in meetings with groups of students. He should talk individually with students with special problems and with those whose scores deviate considerably from the class average.

Profiles

Many test publishers provide cards or leaflets upon which test results can be plotted in *profile* form. These profiles assist students in understanding the results of the tests. They give the student a meaningful picture of his strengths and weaknesses in various areas of a battery of tests. Any test battery, such as the Differential Aptitude Tests (DAT) (20), implies the use of "profiles" as a basis for guidance. Fig. 26 shows a student's eight percentile scores plotted on a chart. The general height, or *level*, of the profile indicates the general ability level. The "jaggedness" of the profile, i.e., the degree of the *scatter* of its various points around the average position of all eight, tells how much the student differs "within" himself. The *shape* of the profile indicates the pattern of his abilities. These three characteristics of the profile may vary somewhat independently of one another. All three must, of course, be taken into account in counseling from profiles. To assist counselors and teachers in using such

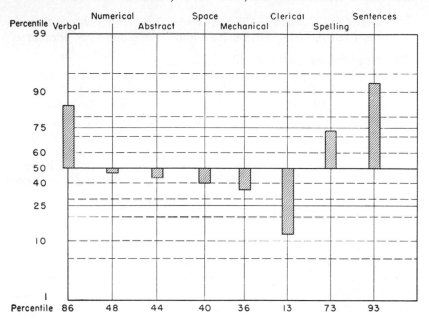

Fig. 26. DAT Profile of Ellsworth Newcomb. (Reproduced by permission of the Psychological Corporation.)

profiles, the authors of the battery have prepared a booklet[5] containing a series of illustrative cases, one of which follows.

Illustrative Case Analysis—Ellsworth Newcomb, Grade 12

Problem

Ellsworth wanted help in changing his career plans, since his low mathematics grades caused him to question his plans for engineering.

Tests

Differential Aptitude Tests. Grade 12.

An *Otis* test. Grade 12. IQ-120.

Ohio State University Psychological Examination. Grade 12. 69th percentile on college freshman norms.

Kuder Preference Record. Grade 12. Highest areas: Literary, Persuasive, Social Service; low areas: Mathematics, Science. (Actual scores not reported.)

[5] G. K. Bennett, H. G. Seashore, and A. G. Wesman, *Counseling from Profiles, a Casebook for the Differential Aptitude Tests,* New York, Psychological Corp., 1951.

Strong Vocational Interest Blank. Grade 12. A ratings: Social Science Teacher, Personnel Manager, Public Administrator, and three sales fields.

Report of counseling in Grade 12

Ellsworth's engineering aspirations had arisen in part from advice given him by a local industrialist. His mathematics grades were A, D, C, and C, indicating difficulty with a subject crucial to engineering. His work experiences had been in selling; he had found this work pleasant and had done well at it. When Ellsworth and his parents reviewed the whole situation, Ellsworth decided to drop his plans for engineering and prepare for business administration. His low Clerical rating was observed but was not considered crucial to the decision. His high verbal ability and language skills, his successful work experience, and his personal qualities argued for this choice. He was later graduated in the second fifth of his class, and he is now in college.

Comments

Open-minded parents can be persuaded by facts—facts from achievement records, from work experiences, from job descriptions, from interest questionnaires, and from aptitude test results. In this case the data added up to a consistent pattern that suggested college-level training but not in engineering. Whether he should study business administration or should complete a general liberal arts course with a social science or language major would be a matter of choice. If he had not wanted to go to college, on-the-job learning in industry or business (perhaps in selling) would have been consonant with his abilities and interests.

One cannot help remarking that while well-meaning, successful persons in the community can be helpful to the school counselor, they sometimes may mislead young people because of their halo as advisers. Most counselors like to enlist the aid of local business and professional men, but the wise choice of such volunteers is not easy. The self-chosen vocational counselor can present embarrassing problems.

Ellsworth solved his problem neatly, partly because of the detailed information yielded by the *Differential Aptitude Tests.* Like the DAT Verbal and Language Usage scores, the OSU [Ohio State University Test] rating indicated college ability. Useful as such a single-score test can be, the DAT and interest test profiles were much more specific in providing a basis for choosing among possible college opportunities.[6]

Fig. 27 shows a sample profile based on results from the California Achievement Tests for a girl in the lower fifth grade. The profile

[6] *Ibid.*

California Achievement Tests

Elementary · GRADES 4-5-6 · **Form W**

DEVISED BY ERNEST W. TIEGS AND WILLIS W. CLARK

Name _Rogers, Elaine C._
Last / First / Middle

Grade _L 5_

School _Central_ City

Date of Test _Nov. 22, 1959_
Month / Day / Year

Teacher or Examiner _Mr. Dow_ (Room _61_) Pupil's Age _10_

Date of Birth _Jan. 18, 1949_
Month / Day / Year

See MANUAL for instructions.

DIAGNOSTIC PROFILE* (Chart Pupil's Scores Here)

TEST	SECTION	POSSIBLE SCORE	PUPIL'S SCORE		
1. READING VOCABULARY	A. Mathematics	12	8		
	B. Science	13	6		
	C. Social Science	12	4		
	D. General	13	6		
	TOTAL (A+B+C+D)	50	24	5.0	40
2. READING COMPREHENSION	E. Following Directions	20	14		
	F. Reference Skills	20	6		
	G. Interpretations	30	17		
	TOTAL (E+F+G)	70	37	5.3	50
	READING GRADE PLACEMENT			5.2	50
3. ARITHMETIC REASONING	A. Meanings	15	9		
	B. Signs and Symbols	15	10		
	C. Problems	15	9		
	TOTAL (A+B+C)	45	28	6.1	80
4. ARITHMETIC FUNDAMENTALS	D. Addition	20	12		
	E. Subtraction	20	9		
	F. Multiplication	20	6		
	G. Division	20	5		
	TOTAL (D+E+F+G)	80	32	5.7	70
	ARITHMETIC GRADE PLACEMENT			5.9	80
5. MECHANICS OF ENGLISH	A. Capitalization	37	10		
	B. Punctuation	34	8		
	C. Word Usage	35	18		
	TOTAL (A+B+C)	106	36	3.9	20
6. SPELLING	TOTAL SPELLING	30	14	5.3	50
	LANGUAGE GRADE PLACEMENT			4.6	30
	Handwriting			5.0	
	BATTERY GRADE PLACEMENT			5.2	50
	CHRONOLOGICAL AGE GR. PL.			5.6	
	ACTUAL GRADE PLACEMENT			5.2	
	INTELL. (M.A.) GRADE PLACE.			5.3	

Grade Placement — 2.0 3.0 4.0 5.0 6.0 7.0 8.0 9.0
Percentile Rank —
Grade Placement

*For an interpretation of green area within Profile, see discussion on Articulation in Part 4 of Manual.

†Column designed for recording Expected Grade Placements, Anticipated Grade Placements, School or Class Averages, etc. See Part 2 of Manual.

Fig. 27. Sample Profile. (Reproduced by permission of the California Test Bureau.)

graphically illustrates grade placement scores—the pupil's achievement in reading, arithmetic, and language. Thus it reveals subject areas in which this girl is strong, typical, or weak, compared to a chosen criterion. The relative positions of the score representations in subsections of each of these three areas make possible a more refined and diagnostic picture of the pupil's achievement in the three major areas. At this point we must interject a caution regarding the interpretation of subtest scores. Because of the limited number of items (10 to 25), scores on the subsections of the test should be used only as guides to indicate pupil difficulties in the major diagnostic areas. The vertical line on the sample profile connects points representing a grade placement of 5.2 (second month of the fifth grade) at the time the test was administered. At first glance this pupil seems to show considerable variability within herself in the different areas and subsections. However, in interpreting any profile the teacher must take into consideration the standard error of measurement, which indicates how much he can expect the pupil's obtained score to vary from her "true" score (see p. 134).

The manual for the test gives the standard error of measurement, in grade placement scores, for the various sections of the test. Although it varies somewhat from section to section, approximately a .5 grade placement score can be used in interpreting all sections. Merely because of the imperfect reliability of the test, the "true" score for this girl can be expected to fall within one standard error (or within one-half grade placement score) above and below the obtained score on any section about two-thirds of the time. Thus, there seems to be a real difference between language and arithmetic achievement, with a weakness in language and especially in the mechanics of English, and a strength in arithmetic, especially in arithmetic reasoning.

Fig. 28 illustrates the procedures of presenting a profile in terms of standard scores in card form, with percentile ranks for a nationwide group norm indicated for strategic levels. The battery of nine tests of the Iowa Tests of Educational Development was given to this eleventh-grade girl. The top of the card shows her scores in standard score form; the solid line in the profile represents them graphically. In this case the average scores for her class were also plotted by a dot-dash line. The dot-dash line indicates that this particular class is quite close to the 50th percentile of the group norm. Thus this girl is above both the average of her class and the national average in Tests 1, 3, 5, 7, and 9, and below both in Tests 2 and 4. Her composite score on Tests 1–8 is slightly higher than the class and national average. Since the probable error of measurement on this test is approximately one standard score, the relative strengths

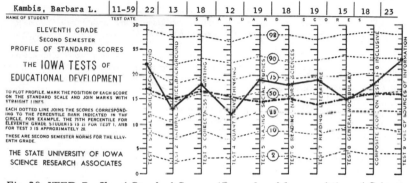

Fig. 28. ITED Profile of Standard Scores. (Reproduced by permission of Science Research Associates.)

and weaknesses of this pupil are readily identified. She is definitely weaker in science and mathematics than in other areas, and below her classmates' average in these areas; but she shows definite strength in the social studies, reading, and using sources of information.

Some test publishers try to provide students with useful information for interpreting test results. Fig. 29 shows the back of an answer sheet for the mathematics test of the Iowa Tests of Educational Development, on which is printed a table of percentile ranks corresponding to given standard scores and a statement to the student explaining what his score means. The standard score of 12, made by the girl in the above illustration, is shown as the equivalent of the 33rd percentile rank for the eleventh grade. Many teachers let students circle their own percentile ranks and take the sheets home for their parents' information.

Some standardized instruments are "self-scoring," in the sense that

PERCENTILES

Score	First Semester				Second Semester			
	9	10	11	12	9	10	11	12
30								99
29				99				98
28				98			99	97
27				97			98	96
26			99	96		99	98	95
25		99	98	95	99	98	96	92
24		97	96	91	98	96	94	89
23	99	96	94	89	98	95	92	85
22	98	93	90	85	96	92	88	80
21	96	91	86	80	94	88	83	76
20	95	88	83	76	92	86	80	72
19	93	85	78	71	89	82	75	65
18	89	80	72	65	85	76	69	58
17	85	73	65	57	80	69	61	53
16	82	67	59	51	75	63	55	47
15	77	62	52	45	70	57	49	40
14	69	52	43	37	62	48	40	34
13	65	47	38	32	57	43	36	30
12	60	43	(33)	28	52	39	31	25
11	50	35	27	22	43	31	25	20
10	44	30	22	18	38	26	20	16
9	39	24	18	15	32	22	16	13
8	31	20	14	12	26	17	13	10
7	25	15	11	9	20	13	10	8
6	19	11	8	7	16	10	8	6
5	14	8	6	4	11	7	5	3
4	9	5	4	3	7	4	3	2
3	6	3	2	1	4	2	2	1
2	3	1	1		2	1	1	
1	2				1			

What your score means

In this day and age, knowing how to solve practical quantitative problems is almost as important as knowing how to read a newspaper. Sooner or later, we all will have to do such things as estimating expenses on home repairs, handling business details, and figuring out costs on insurance and installment buying. This test measures your ability to use arithmetic and mathematics to solve practical problems.

To see how you stand on this test, find your score on the back of this page. Circle this number in the column labelled "Score" at the left. **Read across from your score to the column for your grade and semester. Circle the number in this column.** This is your percentile rank. It shows what per cent of students in your grade all over the country made scores lower than yours. If your percentile rank is around 50, you are about average. This means that approximately half the students in your grade made lower scores than you did.

Ask your teacher to help you decide what to do about improving your score. You will need to study your course grades, scores on other tests, and your plans for the future before deciding what to do.

A high score is a challenge to do better work than the average student. It may mean that you find mathematics especially interesting and should consider a career that requires mathematical ability. You can do extra reading in encyclopedias and college mathematics books. You will probably be interested, too, in reading biographies of famous mathematicians. If you think you want to do mathematical work as an adult, now is the time to prepare for it.

If your score is low, you need to find out *why* it is low. Ask your teachers and your guidance counselor to help you. Do you get the wrong answer because you make mistakes in arithmetic? What kinds of mistakes do you make most often? Is it difficult for you to decide how to set up the problem at the very beginning? Is this the result of poor reasoning or because you didn't read the question carefully?

If you make computational errors, learn how to check your work—and then check and double check it. First see if the answer makes sense and then check that it is exactly right. For example, does $123 \times 14 = 1,722$ or 11,722? Since $100 \times 10 = 1,000$, 11,722 can't be right. Is 1.722 exactly right? Divide 14 into 1,722 to find out.

Learning how to get started at the beginning of a problem is more complicated. You will need plenty of help from your teachers. However, two things usually help in all problem work. First, when someone helps you with a problem, don't be satisfied with just learning *how* to do the problem. Keep working until you know *why* it is done that way. Second, always have the entire problem in mind before you start working it. Working on a problem bit by bit usually leads you up blind alleys. Always remember that practice makes perfect. You will find many quantitative problems in courses and in leisure-time activities. Use every chance you get to develop this important ability.

IBM FORM I.T.S. 1100 B 2508-2

Fig. 29. Score Interpretation on Back of Answer Sheet. (Reproduced by permission of Science Research Associates.)

170

PROFILE LEAFLET

KUDER PREFERENCE RECORD
VOCATIONAL AND PERSONAL

FORMS CH, CM   FORMS AH, AM

FOR BOYS (TURN TO PAGE 2 FOR GIRLS' PROFILE)

You probably completed both forms of the Preference Record—
the **Vocational** and the **Personal**—so you may read and follow
the directions given below. If you completed only one form, follow
the instructions for that form only.

VOCATIONAL

1. In this series of numbers, circle the number that corresponds
to the V-score on the back page of your **Vocational** answer pad:
38   39   40   41   42   43   44.
If your V-score is not in this series, tell your adviser. He may want
you to fill out the **Record** again. If your V-score is circled, go on
to Step 2.

2. Copy the scores 0 through 9 from your answer pad in the boxes
at the top of the chart. Be sure to put score 0 in the box marked 0,
score 1 in the box marked 1, and so on.

3. In each column, find the number that is the same as your score
at the top of that column. Draw a line through the number, from
one side to the other of the column. If your score is larger than
any number in the column, draw a line across the top of the column,
if it is smaller, draw a line across the bottom.

4. With your pencil, blacken the entire space between the lines
you have drawn and the bottom of the chart.

PERSONAL

1. In this series of numbers, circle the number that corresponds
to the V-score on the back page of your **Personal** answer pad:
46   47   48   49   50   51   52.
If your score does not appear in this series, tell your adviser. He
may recommend that you fill out the **Record** again. If your V-score
is circled, go on to Step 2.

2. Copy the scores A through E in the proper boxes at the top of
the profile chart.

3. In each column, find the number that is the same as your score
at the top of the column. Draw a line through the number, from
one side to the other of the column. If your score is larger than
any number in the column, draw a line across the top of the chart;
if it is smaller, draw a line across the bottom.

4. With your pencil, blacken the entire space between the lines
you have drawn and the bottom of the chart.

Now you have a profile of your interests. An interpretation of your
profile will be found on pages 3 and 4.

Fig. 30. Pupil-Made Profile of Interests. (Reproduced by permission of Science
Research Associates.)

TEST SCORE PROFILE

Scores of: _JOE QUAIL_   Sex: _M_
M. or F.

Interpretation: Scores profiled here are **bands** rather than points. The midpoint of each band shows approximately what percentage of students in the norming group earned scores lower than the one profiled. Each band covers two standard errors of measurement, one above and one below the percentile rank score earned. This means that the chances are 2-to-1 that the student's "true" score lies within the range of the band.

If the bands of the student's verbal and quantitative scores overlap, there is probably no important difference between the scores. If the two bands do **not** overlap, the chances are about 5-to-1 that there is a real difference in measured ability present. (See *Manual* for additional information on interpretation.)

Directions for Profiling Scores:

1. Be sure the opposite edge of the profile sheet is folded along the crease so that the circled scores can be read.
2. Copy the encircled scores (verbal, quantitative, and total) in the proper boxes at the bottom of this profile sheet.
3. Fill in the test data required in the heavy black rectangle (test form number, date of testing, grade or class) and the type of norms used; *i.e.*, "Grade 10, public school, end of year," "college freshmen, men, end of year," etc.
4. Place the proper PLOTTING KEY upon the profile so that its bottom edge is even with the guide line near bottom of profile.
5. Move the PLOTTING KEY laterally until the three slots of the norms you want are exactly over the open spaces to the left of the three percentile rank scales: V, Q, and T. (You should *not* see the percentile rank numbers through the slots.)
6. Make a small horizontal pencil mark on the profile sheet (through the slot of the key) for each of the student's three scores, placing each mark exactly opposite the position of the earned score on the PLOTTING KEY. These marks show the percentile rank equivalents of the student's scores.
7. Using the scale on the opposite side of the slot as a measure of length, shade a segment of the column on the profile sheet so that the score mark is exactly in the middle (see directions on PLOTTING KEY). Do this for each of the three scores.
8. Remove PLOTTING KEY and write percentile rank equivalents of scores in the boxes near bottom of profile. (See *Manual* for illustration and full directions for profiling these and other test scores.)

School & College Ability Tests

Form No. _2A_   Date _5/20/58_
Grade or Class _10_
Norms Used _Public School_
END OF YEAR

VERBAL	QUANTI-TATIVE	TOTAL SCORE

Other Tests Administered

Title _ _ _ _   _ _ _ _   _ _ _ _   _ _ _ _
Date _ _ _ _   _ _ _ _   _ _ _ _   _ _ _ _
Form _ _ _ _   _ _ _ _   _ _ _ _   _ _ _ _
Norms _ _ _ _   _ _ _ _   _ _ _ _   _ _ _ _

PERCENTILE RANKS		
80	68	77
SCORES		
Verbal	Quant.	Total
287	295	291

Guide Line

N75R100

Fig. 31. SCAT Profile Illustrating True-Score Bands. (Reproduced by permission of Educational Testing Service.)

172

the student can take the test, score it himself, and construct his own profile. A profile for a test of this type is shown in Fig. 30. The Kuder Preference Record is a self-administered and self-scored interest inventory. After the scoring procedure the pupil makes his own profile according to instructions on the profile sheet. When he fills in and blackens the columns of the various interest areas from the bottom to the top of their corresponding scores, the high and low interest areas are obvious. This pupil's interests are high in mechanical and scientific areas, and lower in the persuasive, artistic, literary, and musical areas. The manuals accompanying this inventory give instructions for interpreting these interest areas.

The Educational Testing Service, publishers of the Cooperative tests, has developed a system of *bands* for improving the interpretation of profiles on some of their tests. The School and College Ability Tests (SCAT) and the Sequential Tests of Educational Progress (STEP) both provide profiles with bands covering two standard errors of measurement, one above and one below the percentile rank score earned. The chances are 2 to 1 that a student's "true" score will lie within the range of the bands. If the bands of a student's verbal and quantitative scores on the profile for SCAT overlap, there is little assurance that the difference between the scores is not due merely to chance. However, if the two bands do not overlap, the chances are about 5 to 1 that there is a real, or nonchance, difference in measured abilities. Fig. 31 illustrates the use of the "true-score" bands in SCAT. Note that although there is an apparent difference between the verbal and quantitative raw scores, there is no assurance of a real difference between the "true" scores for this student, since the two bands overlap.

PRECAUTIONS IN TEST INTERPRETATION

Perhaps most important of all, the teacher should give preference to tests whose norms have been made comparable to those of other tests. Either such tests have all been standardized on one group of pupils, or else their norms have been equated to one another by means of an anchor test.[7] The manuals of the tests that offer this

[7] An anchor test is one to whose norms the norms of other tests are equated.

great advantage in interpretability usually contain information as to this comparability.

Test users should not accept test norms at face value. They should attempt to evaluate all available data concerning the sample of pupils used in deriving them. When selecting standardized tests, educators should give preference to tests standardized on large representative samples of pupils.

Remember that norms are based on frequency distributions and that, in general, half of any group of pupils falls below its average and half above it. A norm is not the "ideal performance" of a group of pupils; it is only the typical performance of typical students at a given time. Hence educators should avoid the fallacy of insisting on "bringing everyone up to the norm." School practices resulting from attempts to get all pupils to be like the "average" have held back many superior students and created emotional problems among the less able. Such practices have caused much criticism of American education through the years; even Benjamin Franklin is reported to have said that "the schools are polishing the bricks and dulling the diamonds."

Many local factors should be taken into account when interpreting the standing of pupils according to norms derived on a nationwide basis. Among these factors are (1) the legal age for entering school, (2) the average age of actually entering school, (3) promotion and retardation policies, (4) rate and selectivity of elimination from school, (5) efficiency of the teaching personnel, (6) the grade placement, time allowances, and general nature of the curricula, (7) the standing of local pupils in mental ability and other aspects related to the one being evaluated, (8) the relative emphasis in the local school on academic, social, and vocational development, and (9) the home background of pupils. The meaning of the derived scores for a given group of pupils can then be interpreted in the light of these factors.

When interpreting the performance of individual pupils or of a class as a whole, the teacher should take into special consideration differences in cultural background of families and communities. There are wide variations in the kinds of experiences pupils have. We can expect that differences in language background, richness of home resources, and intensity of the desire for an education will be reflected in pupil performance.

The performance of pupils also varies with varying emphasis on different aspects of the school curriculum. In some subject-matter areas, such as arithmetic, the teacher usually cannot expect his pupils to progress any more rapidly than the rate at which he presents instructional materials; in other areas, such as reading, there are many opportunities for students to develop skills and knowledge on their own outside the school program. Thus, the performance of individuals and groups should be judged, in part at least, on the basis of the curriculum to which they have been exposed. When the performance of a class or an individual deviates considerably from the norms on standardized tests, reappraisal of the school curriculum and of teaching emphases may be indicated. In many practical situations it is necessary to use norms whose applicability to local conditions is questionable or unknown. To the extent that this is so, the data obtained from them cannot be interpreted meaningfully for individual pupils. There is a way out of this difficulty, however; the teacher may compute *local norms* by the methods outlined in Chapter 3.

A final precaution is to avoid using tests to punish pupils or to foster a spirit of rivalry among pupils, teachers, or schools. Teachers and administrators must keep the welfare of pupils uppermost and be sensitive to the requirements of adequate human relations. Failure to do this in administering and interpreting a testing program has produced negative feelings about tests in both pupils and teachers. Lennon has presented eight specific causes of tension between pupils and teachers:

Improper use of tests, leading to anxiety among pupils and harmful to healthy pupil-teacher relations, stems largely from (1) lack of understanding of the proper role of tests, often accompanied by some insecurity on the part of the teacher herself; and (2) failure to appreciate the emotional problems posed for some children by any ego-threatening procedure.

To be specific:

1. If a teacher looks upon the norm on a standardized test as a goal to be reached by all children, and criticizes those who fail to meet this rigid standard, the pupils will quite naturally come to think of tests as hurdles rather than stepping stones to development.
2. If a teacher in interpreting test results fails to take into account other

relevant information—ability differences, health, status, home background, and the like—she is likely to render an unjust appraisal of a child's work which may well have the effect of discouraging or antagonizing the child.

3. If a teacher overemphasizes tests in her evaluation program, and fails to realize that they cover only a part of the desired outcomes, she runs the risk of placing undue emphasis on certain objectives and of confusing the pupil as to what he is supposed to be learning.

4. If a teacher habitually uses test results as bases for insidious comparisons among pupils, not only is the pupil-teacher relationship damaged, but also the relationships among the pupils.

5. If a teacher berates or scolds a child because of poor performance on a test, she may be building up unfavorable attitudes toward future testing.

6. If a teacher fails to let a pupil know how he did on a test, or give him any indication of how the testing is related to *his* purposes, it is hard for the pupil to make sense of the procedure.

7. If a teacher is herself insecure, and feels threatened by the tests, it is almost certain that her attitude will be communicated to the children. If a school- or system-wide program is in operation, in the planning of which the teacher has had no part, and the purposes of which she does not understand, she is obviously in no position to make clear to the pupils how the testing is likely to do them any good. If the test results are used as a means of appraising teacher competency, the temptation becomes very strong for the teacher to teach for the tests.

8. If a teacher is unsympathetic to a testing program in which she must participate, and makes slighting or sarcastic reference to "these tests that we have to give again," she is certainly engendering a poor attitude on the pupils' part; even young pupils are shrewd enough to sense, however vaguely, that by such behavior the teacher is abdicating her rightful position.[8]

These comments also apply to teacher-administrator relationships and to the school administrator's approach to testing. Using tests for teacher evaluation is quite likely to produce the same type of tensions among teachers as are mentioned above for pupils. In short, proper attitudes toward testing should contribute to good relationships among pupils, teachers, and administrators.

[8] Roger T. Lennon, Testing: Bond or barrier between pupil and teacher, *Test Service Bulletin No. 82,* New York: Harcourt, Brace & World, adapted from *Education,* September, 1954. Used by permission of Bobbs-Merrill Company.

LABORATORY EXERCISES AND DISCUSSION QUESTIONS

1. Why should a teacher's merit not be judged solely on the basis of his pupils' scores on standardized achievement tests? Or on the basis solely of their improvement on such tests?
2. Give reasons for and against informing pupils whether a forthcoming test is to be of the short-answer or the essay type.
3. What working relationships exist in your community between employment services, public and private, and the schools whose pupils must eventually seek jobs through them? How can these relationships be improved?
4. How would you use the results of a testing program to interpret your school to the community? What would you do about the areas in which your school is about "average," outstanding, or below average?
5. The following project may be highly instructive as a major project for some teachers: Set up a plan for organizing a testing program in a school. Assume that you have all levels from kindergarten through high school. The enrollment of the school is approximately 800 pupils: about 70 per elementary grade, and 60 per grade in high school. No systematic testing program has been in effect previously. As director of the program, how would you establish the purposes of the program (list them)? What instruments would you use? How would you go about getting the program planned, installed, and administered? What uses would you make of the test results? Assume that you have a budget of $500 for the first year.
6. How would you deal with a parent who believes that the schools are doing too much testing and not enough teaching and that teachers ought to do what they are paid for doing?
7. As a class project, make a study of the content validity of a standardized achievement test for a given grade level or area of instruction. Devise an "answer sheet" with three columns of responses for each item. Read each item of the test and place check marks in Columns 1 and 2 if you can answer the following questions affirmatively, and a zero if your answer is negative. Indicate the value of the item in Column 3.

> Col. 1: Are the knowledges, skills, and mental processes required to answer this item being taught in my grade (or class) this year?
>
> Col. 2: Should the "average" pupil in my grade (or class) be able to answer this item correctly?

Col. 3: How important are the knowledges, skills, and mental processes required to answer this item correctly? (Mark 4 for very high, 3 for high, 2 for low, and 1 for very low. Add all values on the test and find the average importance value of the test.)

Compare different tests by this procedure.

SUGGESTED REFERENCES

Downie, N. M., *Fundamentals of Measurement*, New York: Oxford, 1958. Chapter 5 contains a brief discussion of the selection, administration, and scoring of standardized tests.

Durost, Walter N., "How to Tell Parents about Standardized Test Results," *Test Service Notebook*, No. 26, New York: Harcourt, Brace & World, 1961, 4p.

Freeman, Frank S., *Theory and Practice of Psychological Testing*, New York: Holt, Rinehart and Winston, 3rd ed., 1962.

In Chapter 6 the author discusses the quantitative and qualitative interpretation of test scores. He points out several areas where caution is indicated and elaborates on clinical aspects of testing.

Lindquist, E. F. (ed.), *Educational Measurement*, Washington: American Council on Education, 1951.

Arthur E. Traxler, in Chapter 10, discusses desirable principles and procedures for administering and scoring objective tests. In Chapter 17, John C. Flanagan presents a thorough analysis of units, scales, and norms for the interpretation of test scores, and the technical procedures and problems in establishing scores and norms.

Seashore, H. G., and J. E. Dobbin, How can the results of a testing program be used most effectively? *Bull. Natl. Assn. Secondary Sch. Principals*, 1958, 42:64–68.

Current deficiencies in educational measurement are the result more of inadequate or improper use of test results than of adequate test instruments. The authors offer suggestions for more effective use of test results.

Stanley, Julian C., *Measurement in Today's Schools*, Englewood Cliffs: Prentice-Hall, 4th ed., 1964.

Chapter 10 discusses the testing program—purpose, selecting appropriate tests, administering, processing, interpreting them, and applying the results.

PART THREE
Evaluation of Classroom Instruction

Identification of educational objectives

Achievement in school consists of moving toward instructional objectives. These objectives must guide both teaching and evaluation. Objectives should be stated in the form of observable pupil changes, understandably and singly, and should be grouped so as to make sense in determining units of instruction and evaluation. Statements of objectives should include only actual guiding purposes, should deal with mental processes as well as with content, and should be determined by individual and social needs.

The achievement of instructional objectives is the degree to which the pupil has moved toward the school's objectives. These objectives are the goals in the direction of which the curriculum seeks to change pupils. Here the curriculum is being defined as *all the experiences used by the school* to attain the aims of education. "Objective" is, of course, a normative concept, carrying value implications as to what is good, and reflecting the purposefulness of the educational process.

What are the objectives of schools, of specific courses, curricula, and teachers? In what ways are these social instrumentalities trying to change pupils? This question, although it constitutes mainly a curriculum problem, is also basic in evaluating educational achievement. For not only the content and methods of instruction but evaluating instruments as well must be determined by the objectives set up. This point of view—that evaluation should be validated against objectives—is so appealing to common sense as to seem platitudinous. Yet it is only since evaluation workers have adopted this point of view that evaluation has begun to escape from stultifying emphasis on one type of objective, memorization of information. Looking to the objectives of instruction for the determiners of evaluation methods has exposed the failure of many evaluation programs to deal with the many objectives long established by curriculum builders. Objectives and evaluation complement each other and are integral parts of the whole instructional program. Objectives define what we are to teach, and evaluation tells us the degree to which our goals are being realized.

SPECIFICITY OF INSTRUCTIONAL OBJECTIVES

Emphasis on objectives as the springboard for evaluating educational achievement has come from evidence concerning the low relationship between achievement of various objectives. Many investigators have believed that acquisition of information in a field is highly related to a person's ability to think in that field and to apply his information.

Research has thrown considerable doubt on this belief, although the results obtained by various investigators have differed. In a study of students taking courses in human biology, physics, chemistry, and basic health, Johnson[1] found that the ability to acquire information was accompanied to a substantial extent by the ability to apply this information. Eurich[2] found that the thirteen subtests of a comprehensive examination designed to measure achievement of thirteen objectives of an English course were so interrelated as to "indicate practically no relationship between achievement in terms of some objectives while between others it is relatively high." Fotos and Remmers,[3] working with objectives and examinations in French courses, obtained high relationships between vocabulary, English to French translation, French to English translation, and the knowledge of verb forms; they reached the conclusion that "the language pattern tends to develop as a whole." In three subject-matter divisions McConnell[4] analyzed tests intended to measure achievement of three kinds of objectives: knowledge of vocabulary, knowledge of facts and principles, and ability to apply facts and principles. He found that differences in what items measured were greater between subject-matter sections (within each of these objectives) than between types of objectives. Hence, the three kinds of objectives differed less among themselves than did the subject-matter divisions.

A different group of researches indicated the specificity of achievement of various objectives by finding low relationships among them. Tyler,[5] who studied numerous courses at Ohio State University,

[1] P. O. Johnson, Differential functions of examinations, *Studies in College Examinations*, Minneapolis: Univ. of Minnesota, Comm. on Educ. Research, 1934, pp. 43–50.

[2] A. C. Eurich, Measuring the achievement of objectives in freshman English, *Studies in College Examinations*, Minneapolis: Univ. of Minnesota, Comm. on Educ. Research, 1934, pp. 50–66.

[3] J. T. Fotos and H. H. Remmers, The functional interrelationships of certain aspects of modern language learning, *Modern Language, J.*, 1934, 18:481–493.

[4] T. R. McConnell, A study of the extent of measurement of differential objectives of instruction, *An Appraisal of Techniques of Evaluation, Symposium*, Washington: American Educational Research Association, February 26, 1940.

[5] R. W. Tyler, The relation between recall and higher mental processes, in C. H. Judd, *Education as Cultivation of the Higher Mental Processes*, New York: Macmillan, 1936, pp. 6–17.

found low correlations among tests on recall of information, tests that demanded the application of principles, and tests of ability to draw inferences from new data. He concluded that students did not develop corresponding degrees of achievement in mere recall and achievement in such higher mental processes as applying principles and drawing inferences. Furst[6] reported low median correlations among 29 measures of achievement of different objectives of general education for high-school and college students over a two-year period of instruction. In the college group the median r's were .312 at the beginning of the period and .347 at the end. In the high-school group the median r's were .229 and .311, respectively. Wittenborn and Larson[7] reported intercorrelations of from .60 to .75 among achievement scores in German reading, vocabulary, and grammar; and correlations of from .50 to .59 between semester grades and these achievement scores.

The differences in these studies in conclusions concerning the specificity of objectives may be due to various factors. (1) Differences in instructional emphases may lead to either a high or low relationship between various objectives. If teachers consistently strive to relate facts and principles to their applications, and to relate practice to theory, there may be higher relationships between achievement of these objectives. (2) The relationship between information and application may vary with the difficulty of the application problems and also with the similarity between the original learning situations and those to which the facts and principles are applied in an examination. Also to be expected is a lower relationship between knowledge tested verbally and applications tested in performance, than between knowledge and applications both measured verbally. (3) The extent of relationship may be a function of the age or maturity of the learner. For example, we might find that the relationship between knowledge of facts and the ability to apply them is higher among college students than among third-grade pupils. (4) Unreliability of the measuring instruments also produces low indices of relationship.

[6] E. J. Furst, Effect of the organization of learning experiences upon the organization of learning outcomes. I. Study of the problem by means of correlation analysis, *J. Exp. Educ.* 1950, 18:215–228; II. Study of the problem by means of factor analysis, *ibid.*, 1950, 18:343–352.

[7] J. R. Wittenborn and R. P. Larson, A factorial study of achievement in college German, *J. Educ. Psychol.*, 1944, 35:39–48.

The practical consequence of these researches for the educator is probably that *each objective must be clearly defined in terms of the measures of its attainment. The attainment of a particular objective cannot be inferred from the measured attainment of another objective.*

GENERAL AND SPECIFIC OBJECTIVES

Educational objectives may, of course, be classified in many ways. One distinction is that between *general* and *specific* objectives. This distinction is not a sharp one but represents a continuum from extreme generality to extreme specificity. General objectives control the general learning situation, such as "a happy and useful life in society" or acquisition of "the ability to reason scientifically."

"Ultimate or general objectives are essentially the same at all levels from kindergarten through Grade 12. Important differences are found only in relative emphasis and in the immediate objectives for the various levels."[8] Specific objectives, on the other hand, are the narrower day-to-day goals, such as "the ability to use the possessive singular correctly," or "the ability to make subjects agree with verbs in number," or "the ability to use the tabular key in indenting for paragraphs," or the "use of the proper form in introducing one person to another."

Both general and specific objectives are necessary in any clear formulation of objectives, since the achievement of general objectives depends upon the contribution made by each specific factor in relation to every other. Fig. 32 shows this interdependence.

Some may argue that excellent teaching practices can exist without the conscious and explicit formulation of objectives. But the clarification of objectives is necessary for the evaluation of teaching practices and pupil achievement, even when it is not essential in instruction. And this clarification usually assists in teaching toward the objectives because of the directive influence of objectives upon the selection of content, activities, and experiences. "Because of important relationships among many subject areas in kindergarten

[8] A Look at Continuity in the School Program, 1958 *Yearb. Assn. for Supervision and Curriculum Develop.*, p. 119.

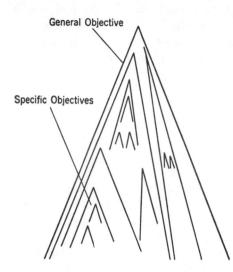

General Objective

Specific Objectives

Fig. 32. Graphic Illustration of Relationship Between General and Specific Objectives.

through Grade 12, objectives involving various subject areas should be stated in such a manner and accomplished in such a way that they reinforce and supplement each other as much as possible, and so that the relationships are readily perceived by the students."[9] The value of any statement of objectives is determined by the extent to which the classroom teacher incorporates it into his thinking and practice.

HOW TO FORMULATE OBJECTIVES

To assist in formulating objectives, we discuss briefly the desirable form and content for statements of objectives. We then give illustrations of objectives for education in general and for specific subjects.

Form for Stating Objectives

1. Objectives should be worded in terms of changes expected in the pupil rather than as duties of the teacher, since attainment of objectives must in any case be evaluated in terms of pupil changes.

[9] *Ibid.*, p. 121.

The following shows the difference between the two ways of stating objectives:

Teacher's objective: To teach the knowledges, skills, habits, and attitudes involving the multiplication table in arithmetic.
Pupil objectives:
Knowledge—To know the multiplication table.
Skill—To be able to apply the multiplication table to problem solving.
Habit—To use smaller numbers as multipliers.
Attitude—To respect the power and value of the multiplication table.

2. An objective should be put in terms of observable changes in the pupil between the beginning and end of his experiences in a defined segment of the educative process. Unless we can tell whether pupils are changed, we shall have difficulty in justifying the objective, however worthy it may appear on philosophical grounds.

3. The terminology of the objective should be clear; its meaning should be defined in terms that pupils, parents, and other teachers can appreciate. Obviously, such clarity often requires much thought and discussion.

4. To prevent confusion and facilitate ready identification of the objective, each statement should refer to only one objective. "To be able to translate French into English and English into French, with correct use of idioms" is not as clear as when these are stated as three separate objectives.

5. Objectives should be grouped for use in guiding pupil activities, in organizing units of work, and in constructing evaluation devices. That is, specific objectives should be grouped under the objective that is general to them.

Content of Statements of Objectives

1. Statements should contain only "real" objectives, not those to which merely lip service is given. Teachers may be tempted to formulate a glib statement rather than to think through their own serious purposes. They should ask themselves whether they intend actually to do something about each objective and about each phrase in the statement of the objective.

2. Objectives should refer not only to the subject matter of a

course but also, and especially, to the mental processes of remembering, reasoning, appreciating, and being interested. And particularly for the higher mental processes, statements of objectives should be comprehensive. The higher mental processes are those to which the individual makes a large contribution through his own conscious effort. Such processes as sensation or mere memory are considered to be lower in the intellectual hierarchy because the individual makes less contribution; he is more "active" when he compares, infers, and abstracts. Deductive and inductive reasoning are more powerful in solving most human problems than is mere recall of facts or the mechanical application of rules to familiar problems.

The classroom teacher will profit from considering and formulating mental process objectives as well as subject-matter objectives. Such consideration will lead to more vital, interesting teaching and presentation of subject matter, in more varied forms, and in forms more recognizable by pupils as relating to their needs. It will also lead to construction of more valid evaluation devices.

3. Both social and individual needs should determine the content of statements of objectives. These needs can be discovered by analyzing the activities and interests of pupils and the society and culture in which they will have to function. A detailed description of methods of curriculum making is out of place here but may be found in books on curriculum development.

ILLUSTRATIONS OF GENERAL OBJECTIVES

Before considering objectives for specific subjects, let us examine attempts to formulate lists of *general* objectives for the work of the schools. Such formulations are, of course, the proper task of educational philosophers, scholars, scientists, administrators, curriculum builders, and other thoughtful citizens. The views of such thinkers, reflecting the social and intellectual forces of their time, have largely determined the nature of the teaching that goes on in the schools.

But those concerned chiefly with the *evaluation* of pupil achievement have also formulated educational objectives. Tyler presented one such formulation, derived from work in constructing achievement tests for several departments of Ohio State University.

Type A. Information, which includes terminology, specific facts, and general principles.

Type B. Reasoning, or scientific method, which includes induction, testing hypotheses, and deduction.

Type C. Location of relevant data, which involves a knowledge of sources of usable data and skill in getting information from appropriate sources.

Type D. Skills characteristic of particular subjects, which include laboratory skills in the sciences, language skills, and the like.

Type E. Standards of technical performance, which include the knowledge of appropriate standards, ability to evaluate the relative importance of several standards which apply, and skill or habits in applying these standards.

Type F. Reports, which include the necessary skill in reporting projects in engineering or reporting experiments in science and the like.

Type G. Consistency in application of point of view, which is most apparent in philosophy.

Type X. Character, which is perhaps the most inclusive, involving many specific factors.[10]

Another list of objectives resulted from a classification of the wide variety of objectives submitted by the thirty secondary schools participating in the Eight-Year Experimental Study of the Progressive Education Association. To observe the effects of a different type of instruction, these thirty schools were freed of the influence of college entrance requirements upon their work by the colleges' agreeing to accept all recommended candidates. Raths[11] was able to classify all the objectives submitted by these schools under the following eight headings:

1. Functional information
2. Aspects of thinking
3. Attitudes
4. Interests, aims, purposes
5. Study skills and work habits
6. Social adjustment and social sensitivity

[10] R. W. Tyler, *Constructing Achievement Tests*, Columbus: Ohio State University, 1934.

[11] L. E. Raths, Evaluating the program of a school, *Educ. Res. Bull.*, 1938, 17:57–84.

7. Creativeness
8. A functional social philosophy

The reader should also consult the *45th Yearbook of the National Society for the Study of Education*,[12] Part I, The Measurement of Understanding, for additional detailed statements of both general and specific objectives in various subject-matter areas. This *Yearbook* emphasizes the importance of teaching and testing for understanding. Separate chapters deal with the measurement of understanding in various major areas of instruction.

ILLUSTRATIONS OF SPECIFIC OBJECTIVES

From the consideration of *general* objectives we now proceed to formulations of objectives within *specific subject matters*. On the one hand is the subject matter—skills, facts, concepts, principles, methods, and so on. On the other hand are the mental processes that can operate upon that subject matter, the behaviors a given teacher will seek to bring about in his pupils in that particular subject-matter field. We can present here only a few formulations of objectives to serve as illustrations of the results of this step in the construction of evaluation devices.

Objectives of Instruction in Reading

Grade I: Reading readiness involves acquisition of the intelligence, visual and auditory perception, language development, background of experience, and social behavior necessary for a child to learn to read. The teacher cannot aim explicitly at some of these objectives, because their attainment is largely a function of certain processes of maturation which we have not yet learned how to affect with specific variations in environment, or of factors like home background, which cannot be readily changed for instructional purposes.

Grade III: Know the sounds of all the letters of the alphabet and of most of the common phonograms. Be able to work out the pronunciation of unfamiliar words without help. Read silently with

[12] Chicago: Univ. of Chicago Press, 1946.

greater speed than is attained in reading orally. Read silently without pointing or lip movements. Like to read, and read widely in varied sources. Be able to read fourth-grade material with satisfactory understanding.

Grade VI: Read widely so as to extend and enrich experience. Continue improvement of basic skills in word recognition and comprehension. Read silently with *much* greater speed than is attained in reading orally. Acquire training in use of books and in the location of information in dictionaries and other reference works. Acquire skill involved in the reading of factual material. Achieve seventh-grade level in reading ability.

Objectives of Instruction in Arithmetic

Some of the essential outcomes that teachers should strive to help pupils accept as reasonable, personal goals in arithmetic are the following:

1. To experience satisfactions that come to individuals who possess an understanding of the meanings and operations in foundational mathematics.

2. To comprehend and appreciate the important contribution of arithmetic to society and personal living.

3. To possess a meaningful mastery of the basic facts in addition, subtraction, multiplication, and division.

4. To understand the relationship and also numerical difference between integers, common fractions, decimal fractions, and denominate numbers.

5. To possess abilities and interest in observing, defining, analyzing, and solving various kinds of problems.

6. To develop ability to estimate and verify answers to mathematical examples and problems.

7. To possess ability in comparing and making judgment values concerning consumer goods.

8. To be able to read and interpret graphs and tables that represent information and facts in the field of consumer economics.

9. To understand different kinds of units of measure and to be able to select and apply with precision appropriate units of measure in various situations.

10. To possess an understanding of the meanings, vocabulary, and operations involved in foundational mathematics.

11. To have developed abilities, values, and interests to motivate continued study of mathematics in secondary school.

12. To possess abilities in understanding the value and application of foundational mathematics in personal and business economics.

13. To understand the important role of mathematical meanings and operations in scientific and technological research and progress.

14. To understand the need for learned competency in using the language and science of arithmetic in responsible citizenship.[13]

For a small unit of arithmetic, the following objectives[14] of the arithmetic of common fractions in Grade 7 illustrate how desired pupil behavior may be defined.

1. Vocabulary

The pupil uses the technical vocabulary of common fractions in such a way as to demonstrate his understanding of the basic concepts.

2. Interest

a. His immediate interest in the topic: He demonstrates a desire to explore situations that call for the addition of fractions.

b. His general interest in mathematics: He demonstrates an increased desire to participate in the class activities and pursue the study of mathematics.

3. Meaning of the operation

a. He explains and otherwise demonstrates an understanding of the principles basic to changing unlike to like fractions.

b. He demonstrates ability to apply the process of addition of whole numbers to common fractions.

c. He demonstrates the ability to extend to common fractions the idea of likeness in addition.

4. Skills

a. He demonstrates speed and accuracy in the addition of common fractions and in skills prerequisite to the process.

b. He solves verbal problems using common fractions.

5. Generalizations

a. He identifies real situations calling for addition of common fractions.

b. He applies what is learned to life situations.

[13] E. T. McSwain and Ralph J. Cooke, *Understanding and Teaching Arithmetic in the Elementary School*, New York: Holt, Rinehart and Winston, 1958, pp. 333–334.

[14] By permission from *Teaching Arithmetic for Understanding*, by John L. Marks, C. Richard Purdy, and Lucien B. Kinney, pp. 343–344. Copyright, 1958, McGraw-Hill Book.

c. He sees the relationship among operations and the dependence of algorisms on the nature of the number system.

Objectives in Secondary-School Language Arts[15]

Language arts teachers throughout the nation accept personal, social, and occupational competence as the goal of education. Attainment of this outcome may be achieved within the limits of the capacity of the individual if his experience with and through the language arts are directed toward:

1. Cultivation of wholesome personal living
   a. Sense of values.
   b. Perspective on one's self and one's time.
   c. Extension of experience so as to be good company *for one's self* as well as good company *for others* through such habits as continued personal reading of high quality and skill in social letter writing and conversation.
   d. Ability to use the cultural resources in one's community including the library, radio, television, motion picture, theater, and public platform.
   e. High degree of competence in the basic skills of reading, writing, listening, and speaking.
   f. Intellectual curiosity and creativeness (so far as possible) in all four of the language arts.
   g. Capacity for logical and critical thinking in expression of ideas and in acceptance or rejection of ideas of others.
   h. Personal integrity in thought and expression.
   i. Intelligent consumption of goods and services because of sensitivity to the denotation and connotation of words; that is, sales resistance without becoming a nuisance as a purchaser, emotional discount for unsubstantiated superlatives in advertisements and sales talks, alert attention to "small print" in contracts, guarantees, and cautions on how to use a product.
2. Development of social sensitivity and effective participation in group life
   a. Sensing values in the current scene and their relation to the contributions of past and future.

[15] Commission on the English Curriculum of The National Council of Teachers of English, *The English Language Arts in the Secondary School*, New York: Appleton-Century-Crofts. Copyright © 1956, Appleton-Century-Crofts, Inc.

    b. Recognition of the dignity and worth of every individual.

    c. Control of one's prejudices so as to avoid giving offense or blocking important group action.

    d. Skill in the language arts of persuasion, cooperative planning, discussion, and decision.

    e. Recognition of the social and psychological factors involved in communication with people of different backgrounds.

    f. A sense of responsibility for critical (as well as imaginative) reading and listening in order to understand and appreciate elements in American culture and in that of other nations.

3. Linguistic competence necessary for vocational efficiency.

    a. Following and giving directions.

    b. Keeping up with technical knowledge in one's occupation.

    c. Maintaining effective interpersonal relationships: employer-employee, employee-employee, employer-public, employee-public.

    d. Developing needed skills in business letter writing, persuasion and exposition, and in techniques of interviewing.

Objectives in Secondary-School Algebra I[16]

Students in algebra should have experiences in:

1. The acquisition of the basic vocabulary
2. Learning to translate quantitative statements into the language of algebra
3. Interpreting the solution of equations where they have significance and in using rules of equality and transformation
4. Solving general verbal problems using as a means of solution the table, graph, formula, and equation
5. Understanding of carefully considered concepts and principles which should lead to fundamental skills and techniques

    a. The four fundamental operations involving positive and negative numbers, algebraic monomials or simple polynomials, and algebraic fractions mainly monomial denominators.

    b. Special products and factoring such as squaring a binomial, finding the product of the sum and the difference of two terms, factoring a polynomial containing a common monomial term, factoring trinomials of the form x^2 plus bx plus c, and factoring the difference of two squares.

[16] *Guide to Secondary Education in Oregon for School Years 1957–1959*, Salem: Superintendent of Public Instruction, State Department of Education, 1957, pp. 141–142.

    c. Powers and roots, involving the laws of exponents and their use, square roots of positive numbers, and fundamental operations involving radicals of the monomial type.

6. The study of relationships and of dependence
    a. Interpreting tables of related number pairs.
    b. Making graphs based on tables of related number pairs and using graphs in the solution of problems.
    c. Using formulas as means of expressing relationship or dependence.
    d. Equations involving the solution of equations of the first degree in one unknown, fractional equations, equations of the form ax^2 equals b, and simple radical equations.
    c. Using equations in the study of proportion and of variables.

TAXONOMY OF EDUCATIONAL OBJECTIVES: COGNITIVE DOMAIN

As the reader looked over the foregoing lists of general and specific objectives, he may have been impressed with the variety and ambiguity of the terms used. For example, what is meant by "information" and "knowledge"? Are these the same or should some distinction be made in them? Similarly, what is meant by "reasoning" as against "scientific method"? When two curricula or statements of objectives contain a given term, does it have the same meaning? When teachers make up a statement of objectives, can they feel satisfied that they have thought through all the important possibilities? Or may they wonder whether they have not overlooked, through accident or personal blind spots, some of the objectives with which they should be concerned? Concern about some of these inconsistencies in meanings has led to the development of a taxonomy.

In 1949, a group of college and university examiners organized a "Taxonomy Group." Over several years this group worked toward a comprehensive classification of educational objectives to be used for several purposes, such as the following:

1. To facilitate communication among teachers, examiners, and other educational workers.
2. To set up a comprehensive, systematic list of the types of behavior at which educational procedures may aim.

3. To provide a source of hypotheses and questions for methods of developing curricula, teaching methods, and testing techniques.
4. To arrange educational behaviors, or objectives, from simple to complex.
5. In general, to lay bare many of the hitherto concealed assumptions underlying the statements of objectives that educators have developed in the past.

The following brief description of the taxonomy[17] is intended merely to introduce the reader to this highly significant development.

Three Domains

In the first place, the Taxonomy Group identified three major "domains" of objectives—the Cognitive, the Affective, and the Psychomotor. The affective domain includes attitudes, appreciations, emotional and social adjustment, and the like. The psychomotor domain will presumably deal with types of small and large muscle skills and coordinations such as those involved in surgery, physical training, mechanical work, and clerical trades.

The Cognitive Domain

Within the cognitive domain, the taxonomy provides for two major classes—knowledge, and intellectual skills and abilities.

Knowledge. The first of these major classes—1.00: Knowledge—has in turn been defined as follows:

Knowledge as defined here includes those behaviors and test situations which emphasize the remembering, either by recognition or recall, of ideas, material, or phenomena. The behavior expected of the student in a recall situation is very similar to the behavior he was expected to have during the original learning situation. In the learning situation the student is expected to store in his mind certain information and the behavior expected later is the remembering of this information. Although some alterations may be expected in the material to be remembered, this is a relatively minor part of the knowledge behavior or test. The process of

[17] Benjamin S. Bloom, Max Engelhardt, Edward Furst, Walker Hill, and David R. Krathwohl, A *Taxonomy of Educational Objectives—The Cognitive Domain*, New York: Longmans, Green, 1956.

relating and judging is also involved to the extent that the student is expected to answer questions and problems which are posed in a different form in the test situation than in the original learning situation.

In the classification of the knowledge objectives, the arrangement is from the specific and relatively concrete types of behaviors to the more complex and abstract ones. Thus, the knowledge of specifics refers to types of information or knowledge which can be isolated or remembered separately, while the knowledge of universals and abstractions emphasizes the interrelations and patterns in which information can be organized and structured.

While it is to be recognized that knowledge is involved in the more complex major categories of the taxonomy (2.00 to 6.00), the knowledge category differs from the others in that remembering is the major psychological process involved here, while in the other categories the remembering is only one part of a much more complex process of relating, judging, and reorganizing.

Following this definition, knowledge is broken down into types such as the following:

1.10: Knowledge of Specifics—the recall of specific and isolable bits of information

1.11: Knowledge of Terminology—of referents for specific verbal and nonverbal symbols

1.12: Knowledge of Specific Facts—of dates, events, persons, places, sources of information, etc. . . .

1.22: Knowledge of Trends and Sequences—of the processes, direction, and movements of phenomena with respect to time . . .

1.24: Knowledge of Criteria—of the criteria by which facts, principles, techniques, and procedures are employed in a particular subject . . .

1.32: Knowledge of Theories and Structures—of the body of principles and generalizations, together with their interrelations, which present a clear, rounded, and systematic view of a complex phenomenon, or field

The Taxonomy Group has also developed illustrative objectives and test items for each of the categories of knowledge. For example, 1.11: Knowledge of Terminology includes such objectives as "Ability to define technical terms by giving their attributes, properties, or relations" and "Knowledge of the vocabulary of the fine arts sufficient to be able to read and converse intelligently." An illustrative test item in this field is found on the following page.

A synapse can best be described as:

1. a mass or layer of protoplasm having many nuclei but lacking distinct cell boundaries.
2. a lapse of memory caused by inadequate circulation of blood to the brain.
3. The pairing of maternal with paternal chromosomes during maturation of the germ cell.
4. the long cylindrical portion of an axon.
5. the point at which the nerve impulse passes from one neuron to another.

Intellectual Skills and Abilities. The second major heading of the cognitive domain—intellectual skills and abilities—includes the following categories of objectives, each of which, with its sub-categories, is carefully defined. Each is also illustrated with objectives and test items from actual subject-matter fields.

2.00 Comprehension
    2.10 Translation
    2.20 Interpretation
    2.30 Extrapolation
3.00 Application
4.00 Analysis
5.00 Synthesis
6.00 Evaluation

The interested reader is referred to the *Taxonomy* itself for a wealth of additional definitions, illustrations, and sample test questions.

TAXONOMY OF EDUCATIONAL OBJECTIVES: AFFECTIVE DOMAIN

The Taxonomy Group of college and university examiners continued its work during an eight-year interval and has recently published a book on classifying educational goals in the affective domain.[18]

[18] David R. Krathwohl; Benjamin S. Bloom, and Bertram B. Masia, *Taxonomy of Educational Objectives: The Classification of Educational Goals, Handbook II: Affective Domain*, New York: McKay, 1964. pp. xiv + 196.

The problems of classification in this domain proved to be much more recalcitrant than those of the cognitive domain, particularly with respect to finding a single continuum, like that of complexity in the cognitive domain, to which to order affective objectives. The key concept chosen for classification in the affective domain is *internalization*.

In studying the history of several major college general education courses the authors found that typically the original statement of objectives gave about equal emphasis to cognitive and affective goals. But over a ten- to twenty-year period they found a rather rapid dropping of the affective objectives.

"It was evident too that there is a characteristic type of *erosion* in which the original intent of a course or educational program becomes worn down to that which can be explicitly evaluated for grading purposes and that which can be taught easily through verbal methods (lectures, discussions, reading materials, etc.)" (p. 16). This erosion, they judge, is further enhanced by inadequacy of appraisal techniques and especially as a function in our culture of viewing beliefs, attitudes, values and personality characteristics as private matters.

Nevertheless, affective behavior—characterized by feeling tone, emotion, acceptance or rejection—fundamentally determines the self-actualization of the individual in his society and his interpersonal and intergroup relations, hence the health and stability of the society. For notable examples of affective behavior we need only point to civil rights demonstrations and much "cold war" behavior.

With *internalization* as the ordering concept the authors of *Handbook II* have developed the taxonomy with degrees of increasing internalization. We indicate only the major rubrics here. Each has several identifiable subcategories, analyzed and elaborated with illustrative operational measurement techniques.

1.0 Receiving (Attending)
2.0 Responding
3.0 Valuing
4.0 Organization
5.0 Characterization by a Value or Value Complex

Objective 3.3, "Devotion to those ideas and ideals which are the foundation of democracy," can be illustrated, to give only one example by an item from a Purdue Opinion Panel poll report:[19]

"Pupils of all races and nationalities should attend school together everywhere in this country."
— Agree
— Undecided; probably agree
— Undecided; probably disagree
— Disagree

Handbook II: Affective Domain describes a variety of measurement techniques and illustrative examples. You, the reader, if seriously concerned with measurement and evaluation of the achievement of educational objectives, will find this *Handbook* a very important educational tool.

STUDENT PARTICIPATION IN EVALUATION

Should teachers and school administrators make all decisions concerning content and procedures in evaluation? Or should students participate in such decisions? Modern psychology and democratic social values agree that important educational objectives can be achieved by having students participate. Many individual teachers and school systems have increasingly been placing responsibility on students for evaluating their own achievement. Nor is this restricted to any particular level of education; it is being done from the first grade to the university.

An example of such participation in the first grade is given in the following:[20]

In one school, the first grade children attempted to evaluate their own level of development with respect to points that *they* as a group felt to be important. Since they thought that their parents would be interested, they reported to them, too. The teacher worked with each child to help him get a reasonably correct concept of his performance level before the group finished the project. Here is the report as they developed it.

[19] From Poll Report No. 61, Vol. 20, No. 1, 1960, by R. D. Franklin and H. H. Remmers.
[20] F. E. Harris, *Three Persistent Educational Problems: Grading, Promoting, and Reporting to Parents*, Lexington, Kentucky: Bulletin of School Services, College of Education, University of Kentucky, 1953, 24:28–29.

Dear Father and Mother,
This is my report to you. All the children helped decide the things to report on.

1. I am a quiet worker. ....
2. I am a good listener. ....
3. I remember my jobs. ....
4. I finish my work. ....
5. I let other people have turns. ..
6. I keep my hands at home. .....
7. I work to make the First Grade a nice place. ....
8. I am a good helper. ....

9. I try to be a nice person in the rest room. ....
10. I walk in the halls (not run). .
11. I try to be kind. ....
12. I am a good neighbor in groups.
13. I cross streets safely. ....
14. I am fair when I play.
15. If I stay for lunch, I try to be a good helper. ....

Signed

....

....

An illustration at the college level is provided by a course taught by one of the present authors. After considerable discussion of the objectives to be achieved in the course, the students decided that one desirable activity for themselves would be to specify these objectives in detail, design appropriate test exercises to evaluate their achievement, administer the tests, score and interpret them, and finally report the results to the class. During the first four weeks of the course the 33 students read the textbook fairly rapidly, after which they divided themselves into 11 committees of three each. Each of these committees was responsible for one periodical test, so that each student in the course took 10 tests at weekly intervals. This procedure proved to be highly motivating. Indeed, the instructor's chief function often became that of umpire when the wording of a particular item was hotly challenged by one or another of the students who had missed it. Moreover, a healthy group rivalry developed not only as to item wording but also as to completeness of reporting the results, including estimating the reliability of the test, reporting the number of times each item was missed, and making recommendations for turning the test results into grade equivalents.

Obviously, this general procedure can be applied, with innumerable modifications, in any subject-matter area and at all levels. The instructor tends to become a resource person rather than the sole purveyor of wisdom. In the example just cited, some of the committees asked the instructor to review their questions before they were administered; others did not. Thus the amount of control exercised by the teacher varied considerably.

Recent years have seen increasing attention given to the notion of "self-evaluation"—the pupils themselves carrying out all steps in evaluation. Usually this concept is linked to a pattern of education such as the following. Pupils determine to a large extent, with the guidance of their teachers, what they will undertake to learn. They identify the problems with which they wish to concern themselves. These problems may take the form of traditional subjects and be recognizable as problems in arithmetic, physics, or geography. Or more likely, they may cut across traditional subject-matter lines, as when pupils attack the problem of preventing the sewers in their neighborhood from overflowing after a heavy rain and find themselves concerned with the physics of fluids, sanitary engineering, politics, public opinion, taxation, and health.

Whatever form the problem may take, many educators insist that more of the responsibility for identifying and selecting the problems that pupils will work on should be given to the pupils themselves. Pupils will need help, of course, in identifying and solving their problems. They will get this help from their teachers. They will need to learn how to use reading and community resources effectively in identifying and solving their problems. They will learn to keep personal educational records to facilitate their learning. They will learn to work together in groups in identifying and solving their problems. And they will develop improved reading skills of a kind necessary for problem solving and perhaps different from those previously used in school. Above and beyond these is the necessity for developing skills in self-evaluation.

Why has such an educational program, including self-evaluation, been proposed? (1) It fits in with the idea of making learning more significant by giving greater responsibility to the learner. Motivation will be stronger and more genuine when pupils work on problems that they themselves have identified and selected as significant to themselves. Their "ego involvement" in the learning process and the transfer of what they learn in school to out-of-school life will be greater when they have acquired skill in identifying and solving their own problems. The ability to continue learning and to teach oneself should be greater in adults who have had to develop the necessary skills during their school days. And if the process is to be truly significant, it must be accompanied by self-evaluation whereby the students themselves largely determine what is to be evaluated and how the evaluation is to be carried out.

(2) The idea of self-evaluation also stems from the concern of educators with the democratic process. If schools are to produce adults who live democratically, the school organization should exemplify the tenets of democracy. Many educators conclude that schools in which the pupils have no voice in determining on what grounds they are to be evaluated or how the evaluation is to be made, are not furthering the democratic ideals that teachers profess.

But, the reply goes, there must be realistic and severe limits to how far self-determination can be allowed to go. Democracy does not mean that everyone is qualified to do anything, that everyone can have responsibility and authority for every phase of the educative process. The patient on the operating table, to use an extreme analogy, does not have and does not want the right to discuss with the surgeon whether he should have an appendectomy or how it should be done. By the same logic, the six-year-old child is not qualified to have a voice in deciding what he should study, or how. Indeed, at all levels of education, it is the teachers and other mature citizens who should primarily determine the curriculum. For them to give away any important share of this responsibility to the "consumers" of education would amount to their failing to put their superior training and competence to full use. For pupils to have any large share in evaluating their own achievement would amount to the blind leading the blind. To introduce value-laden terms like democracy into a discussion of these issues, it is charged, is to becloud the issue. What we need are the educational methods, under any label, that lead to the greatest achievement of the most valid educational objectives by the greatest number of pupils. Teachers are the agents of society, selected and trained to be highly qualified in determining what pupils need to learn and how they can learn it, and in evaluating pupils to determine how well they have learned.

It is exactly at this point that many teachers in recent years have taken the position that (a) democratic ways of living must be learned in schools as well as elsewhere; (b) the best and perhaps the only way to learn democratic ways of living is by experiencing a democratic way of life including a democratically organized system of education; (c) the boredom, inertia, and ineffective learning that characterize many pupils in present-day schools result from teaching that is not attuned to their needs and concerns; (d) the remedy for the inadequacies of our schools in training for democratic living and in teaching pupils the other things they need lies in destroying the teachers' monopoly in curriculum building and evaluation.

This is not the place for any full discussion of alternative approaches to curriculum building, classroom management, and the organization of learning in modern schools. But so far as these approaches imply the need for self-evaluation, we must consider them here. Is self-evaluation desirable? Our answer must be affirmative, but qualified as follows:

1. Self-evaluation by pupils must be "taken seriously" by teachers if it is to have optimum effect on learning. Evaluations of pupil achievement have always been used as bases for the distribution of rewards (high marks, honors, admissions, prizes, and the like) and deprivations. If self-evaluation is taken seriously, it should be similarly used as bases for distributing rewards. Whatever these rewards and deprivations may be in more democratically oriented, pupil-centered, problem-process systems of education, some analogue of them, perhaps more intrinsic than grades and marks, must exist. If not "taken seriously" as bases for rewards, self-evaluation will lose whatever good effect it can have on the learning process.

2. Self-evaluations should be as valid as possible. The teacher will need to guide and train pupils to make valid self-evaluations. He cannot rely solely on pupils' feelings of satisfaction or dissatisfaction with their performance and achievement. The mere fact that a pupil feels he has achieved an objective is no evidence of the desirability of the learning process he has completed. People tend to feel satisfied with the results of their visits to fortune-tellers, or quacks of other kinds. The unsupported statements of students are insufficient evidence that they have achieved new understanding.

How much the learning process can be pupil-oriented may depend on how much the educational achievement serves as a "gateway" to highly desired goals. When achievement in a curriculum constitutes the path to higher, more rewarded positions in society, self-determination and self-evaluation of learning are less usable as bases for rewards and deprivations. We can see this in professional education. The kinds of preparation needed for entering medical or legal practice cannot be determined by the student as much as can general education in the fifth grade. In the former case, society must set standards to govern the competition for admission. For its own protection society must enforce these standards by systems of evaluation that are anything but "self-evaluation." In the fifth grade, on the other hand, what a pupil learns and how he goes about learning it may be more realistically left in his own hands to some extent. His self-evaluation of his learning does not here result in regulation of social mobility.

In short, the feasibility of self-evaluation depends on the extent to which achievement of instructional objectives is a vehicle to social rewards for which there is competition. There can be wider distribution of the rewards to which high achievement in the fifth grade leads than of those to which adequate achievement in medical school leads. Realistic understanding of the feasibility of self-evaluation in American education, it seems to us, must take such competition into account.

LABORATORY EXERCISES AND DISCUSSION QUESTIONS

1. In what ways was the curriculum of the high school you attended shaped by the needs of the society and community it served? In what ways was it shaped primarily by the needs of the individual student?
2. Under what conditions would it be desirable for a teacher to use the same tests year after year, improving them by whatever experience and statistical means are available, instead of constructing or selecting entirely new ones each year?
3. Why are there variations between state and community school systems in instructional objectives for nontool subjects such as American history? How do these variations affect the applicability of standardized tests?
4. What are the responsibilities of a primary-grade teacher in the area of measurement and evaluation? Compare these with the responsi-

bilities of a teacher of mathematics and a teacher of vocational education in high school.

5. Compare measurement in arithmetic with measurement in the social studies, biology, reading, music, and art. What are the important similarities and differences?

6. What changes in emphasis in educational objectives do you think have been taking place over the last twenty-five years? What evidence can you cite to support your answer? How have these changes affected educational measurement?

SUGGESTED REFERENCES

Bloom, Benjamin S. (ed.), *Taxonomy of Educational Objectives*, New York: Longmans, Green, 1956.

A discussion of the problem of classifying educational objectives in a systematic way. Contains a wealth of definitions and illustrative material useful in test construction.

Furst, E. J., *Constructing Evaluation Instruments*, New York: Longmans, Green, 1958.

Chapters 2 and 3 present excellent discussions of objectives and behavioral definitions, by one of the authors of the *Taxonomy of Educational Objectives*.

Green, John A., *Teacher-made Tests*, New York: Harper & Row, 1963.

In Chapter 1 the author discusses the principle that measurement objectives must parallel instructional objectives.

Krathwohl, David R., *et al.*, *Taxonomy of Educational Objectives: The Classification of Educational Goals, Handbook II, Affective Domain*, New York: McKay, 1964.

A discussion of a much neglected area of measurement and evaluation with many conceptual and operational definitions useful in constructing measures in the areas of feeling, emotion, beliefs, interests, attitudes, and values.

Thomas, R. M., *Judging Student Progress*, New York: Longmans, Green, 1954.

In Chapter 15, the author presents a survey of the teacher's job for the year. He shows how a chart of objectives can be developed, stating the objectives clearly in terms of pupil behavior, the general methods to be used, and the types of evaluation devices desired. This is accompanied by illustrations for the elementary grades.

Travers, Robert M. W., *How To Make Achievement Tests*, New York: Odyssey, 1950.

This brief book of 176 pages provides teachers with techniques for defining educational goals and developing tests to evaluate them.

Wrightstone, J. W., J. Justman, and I. Robbins, *Evaluation in Modern Education*, New York: American Book, 1956, pp. 94–98.

An excellent discussion of objectives and an illustration of a specifications chart.

CHAPTER 8

Constructing teacher-made tests

Objectives and Evaluation Devices

Type of Evaluating Device

Essay vs. Short-Answer Testing
Reliability of Grading or Scoring
Extensiveness of the Sampling of Achievement
Possibility of the Pupil's Guessing or Bluffing
Pretest, or Motivational, Effects on Pupil Achievement
Posttest, or Instructional, Effects on Pupil Achievement
Labor of Construction
Labor of Scoring and Grading
Cost of Administration
Attitudes of Pupils Toward the Two Types of Tests
Intellectual Pleasure and Professional Growth Derived by the Teacher
Distorting Effects on Manifested Achievement
Fitness for Evaluation of Complex Achievement
Summary Comparison

Constructing and Grading Essay Tests
Types of Essay Questions
Suggestions for Constructing Essay Tests
Suggestions for Grading Essay Tests
Percentage Passing. Check-List Point-Score Method. Projective Interpretation
Further Aids in Grading Essay Tests

Constructing Short-Answer Tests
Table of Specifications
Composing Test Items
Types of Test Items
Simple-Question Items
Supply-Completion Items
Constant-Alternative Items (True-False and Others)
Changing-Alternative Items (Multiple-Choice)
Matching Items
Analogies
Rearrangement Items

Arranging and Administering Short-Answer Tests
Assembling Items into Parts
Editing the Items and Arranging Them in Order of Difficulty Within Parts
Arranging Items for Easy Scoring
Preparing the Scoring Key
Directions to the Pupil
Directions to the Test Administrator

Improvement of Objective-Type Tests
Item Analysis
Procedures for Making a Simple Item Analysis

Product and Procedure Evaluation (Manipulative-Performance Tests)
Analyzing the Product into Specific Features
Scoring Specific Features
Illustrative Product and Procedure Evaluation Devices
Measuring Scale for Handwriting. Check list for Use of Microscope. "Setups" for Evaluating Shop Procedures

Open-Book Examinations

Oral Examinations

Let us assume that the objectives of instruction have already been stated in accordance with the procedures in Chapter 7. At this point, then, the teacher has a set of objectives (in the form of grouped, unitary, understandable statements about observable changes in pupils) toward which instructional effort is actually directed, which involve both subject matter and mental processes, and which have been determined on the basis of social and individual needs.

From this point onward, the construction of evaluation devices requires answers to the following questions:

1. At what objective or group of objectives is the evaluation device aimed?
2. Which of the following types of devices is best suited for evaluating the achievement of these objectives?
   a. Devices involving symbols (verbal, mathematical, musical, etc.)
   b. Devices involving "real things" rather than symbols
   c. Devices involving direct observation of behavior or performance
3. If a device involving language is chosen, should it be an essay test or a short-answer test?
4. If an essay test is to be used, how should it be constructed?
5. If a short-answer test is chosen, should it be an externally made, standardized, purchasable test, or a teacher-made test? (Refer to Chapter 4 for a discussion of this question.)
6. If a teacher-made short-answer test is chosen, what types of questions should be used and how should they be apportioned and composed?
7. If an externally made, standardized short-answer test is to be used, how should it be chosen from among the many available? (This question was discussed in Chapter 5 with respect to the school testing program. The same consideration should be given to using a standardized test for evaluating classroom instruction according to local objectives as for the school testing program.)
8. If a nonlanguage product or procedure device is to be used, how should it be constructed?
9. What is the place of open-book examinations?
10. Should oral examinations be used? If so, where and when?

OBJECTIVES AND EVALUATION DEVICES

Different objectives require different evaluation devices. Not all the different kinds of class achievement can be evaluated by the same type of device. Hence, after the objectives have been formulated, the next step in constructing an evaluation device is to match each objective, or set of objectives, with an appropriate kind of evaluation device. Tyler has well illustrated this procedure of singling out an objective so that evaluation devices may be constructed to fit its requirements.

Each of the eight objectives set up for elementary courses in zoology was defined in terms of the behavior expected of students. In defining the first objective, a fund of information about animal activities and structures, the specific facts and general principles which the student should be able to recall without reference to textbooks or other sources of information, were indicated. The second objective, an understanding of technical terminology, was defined by listing the terms which the student himself should be able to use in his own reports, and another list of terms which he would not be expected to use, but should be able to understand when he finds them in zoological publications. The third objective, an ability to draw inferences from facts, that is, to propose hypotheses, was defined by describing the types of experiments which an elementary student should be able to interpret. The fourth objective, ability to propose ways of testing hypotheses, was defined by listing the types of hypotheses which an elementary student should be able to validate by experiment, or to propose ways of validation. The fifth objective, an ability to apply principles to concrete situations, was defined by listing the principles which elementary students should be able to apply, and types of concrete situations in which the student might apply these principles. The sixth objective, accuracy of observation, was defined by listing the types of experiments in which the elementary student should be able to make accurate observations. The seventh objective, skill in the use of the microscope and other essential tools, was defined by describing the types of microscopic mounts and types of dissections which elementary students should learn to make. The eighth objective, an ability to express effectively ideas related to zoology, was defined by indicating the nature of the reports, both written and oral, which zoology students are expected to make and the qualities demanded for these reports to be effective.[1]

TYPE OF EVALUATING DEVICE

Which of the following three types of devices is best suited to evaluate the achievement of these objectives: those involving (1) verbal and/or mathematical language, (2) concrete objects rather than symbols, or (3) direct observation of performance?

[1] R. W. Tyler, *Constructing Achievement Tests*, Columbus: Ohio State University, 1934, p. 8.

These types may be illustrated by referring to Tyler's objectives, quoted above. Devices involving language (by language we mean any system of communication using symbols) apply to the first, second, third, fourth, fifth, and eighth objectives. Devices involving concrete objects apply to the seventh objective, skill in using the microscope and other essential tools, since this skill is reflected in the quality of the microscopic mounts and types of dissection made by the students. Devices involving direct observation of behavior also apply to the sixth and seventh objectives, since the evaluator directly observes the student's behavior, the movements of his body and eyes, the position and vantage points adopted, the skill in manipulating instruments.

The device involving language is represented by the paper-and-pencil test, the most frequently used type of evaluation device. The preponderance of written language or paper-and-pencil devices in the evaluation of achievement merely reflects how important language is in the school curriculum and in our civilization.

Devices involving nonsymbolic materials are usually in the form of a check list or rating scale upon which may be indicated the presence or absence, or degree of quality, of the salient features of the product. Typical products are those which pupils turn out in art courses, chemical laboratories, home economics laboratories, woodwork and metalwork shops—drawings, precipitates, pies, dresses, chairs, book ends, wrenches.

Devices involving behavior enable an observer to evaluate on a rating scale or check list a pupil's achievement of desirable ways of moving or speaking. Typically observed under this heading are clarity of speech, posture, habits of recitation in class, physical education achievement, and efficiency in handling scientific apparatus.

Obviously, in most cases, teachers will find devices involving language best suited to their instructional objectives. Thus, our major interest will be in paper and pencil types of measurement.

ESSAY VS. SHORT–ANSWER TESTING

If a device involving language is chosen, should it be an essay test or a short-answer test? Let us compare the merits and limitations of both types of test, primarily for the purpose of reviewing the kinds of arguments that have been introduced during decades of controversy. The various points are not necessarily taken up in order of their importance.

Reliability of Grading or Scoring

In general, the short-answer test can be graded more reliably, or consistently, than the essay test. This means that a given short-answer test paper will have the same score no matter who grades it or how many different occasions the same person grades it, if we disregard clerical errors. On the other hand, different people or the same person at different times will not grade essay tests in the same way. The variability in grading is readily apparent in Table 10, listing the grades assigned to each of ten student essays which from 30 to 47 readers read and graded.

Table 10. Grades Given to Student Essays by 47 Raters

Paper	A	B	C	D	F	Totals
1	0	1	17	13	8	39
2	0	1	28	11	7	47
3	1	6	33	5	2	47
4	1	2	30	8	5	46
5	2	10	32	3	0	47
6	5	14	24	3	1	47
7	0	9	15	3	3	30
8	2	9	19	13	3	46
9	1	1	9	15	21	47
10	1	3	20	14	6	44
N	13	56	227	88	56	440
%	3	13	51	20	13	100

SOURCE. From P. L. Dressel, *Evaluation in the Basic College*, New York: Harper & Row, 1958. (Not all papers were read by all raters.)

Pidgeon and Yates[2] administered a number of essay-type English examinations on different occasions to groups of eleven-year-old

[2] D. A. Pidgeon and A. Yates, Symposium: The use of essays in selection at 11:IV. Experimental inquiries into the use of essay type English papers, *Brit. J. Educ. Psychol.*, 1957, 27:37–47.

children. Seven examiners marked the scripts, and a complex experimental design enabled a variety of statistical analyses to be carried out. "The results of the experiments that we have outlined . . . show that even in ideal conditions, which cannot in practice be contrived—that is, with a faultless system of marking—papers of this kind do not achieve the level of reliability that is maintained by objective tests, nor do they achieve the same degree of validity."

The unreliability of rating essay tests has been demonstrated repeatedly by many experiments. All these investigations found that scores on essay tests, *graded according to the usual methods* by different graders, vary widely. A large amount of this variation may be due not only to the unreliability of scoring, but also to a difference in the standards required for various grades.

Among other factors possibly responsible for unreliability in grading essay tests are psychological factors, influence of handwriting, and the order in which the papers are read. Psychological factors, such as fatigue, affect ability to distinguish between degrees of merit. As a test grader reads through a large pile of papers there are systematic changes, resulting from factors which, although varying for different graders, grossly affect the test scores. Test papers identical in content receive different grades when there are differences in the quality of handwriting. The order of reading test papers sometimes leads to different grades for papers of comparable content. A mediocre test paper read immediately after a very superior one may seem poorer than it is; if it were read after a very inferior one, it would seem much better.

Extensiveness of the Sampling of Achievement

The usual short-answer test containing, say, fifty items or questions draws upon a far wider range of pupil achievement than does the typical essay test containing less than fifteen questions. Consequently, with short-answer tests there is less danger that chance variations in preparation and achievement will have a great effect on test scores. Such effects occur when pupils do or do not happen to guess correctly which of a small number of essay questions will be asked. Furthermore, the more extensive coverage that short-answer tests make possible may produce less variation among teachers in the content selected for tests. On the other hand, it can be argued that each essay question usually elicits a larger sampling of achievement than each short-answer question. Which sampling is larger hence depends on how the two kinds of tests are used.

Possibility of the Pupil's Guessing or Bluffing

The restricted number of alternatives which multiple-choice tests present are often considered to let a pupil achieve a higher score than is warranted by his true achievement. That is, in a test of one hundred items each presenting two choices, pupils could on the average make fifty correct responses by following the advice of a tossed coin. Various statistical formulas have been offered to correct for this chance factor. Such mechanically applied statistical corrections cannot entirely eliminate the problem of guessing, since they are based on theorems of probability or on statistical studies of average effects, neither of which can correct for the *individual* pupil's spurious achievement through guessing.

Nonetheless, as the logic of estimating test reliability shows, when a test has adequate reliability we know that the factor of chance success is negligible. Chance success on multiple-choice items, if the test is reliable enough, will not greatly affect the rank order of pupils.

The essay test, however, may be similarly weakened if not well constructed and graded. A pupil may often gain an advantage from the positive effect on grades of such factors as speed of writing, good literary style, and ability to "free-associate" around a question. Here, however, valid, constant scoring standards can counteract the effect of bluffing or guessing in the case of *individual* students.

Pretest, or Motivational, Effects on Pupil Achievement

Does expecting a short-answer instead of an essay test have a different effect on a pupil's preparation and achievement? Students certainly think so when they insist on knowing whether they will have an essay or short-answer test. Several experiments have attempted to answer this question. Some of them have shown that the short-answer test directs attention to detail and exact wording, whereas the essay test encourages study methods involving organization, perception of relationships, and personal reactions. Others have shown that the true-false, multiple-choice, completion, and essay tests are equally good for motivating the learning of facts. Some studies show significant differences between the essay and the objective-type tests, but others show no significant differences when subsequent retention of the subject matter was tested. The conclusion on this issue probably cannot be general. It depends on what kinds of essay and short-answer tests students have experienced in the past, what expectations they have developed concerning such tests, and the mental processes required by the content of the test items.

Posttest, or Instructional, Effects on Pupil Achievement

We can break this question down into (1) the suggestive effect, if any, of the untrue material included in short-answer tests and (2) the potentialities of the two kinds of test for increasing various kinds of achievement. Negative suggestion refers to the possibility that the false statements in true-false tests and the incorrect alternatives in multiple-choice tests may implant misinformation in the minds of pupils. That is, students may retain the false elements of tests and later on believe them to be correct. Research has shown that the small amount of negative suggestion is fully offset by an even greater positive suggestion, leaving a positive net effect. So, on the whole, pupils learn more than they lose by taking true-false tests.

The value of the two types of tests for instructional purposes can have two forms. One such value for the essay test is urged forcefully by Krey:

There is one skill which may, indeed has been, seriously impaired by the excessive use of the new-type tests. This is skill in expression, the ability to set forth some topic in social science clearly, convincingly, and agreeably. Teachers in college have begun to remark that students who come to them from school systems in which the new-type test has been used almost exclusively for a number of years are unable to express themselves cogently either orally or in writing. In school systems in which the new-type test has been used extremely, it has been possible for students to avoid writing a single complete sentence except in courses in English composition. Inasmuch as coherent and cogent composition is still one of the most widely used, as it is one of the most valuable, skills in social science, it would seem essential to continue to use the essay-type examination, if for no other reason than to afford practice in this skill.[3]

Although Krey applies his argument only in the social sciences, his point of view has been upheld in many other subject-matter fields. Granted the importance of the skills he mentioned, the essay test becomes essential as a motivator and instructional device for the development of those skills. However, ability to write "coherent and cogent composition" is so important that it should by no means be left to incidental learning while taking an examination. On the contrary, it should be carefully provided for in the instructional program and be separately evaluated.

Short-answer tests may also be of instructional value, as shown by a study by Curtis and Woods,[4] who compared the teaching values of four common practices in correcting examination papers. The four methods were as follows:

1. Pupils corrected own papers while teacher read the correct answers. Free discussion followed.
2. Teacher checked incorrect items but made no corrections. Papers were later returned and discussed item by item.
3. Teacher carefully wrote in all corrections. Papers were later returned and discussed item by item.
4. Teacher carefully wrote in all corrections. Papers were later returned but only the questions pupils asked were discussed.

On the next day and again after six weeks, the test containing one hundred items in various short-answer forms was repeated without warning. The first method, in which the teacher is least active and the pupils most active, resulted in the greatest improvement in scores.

A process of using "testing" for teaching has lately received considerable attention. Skinner[5] has developed "teaching machines" in which materials are presented much like tests of the short-answer type. Although the teaching machines are not intended as tests or

---

[3] T. L. Kelley and A. C. Krey, *Tests and Measurements in the Social Sciences*, New York: Scribners, 1934.

[4] F. D. Curtis and G. G. Woods, A study of the relative teaching values of four common practices in correcting examination papers, *Sch. Rev.*, 1929, 37:615–623.

[5] B. F. Skinner, Teaching machines, *Science*, 1958, 128:969–977.

evaluation devices, they warrant mention at this time. According to Skinner:

> Sets of separate presentations or "frames" of visual material are stored on disks, cards, or tapes. One frame is presented at a time, adjacent frames being out of sight. In one type of machine the student composes a response by moving printed figures or letters. His setting is compared by the machine with a coded response. If the two correspond, the machine automatically presents the next frame. If they do not, the response is cleared, and another must be composed. The student cannot proceed to a second step until the first has been taken. A machine of this kind is being tested in teaching spelling, arithmetic, and other subjects in the lower grades. . . . For more advanced students—from junior high school, say, through college—a machine which senses an arrangement of letters or figures is unnecessarily rigid in specifying the form of response. Fortunately, such students may be asked to compare their responses with printed material revealed by the machine. In the machine . . . material is printed in 30 radial frames on a 12-inch disk. The student inserts the disk and closes the machine. . . . All but one corner of one frame is visible through the window. The student writes his response on a paper strip exposed through a second opening. By lifting a lever on the front of the machine, he moves what he has written under a transparent cover and uncovers the correct response in the remaining corner of the frame. If the two responses correspond, he moves the lever horizontally. This movement punches a hole in the paper opposite his response, recording the fact that he called it correct, and alters the machine so that the frame will not appear again when the student works around the disk a second time. . . . The student proceeds in this way until he has responded to all frames. He then works around the disk a second time, but only those frames appear to which he has not correctly responded. When the disk revolves without stopping, the assignment is finished.

Short-answer tests can have instructional value when they are used so as to provide practice. Thus both the essay and the short-answer test can have positive effects on achievement, each in its special way. The instructional value of the essay test involves the highly important ability to marshal and organize ideas with a minimum of outside help; the instructional value of the short-answer test can be aimed at the wide variety of other objectives that can be tested in this form.

Labor of Construction

To make an essay test in its *usual* form requires far less effort than the short-answer test does. This follows from the differences between the two types of tests in the number and precision of the questions put to the pupil. As shown in the following sections, good short-answer test items can be composed only by giving thoughtful and detailed attention to instructional objectives, and by applying much general intelligence. Essay test questions are usually fewer, less specific in content, and less carefully composed with regard to subtle psychological values. Furthermore, it is possible to accumulate short-answer test questions from year to year; they merely require editing to keep them up to date. This accumulation increases (1) the sampling of the subject matter, (2) the flexibility of testing for special purposes, (3) the possibility of constructing "equivalent" forms of tests for determining reliability, and (4) the ease of constructing short-answer tests.

Labor of Scoring and Grading

Here the short-answer test is superior because it can be scored quickly and little skill is required. Although an essay test can be constructed in less than one hour, grading it may require perhaps ten hours. A short-answer test may require ten hours for construction and perhaps one hour for scoring. The essay test require expert knowledge for both construction and grading, whereas a short-answer test requires an expert only for its construction. Although these illustrative time estimates would probably never apply in a real case, it is clear that there is little difference between the two types in the total quantity and quality of the work involved, unless the number of pupils tested is far greater than is usual in the average classroom. In this case, the short-answer test has a major advantage because of its easy scorability.

Cost of Administration

Short-answer tests usually are reproduced by mimeograph or a similar method, so that each pupil will have a copy. Essay tests, on the other hand, can be written on the chalkboard or dictated orally. The importance of these factors depends on the availability of reproducing devices to the classroom teacher. Since most present-day schools have such devices, this consideration should probably not affect the teacher's choice between the two types of tests.

Attitudes of Pupils Toward the Two Types of Tests

The evidence on pupil attitude has differed. Some investigators report that pupils prefer essay tests, and others report a preference for the short-answer test. Some claim that pupils, realizing that marks on essay tests are relatively unreliable, consider them unjust and prefer short-answer tests for the reliability of scoring which they insure. However, Jones[6] found that the statement, "I think one's ability is far better shown through discussion questions than through short objective questions," was agreed to by 68 percent of the students in colleges which gave senior comprehensives, and 55 percent of the superior students in other colleges. Alumni taking both types of examinations offered even more favorable comments on the essay test, because they felt that it was more important to be able to discuss an issue than merely to check it.

Since attitudes are learned, students' feelings on this issue will depend on their experience with the two kinds of tests. Teachers can probably shift these attitudes in either direction according to the skill and wisdom they apply to using the two in their classrooms.

Intellectual Pleasure and Professional Growth Derived by the Teacher

Most of the work in short-answer testing goes into the construction of the test, whereas most of the work in essay testing goes into grading the test. How do the two types compare as far as pleasure in the work is involved? Vernon's preference is one with which most teachers will agree: ". . . The setting of a new-type test is a fascinating occupation, which can be done in odd moments throughout the year; and the marking is simply a routine matter which involves no

[6] E. S. Jones, The relationship of examinations and instructions, Proc. 1936, Institute for Administrative Officers of Higher Institutions.

mental strain. By contrast, the marking of large numbers of essay-type scripts in psychology is the most trying work that he has ever had to do."[7]

Constructing short-answer tests probably results in greater professional growth for the teacher than does constructing essay tests. The need for thinking through instructional objectives, for intensive attention to subject matter, for sophistication in the logical theory of measurement, for insight into pupil difficulties and errors is greater in short-answer testing. In satisfying these needs the teacher should acquire desirable skills that carry over into all phases of teaching.

Torbet[8] studied the attitudes of a selected group of 150 secondary-school teachers in Colorado—50 English, 50 mathematics and science, and 50 homemaking and shop—on general testing issues, issues related to the mechanics of testing, and issues in which personality played a predominant role. According to his findings:

> Teachers clearly agreed with expert opinion on the value of testing in the educational program; on returning test papers and explaining the answers for instructional purposes; on the necessity of goals for testing; and on selecting important points in the instruction for testing. . . . The areas of disagreement with the experts suggest that the overall mental hygiene aspect of testing needs attention. Teachers seldom mentioned the pupils in test evaluation. On the contrary, it appeared that testing was an onerous task to teachers and an authoritarian weapon in their hands to compel obedience of pupils. There were, however, many individual exceptions to this generalization. . . . The majority of teachers interviewed did not seem to understand the mechanics of good testing.

Distorting Effects on Manifested Achievement

Here we are concerned with whether essay tests and short-answer tests introduce factors between the teacher and pupil performance that distort the expression of achievement, just as colored glasses change things. Do essay tests involve behavior on the part of the pupil that colors his achievement? Do short-answer tests elicit be-

---

[7] P. E. Vernon, *The Measurement of Ability*, London: Univ. of London Press, 1940, p. 247.

[8] David P. Torbet, The attitude of a select group of Colorado secondary school teachers toward informal teacher-made tests as measured by a projective interview, *J. Educ. Res.*, 1957, 50:691–700.

havior that reflects not only achievement but also intelligence and test sophistication that operate to provide him with correct answers even when he does not really have the achievement at which the test is aimed? Essay tests measure ability in expression, breadth of vocabulary, speed of writing, and other aspects of pupils that may be irrelevant to a particular kind of achievement. The "halo" effect of the teacher's general impression of a pupil also comes between the pupil's achievement and the teacher's evaluation of it.

Short-answer tests, however, are not necessarily free from this distortion. A pupil must be able to follow the instructions given in a test and then manipulate his knowledge and intellectual resources in such a way as to fit them to the requirements of the question. Ebel has presented an excellent summary[9] of the "irrelevant cues" that may twist the achievement of a pupil below or above its true value. Short-answer testing requires skill in anticipating the mental devices that enable a pupil to obtain a higher score on a test than his achievement warrants. The methods of phrasing test questions that minimize this distortion are discussed later in this chapter. Here we note only that short-answer tests as well as essay tests can distort what they are testing.

Fitness for Evaluation of Complex Achievement

It is frequently charged that short-answer tests measure only small elements of achievement in the form of details of information and collections of facts, and that essay tests are needed to evaluate general understanding, interpretation, capacity for organizing and formulating knowledge, and other complex mental operations. This belief is reflected in the findings concerning differences in the way pupils prepare for the two kinds of tests.

Short-answer tests *can*, however, be designed to get at these complex types of achievement. The yearbook, "The Measurement of Understanding,"[10] described in detail the techniques that can be used to evaluate higher mental processes in various school subjects. Ebel's chapter, "Writing the Test Item,"[11] also gives specific illustra-

[9] R. L. Ebel, Writing the test item, chap. 7 in E. F. Lindquist (ed.), *Educational Measurement*, Washington: American Council on Education, 1951, pp. 221–223.

[10] W. A. Brownell, *45th Yearb. Natl. Soc. Stud. Educ.*, 1946, Part 1.

[11] R. L. Ebel, *op. cit.*, chap. 7.

tions of test items for measuring complex understanding. Many of these techniques involve short-answer testing. The success of these authors in devising and describing such techniques indicates that essay tests have no monopoly on the possibilities of evaluating complex achievement.

The following statement by Freeman sums up our own position: "I suggest that we recover our balance, confining objective tests to those uses to which they are fitted, and restoring the free expression of thought to the position which it deserves."[12]

Summary Comparison

The accompanying tabulation summarizes the advantages of essay and short-answer tests. A plus sign indicates the type judged to be superior as far as the factors listed are concerned.

Factor	Essay	Short Answer
Reliability of scoring		+
Adaquacy of sampling student achievement		+
Labor required to prepare	+	
Labor required to score		+
Providing opportunity for student to select, or ganize, and integrate	+	
Providing opportunity to test effective writing ..	+	
Possibility for bluffing, "writing around the topic"		+
Opportunity for guessing	+	
Freedom from distortion of grading by skill in expression and quality of handwriting		+

CONSTRUCTING AND GRADING ESSAY TESTS

Once we have decided to restrict the use of the essay test to the type of evaluation for which it is best suited, we have the task of defining achievement in terms of mental processes—ways in which subject matter may be handled. The operation of a mental process assumes the presence of some material or subject matter to be

[12] F. N. Freeman, The monopoly of objective tests, *Educ. Forum*, 1946, 10: 389–395.

processed or handled by the pupil. To find out whether he has the knowledge or "raw material" it is usually sufficient to use the short-answer type of test. This does not mean that short-answer or "objective" tests must be restricted to the testing of factual information but rather that they are better suited for this purpose than essay tests. The essay test has long been used in a confused way for the simultaneous testing of both factual information and the ability to handle or process this information in various ways. Failure to restrict essay testing to the purposes for which it is best suited has resulted in lower validity and efficiency of evaluation.

One reason for failing to use the essay test only where it is suited is that teachers have been unfamiliar with the short-answer forms of test items. Another is that they have not been sufficiently aware of the many types of essay question and of the need for framing questions that will require the mental processes called for by instructional objectives. The latter reason may be largely eliminated if teachers become familiar with types of question like those presented by Monroe and Carter.[13] These authors listed twenty types of "thought" questions. This list cannot claim to be exhaustive, composed of mutually exclusive items, or based on experimental research; but it should prove suggestive to teachers who wish to realize the full potentialities of the essay question. We must remember that the question alone does not determine the mental processes required or elicited. How the subject matter has been taught and how the student has learned also make a difference. The same question may require "thought" from one student, memory from a second, and other mental processes from a third. The thought question for a given student today may be a memory question for the same student tomorrow.

Types of Essay Questions

On the following page is Monroe and Carter's list of types of essay questions, with an illustration of each type drawn whenever possible from these authors.

[13] W. S. Monroe and R. E. Carter, *The Use of Different Types of Thought Questions in Secondary Schools and Their Relative Difficulty for Students*, Bull. 14, Bureau of Educational Research, College of Education, University of Illinois, 1923.

1. Selective recall—basis given
   What do New Zealand and Australia sell in Europe that may interfere with our market?
2. Evaluative recall—basis given
   Which do you consider the three most important American inventions in the nineteenth century from the standpoint of expansion and growth of transportation?
3. Comparison of two things—on a single designated basis
   Compare Eliot and Thackeray in ability in character delineation.
4. Comparison of two things—in general
   Compare the early settlers of the Massachusetts colony with those of the Virginia colony.
5. Decision—for or against
   In which in your opinion can you do better, oral or written examinations? Why?
6. Causes or effects
   Why has the Senate become a much more powerful body than the House of Representatives?
7. Explanation of the use or exact meaning of some phrase in a passage
   Tell how a siphon works.
8. Summary of some unit of the text or of some article read
   Tell briefly the contents of the Declaration of Independence.
9. Analysis (the word itself is seldom involved in the question)
   What characteristic of Silas Marner makes you understand why Raveloe people were suspicious of him?
10. Statement of relationship
    Why is a knowledge of botany helpful in studying agriculture?
11. Illustration or examples (your own) of principles in science, language, etc.
    Illustrate the *incorrect* use of a relative pronoun with a parenthetical phrase.
12. Classification (usually the converse of number 11)
    Group the following words according to their part of speech and name each group: red, boy, run, house, in, with, small, slowly, ball, etc.
13. Application of rules or principles in these situations
    If you sat halfway between the middle and one end of a seesaw, would a person sitting on the other end have to be heavier or lighter than you in order to make the seesaw balance in the middle? Why?
14. Discussion
    Discuss the Monroe Doctrine.

15. Statement of aim—author's purpose in his selection or organization of material
    What was the purpose of introducing this incident?
16. Criticism—as to the adequacy, correctness, or relevancy of a printed statement or a classmate's answer to a question on the lesson
    What is wrong with the following menu? [Menu is given below.]
17. Outline
    Outline the steps required in computing the square root of a five-figure number.
18. Reorganization of facts (a good type of review question to give in training in organization)
    The student is asked for reports where facts from different organizations are arranged on an entirely new basis.
19. Formulation of new questions—problems and questions raised
    What else must be known in order to understand the matter under consideration?
20. New methods of procedure
    How would you change the plot in order to produce a different effect?

It should be clear—especially from the discussion of the various kinds of short-answer questions later in this chapter—that some of these types—among them 1, 2, 11, 12, and 19—can be formulated in short-answer form, such as completion or simple-recall items.

Suggestions for Constructing Essay Tests

1. Use essay questions only to evaluate achievement of the instructional objectives that short-answer forms do not test as well or better.

2. Phrase the questions so they will require as precisely as possible the specific mental processes operating on specific subject matter that are embodied in the instructional objective at which the questions are aimed.

3. Sometimes the teacher uses an essay test question as a "projective technique," and gives the student no information about what basis to use in answering it. The student is encouraged to choose and defend his own interpretation of a question, and is allowed a

free and extended response. The teacher can sometimes in this way gain improved insight into a student's abilities, difficulties, and ways of thinking and thus have a basis for guiding his learning.

4. Unless you are using the essay test as a projective technique, phrase the questions so as to give as many hints concerning the organization of the pupil's answers as are not inconsistent with the instructional objectives at which the questions are aimed. The teacher should not ask pupils merely to discuss a specific topic but should give them the basis of discussion. He should not give any hints concerning the organization of answers, of course, if part of the objective at which the question is aimed is ability to distinguish the relevant bases for discussion. Such "structuring" really increases the number of questions or subquestions in an essay examination and reduces the length of the answer to each question. As such, the more structured the essay question becomes, the more it resembles short-answer test items. Carried to an extreme, structuring robs the essay question of its unique value in testing the pupil's ability to organize and express his answers. Each teacher must therefore maintain some balance between openness and structure in essay questions. He can attempt to elicit as much organizational effort from the pupils as possible while giving them a common set of reference points that will make their answers comparable.

5. Should you permit choice among questions? Some writers hold that only by requiring all pupils to answer all questions can their achievement be compared. It is almost impossible to equate optional questions for difficulty without an elaborate pretesting program. Hence the teacher who permits a choice among optional questions can never know whether all the pupils have taken a test that is equally difficult. Nor can pupils be relied on to choose essay questions from a series of optional questions that will enable them to show their achievement in the best possible light. Some pupils may think that choosing more difficult questions will make the teacher more lenient to them, but others in the same classroom will not reason this way.

On the other hand, it sometimes seems that allowing choice among questions makes the test fairer. Students can better show their strengths according to their different backgrounds. In a sense, students may be made to take the "same" test more effectively if they are allowed to choose among questions or topics according to their special interests, than if all are forced to write on the same topic.

6. Plan the questions so that the pupil can actually give adequate answers to all of them within the alloted time if he has the required achievement. The questions should be arranged in order of increasing difficulty to promote a better distribution of working time and better morale while taking the test. Pupils of mediocre or low achievement may become discouraged if they are confronted with the more difficult questions at the beginning of the test. Time will be lost which they could more profitably employ on the easier questions. Furthermore, only the better pupils are differentiated from one another by the more difficult questions. The weaker pupils coming to the difficult items at the end of the test already have had an opportunity to indicate their full achievement; hence discouragement and loss of working time will have no adverse effects on them.

Suggestions for Grading Essay Tests

We shall discuss three methods of grading essay tests: (1) the percentage-passing method, (2) the check-list point-score method, and (3) projective interpretation.

Percentage Passing. The percentage-passing method involves giving each question a definite value and marking every answer to that question on the scale of 100. Some arbitrary percentage, such as 60 or 70, is commonly chosen as the dividing line between "passing" and "failing." "Passing" is usually vaguely defined in such terms as "able to meet minimum standards at this grade level." This grading method is still used in some school systems for report-card grades. Its major disadvantage is that the standard of "passing" varies widely from teacher to teacher. Also it permits such a wide range of scores —from zero to 100—that it gives a spurious notion of how finely teachers can discriminate between qualities of performance. Furthermore, it is usually not accompanied by any system for analyzing answers into specific features. A definite and unambiguous criterion of excellence of response is usually not available.

The shortcomings of this method have been brought out by many studies of the reliability of grading essay questions, for this is the method usually used in these studies. (See the discussion of the reliability of essay test grading on p. 213.) As these studies have shown, wide fluctuations in grades given a single paper by different teachers may be expected in most cases where this method is used.

Check-List Point-Score Method. The check-list point-score method requires analyzing the ideal response to the essay question into a series of features or points, each specifically defined. The pupil's answer is then judged with respect to each feature and a point is awarded if the feature is present in the response.

An illustration of this method is the way the College Entrance Examination Board graded the following item on the interpretation of sight passages:[14]

A metaphor is a transfer of meaning, one thing or act being named or implied when another is meant. It is the commonest and most serviceable figure in language. . . . There is at least one metaphor in each of the following passages. Indicate the metaphors in each passage and translate them in such a way as to show your understanding of the author's use of them. Allow about twenty-five minutes for this question. The model below is intended to suggest the kind of an answer expected. [Model omitted.]

1. "Poverty is the banana skin on the doorstep of romance," P. G. Wodehouse.

The pupil's answers to questions in this series were to be marked on a maximum of five points:

Adequate comprehension of the passage as a whole, 1 point
Explicit indication of the principal metaphors (banana skin and doorstep), 1 point
Adequate translation of these terms, 1 point
More than merely adequate understanding of the passage (i.e., recognition of Wodehouse's humorous purpose), 1 point
Composition—to all answers not incoherent or marred by serious grammatical errors, 1 point

[14] E. S. Noyes, Recent trends of the comprehensive examination in English, *Educ. Rec., Suppl. 13*, 1940, 21:107–119.

For example, the following response would receive credit for only the fifth point: "In this sentence Wodehouse means the banana skin to be an aid rather than a hindrance to romance. By this Wodehouse shows that a person does not stop to think about falling in love merely because of poverty." The pupil failed to comprehend the meaning of the passage, indicated only one of the metaphors, mistranslated that one, and lost the fourth point for not having more than a merely adequate comprehension. He received the fifth point because his answer was reasonably grammatical, had no misspellings, and was properly punctuated.

The following answer received credit for all points except the second: "Wodehouse is humorously saying that poverty is the danger that romance faces at its beginning." The student scored the first point because he clearly understood the passage, lost the second for failure to indicate the metaphors explicitly, and won the third for translating both metaphors, the fourth for recognizing the humorous purpose, and the fifth for composition.

In grading by this method the teacher must work out a rigorous, explicit analysis of the things desired in the pupil's response. He should write out an answer that contains all these ideas. Perhaps he should also make another list of ideas not regarded as acceptable for credit.

Projective Interpretation. In considering essay tests as projective techniques, Sims[15] has suggested the following procedure:

1. Use an inductive method; only after inspecting the answers should you work out a point of view for interpreting them. (If you can predetermine the right answer, use a short-answer test.)
2. Distinguish between manifest and hidden content, between results of the curriculum and the manifestations of general personality, between the answers and the inferences from them. Style, omissions, rationalizations, or attitudes can be as revealing as what is consciously written in a paper.
3. Identify clearly and exactly what you are looking for, and develop an organized method for inferring from the data. (Presumably this im-

[15] V. M. Sims, The essay examination as a projective technique, *Educ. Psychol. Meas.*, 1948, 8:15–31.

plies techniques like those described for the check-list point-score method.)

4. Read the papers for what they reveal about the learning of individual students rather than for simple counts of objective facts. This usually will give you clues and suggestions for further work with individual students.

5. If it is necessary to determine marks or grades, identify the most frequent pattern of response as the basis for one mark and classify the deviates into categories of marks above and below it. If possible, develop check sheets, rating scales, or sets of objective questions for the reader to use in evaluating answers. (This is also similar to the check-list point-score method.)

6. Avoid overly broad generalizations. Since essay tests are limited samples of behavior, conclusions about personality based on them should be tentative.

Projective techniques for appraising personality require years of scientific effort before they become established as trustworthy. Some projective techniques, such as the Rorschach inkblots (requiring specially trained clinicians), are still not completely validated after decades of research. Some psychologists hold that essay tests can be considered projective techniques in only a figurative sense until they have been systematized and validated. But they can give insight into personality and achievement that is not available by any other means.

Further Aids in Grading Essay Tests

The following are also suggested as ways to improve grading essay examination papers:

1. Grade papers without knowing whose paper you are grading. Factors such as teacher-student relationships can thus be largely eliminated and the paper graded solely on its merit. A teacher's prejudice for or against a pupil cannot then affect the grade he gives the paper. The teacher can secure anonymity by having the pupils write their name on the back of the examination paper, or by assigning numbers to the pupils in such a way that they are unknown to him, and later having each pupil put his name opposite the appropriate number.

2. Grade only one question at a time. In this way the teacher

can compare one pupil's answer to a given question more easily with all the other answers to the question. This procedure requires the teacher to keep only one list of points in mind at a time; he does not have to waste time continually refreshing his memory about the points required in other questions.

3. Wherever possible, have papers graded by more than one person, especially in important examinations that determine promotion, graduation, and so on. As much as possible, the graders should have the same standards and consider the same points. Whenever two graders disagree sharply, a third grader should read the papers, rather than having the first two graders arbitrate; in the latter situation the grader with the more dominant personality may determine the grade.

4. Make special provision for considering sentence structure, paragraphing, writing ability, spelling, and so forth. Should these factors affect the student's score on an essay examination that is primarily concerned with other instructional objectives? It will, of course, require a conscious effort on the part of the teacher to prevent himself from being influenced adversely by poor spelling and grammar, or, on the other hand, influenced favorably by neat handwriting, extensive vocabulary, and fine prose. Although all these factors in answers to essay questions may be positively related to pupil's achievement of other objectives, they are, strictly speaking, often irrelevant to the specific kinds of achievement at which the essay test is aimed. In any case, the teacher should consciously make a decision on this point.

CONSTRUCTING SHORT-ANSWER TESTS

Short-answer test construction involves the following steps: (1) Draw up an outline or table of specifications, indicating in terms of subject matter and mental processes the instructional objectives whose achievement is to be evaluated. (2) Compose the individual items or questions so that they correspond with specific items in the table of specifications. (3) Arrange these items in proper order and form, prepare directions for the pupils taking the test, prepare the scoring key, and arrange other mechanical features of the test. We shall describe each of these steps in turn.

Table of Specifications

The table of specifications draws its material from the statement of instructional objectives. It differs from the statement of objectives in that it is designed to aid in test construction rather than in teaching. The table of specifications for an achievement test will contain only the objectives that can be evaluated by the test; it will omit those whose achievement cannot be evaluated by a device involving symbols in the form of a teacher-made short-answer test.

The table of specifications should contain some indication of the relative importance of each of the various instructional objectives. The subdivisions of the table of specifications should, of course, be made on more than one basis so that no important points of view will be omitted or unduly emphasized.

Table 11 shows how specifications might be drawn up for an examination in physical science. The teacher and students in the course could probably express their ideas as to the proper emphasis on various objectives by means of such a table. The actual number of items will probably change as test construction goes on. The teacher will get new ideas about points that the pupils should understand or know. He will also probably find that his efforts to make up meaningful questions are unsuccessful in some areas; in these areas the number of items may be reduced. In short, the table of specifications *interacts* with the process of writing the questions; each influences the other. The table of specifications keeps the teacher aware of the emphasis he is building into his test.

By tallying each item, as it is prepared, in the appropriate subdivision in the table of specifications, the teacher can keep the distribution of the items in agreement with the emphasis determined by the statement of objectives. The number of items for a given objective should be roughly proportional to the desired contribution of that part of the test to the total score. Since this is only a rough approximation, however, test makers need not show the exact number of items in the tables of specifications. The actual weighting of a given part of the total test score can be determined only approximately by the number of items allotted to that part.

Table 11. Table of Specifications

Objectives	The Universe and Solar System, Scientific Method	Origin and Composition of Earth, Rocks—Minerals	Atmospheric Movements, Clouds, Weather	Atomic and Kinetic Theory, Gas Laws, Heat
		Content		
Numbers of lectures	4	5	3	6
Number of laboratory periods	1	4	1	3
Total time in each area	5	9	4	9
I. Knowledge and understanding of				
A. Scientific facts and terminology	5	12	3	4
B. Principles, laws and theories	2	3	2	4
C. The mathematical treatment of physical concepts	1	...	1	2
D. Theoretical assumptions and valid experimentation	1	1	...	4
E. Definitions and generalizations	2	4	2	2
II. Skills and abilities in				
A. The solution of mathematical problems	1	...	...	4
B. The application of principles to familiar problem situations	2	4	1	3
C. The application of principles to new problem situations	1	2	1	4
D. Laboratory procedures and techniques	...	2	...	1
E. The formulation of generalizations from specific facts	2	2	1	2
F. The interpretation and use of data, tables, and pictorial material	1	3	3	3
Totals	18	33	14	33

SOURCE. From *Comprehensive Examinations in a Program of Gen-*

for a Physical Science Examination

	Content							
Mathematics, Variation, Functions, Right Triangles	Weathering, Erosional Agents, Deposition of Sediments, Field Trip	Mechanical Energy, Gravitation, Forces and Motion	Electrical Energy, Statics, Magnetism, Electrical Effects	Chemical Energy and Changes, Acids—Bases	Earth Movements, Diastrophism, Vulcanism, Isostasy	Wave Motion, Light, Sound, Electromagnetic Radiation	Metals, Non-Metals, Fuels, Carbon Compounds, Periodic Chart	Total Number of Items
5	3	3	6	5	3	5	5	. . .
4	1	3	2	5	0	5	1	. . .
9	1	6	8	10	3	10	6	
2	6	3	6	8	2	8	4	63
2	4	3	3	4	2	4	3	36
. . .	. . .	2	2	2	. . .	2	2	14
. . .	. . .	2	2	3	. . .	3	2	18
2	2	2	2	3	2	3	2	28
6	. . .	3	4	4	. . .	4	. . .	26
2	2	3	2	2	2	4	3	30
2	2	2	2	4	1	2	1	24
. . .	. . .	1	2	3	. . .	1	1	11
. . .	2	2	1	2	. . .	3	. . .	17
4	2	2	2	3	2	4	4	33
20	20	25	28	38	11	38	22	300

eral Education, East Lansing: Michigan State Univ. Press.

Composing Test Items

The next step is to compose the individual items. Short-answer items can take many forms: true-false, multiple-choice, completion, and matching, among others. Which form the teacher should use for testing the particular objective is a matter of psychological insight into the mental operations required. But the fitness of any form of test item for testing a particular objective or mental operation depends not only on the form of the item but also on how it is applied. True-false or multiple-choice items may test merely memory but they can also be designed to test interpretation, organization, ability to infer, and other mental processes.

Before we discuss the form of short-answer test items, it will be profitable to consider some of the principles that apply to all of them. Some of these principles call merely for common sense, but their discussion is justified by the frequency with which teacher-made tests violate them. Others reflect the research and experience of test experts and would not be apparent to novices.

1. Avoid obvious, trivial, meaningless, and ambiguous items.
2. Observe the rules of rhetoric, grammar, and punctuation.
3. Avoid items that have no answer upon which all experts will agree.
4. Avoid "trick" or "catch" items, that is, items so phrased that the correct answer depends on obscure key words to which even good students are unlikely to give sufficient attention.
5. Avoid items which contain "irrelevant cues." These are items so phrased that the correct answer may be determined merely by using intelligence without real knowledge of the achievement at which the item is aimed. The kinds of irrelevant cues which may occur vary with different types of test items and will be discussed specifically in connection with each type. Illustrative of an irrelevant cue is the following:

    Man is an (1) plant, (2) reptile, (3) animal, (4) bird.

    The irrelevant cue here is the article "an," which indicates that the correct answer must begin with a vowel.
6. Avoid items that furnish the answers to other items, because this will render one of the items useless for evaluation purposes.

Types of Test Items

Ebel has distinguished two major types of short-answer test items: the *supply* and the *selection type*.[16] In the past these were called "recall" and "recognition" types, respectively. But the latter terms imply that all items measure merely either of these two kinds of memory. Since this is untrue, it is better to use the terms "supply" and "selection," which tell whether the pupil must supply the words, numbers, or other symbols for his answer or select his answer from given alternatives.

What is tested by a specific type of test item depends not only on what it gives to the pupil and what sort of response it requires of him, but also on how the particular material has been taught. Questions requiring interpretative thinking by pupils in one classroom may require only rote memory from pupils in a classroom in which the desired response has been taught explicitly.

In constructing test items the teacher must therefore ask himself such questions as: "What type of test item is best suited to evaluate the French vocabulary of my pupils in the light of how they have learned vocabulary?" "What type of test item is best suited for evaluating my pupils' ability to reason arithmetically?" "What type of test item is best suited to evaluate my pupils' understanding of the relative importance of the various causes of the American Revolution?" In answering these questions he will employ all his psychological insight into the teaching situation, the pupils' learning, and the relationship of both to instructional objectives.

The *supply type* includes the following kinds of short-answer test items:

1. Simple question: very short essay-type
2. Completion: very short essay-type

The *selection type* includes the following kinds of short-answer test items:

3. Constant alternatives, i.e., items requiring choice between constant alternatives, such as

[16] R. L. Ebel, *op. cit.*, p. 193.

a. True-false, yes-no, right-wrong, synonym-antonym, agree-disagree (two alternatives)
b. True-false-doubtful, true-false-converse (three constant alternatives)
c. True or false with corrections
d. True or false for a series of statements based on a given topic or body of material
e. True or false with inferences
f. True or false with qualifications
g. True or false with diagrams
h. Check list for a given characteristic
i. Master list of characteristics, explanations, evaluations, etc.
4. Changing alternatives (multiple-choice), i.e., items requiring choice between changing alternatives on the basis of which one is the
a. Correct or best answer
b. Incorrect or worst answer
c. Common principle or most inclusive
d. Most dissimilar
e. Result from among causes
f. Cause from among results
5. Matching
a. Simple matching
b. Compound matching
6. Analogies
7. Rearrangement
a. Chronological order
b. Logical order
c. Ranking
d. Pied outlines

As we take up each of these in turn, we shall provide definitions and illustrations, discuss advantages and limitations, and suggest how best to use it.

Simple-Question Items

Simple-question items are usually in the form of a direct question, a specific direction, or a "stimulus," to which the pupil responds with a word, a number, a phrase, or a sentence. Illustrations:

What are the two main gases found in air? _____   _____
Who was the first President of the United States? _____
Explain in one sentence or phrase what connection each of the following people had with Abraham Lincoln.
Stephen A. Douglas _____
Chester A. Arthur _____
Ulysses S. Grant _____
Dred Scott _____

Advantages and Disadvantages. The advantages of this type are: It eliminates almost entirely the possibility of guessing. It is a "natural" form of question, requiring little adaptation by the pupil. It is easily prepared. This type of item is particularly useful in problem-solving situations in mathematics and the physical sciences, where the result of a complex reasoning and computational process can be expressed in a few symbols.

The disadvantages include the following: Scoring is not as completely objective as that of the selection type of item. Almost inevitably certain pupils make responses that only expert judgment can distinguish from the correct answers in the scoring key. In subjects other than mathematics and the physical sciences, the simple-question item tends to become too much a matter of identifying, naming, and associating facts; interpretative, inferential handling of complicated concepts may be slighted. This type of item is relatively unfit for testing understanding of definitions or other achievement that cannot be expressed in a single, unique word, phrase, or number.

Suggestions for Improving Simple-Question Items

1. *Require short, definite, clean-cut answers.* Only in the degree which this suggestion is followed will objectivity of scoring be possible. Example:

Faulty: What kind of process is evaporation? ....   _____
Improved: To what does a liquid change when it evaporates? ..   _____

2. *If several correct answers (synonyms) are possible, count each one correct.* Example is found on page 240.

What method is used to preserve meats which are transported over long distances? .... —————

Here the correct answer may be "refrigeration," "cooling," "icing," "canning," "cold-packing," "pickling," or "smoking." In scoring this item, count each of these responses right, or change the item to restrict the correct answer to only one of these.

3. *Decide whether spelling should be disregarded or given a separate score.* It is usually preferable to distinguish accuracy in spelling from knowledge of the correct response as a separate instructional objective and evaluate it separately.

4. *Minimize the use of textbook expressions or stereotyped language in phrasing the questions.* Such phrasing rewards and motivates rote memorization of the textbook, which is not always associated with real understanding independent of textbook terminology.

5. *Specify the terms in which the response is to be given.* Failure to observe this results in responses all of which may be correct but evade the issue at which the item is aimed. Example:

Faulty: Where is the world's tallest building located? ...... —————
Improved: In what city is the world's tallest building located? —————

In the first case the correct answer could be anything from "North America" to "the Atlantic seaboard." The second example forces the pupil to face the issue. With computational problems indicate how precise (e.g., to how many decimal places) the answer should be and whether or not units are required.

6. *In testing for a knowledge and understanding of definitions it is often better to provide the term and require a definition than to provide a definition and require the term.* This requires a higher level of achievement. Since definitions cannot usually be phrased in the form of a "short answer," it is obvious that the simple-question type of test item is rather unfit for testing understanding of definitions. Example:

Faulty: What is the general term for vertebrates whose females suckle their young? .... —————
Improved: Define "mammal." ——————————————

Other types of test items, such as the multiple-choice, are probably better adapted to testing this kind of achievement.

7. *Direct questions are probably preferable to incomplete declarative sentences.* Especially for younger and less "test-sophisticated" pupils, the direct question is preferable because it is more similar to ordinary discourse. Example:

Faulty: America was discovered in the year .... _____
Improved: In what year was America discovered? .... _____

8. *Hints concerning the correct answer, in the form of the first letter of a word, or a number indicating the number of letters in a word, should generally not be given.* Such hints may confuse students when the answer upon which they have decided does not coincide with the given hint, although it is a correct synonym. Guessing and responses to superficial cues may also result from this practice.

9. *The space for the response should usually be at the right of the question.* Most pupils prefer this placing, probably because the right-handed pupil does not have to cover the question while writing his answer.

10. *Allow enough space for the response to permit legible writing.* Allow more space for younger pupils.

11. *Arranging the answer spaces in a column at the right-hand margin of the page makes scoring more convenient.*

Supply-Completion Items

Supply-completion items require the pupil to "write in" a word which has been omitted from either an isolated statement or connected discourse. Examples:

The joule is a unit of .... _____
Most automobile engines are _____ cycle engines.
The mother called to her child, "Please go to the store and _____ me some apples."
The greatest nation of the western hemisphere is _____, the head of which is the _____, who exercises the chief _____ power of the government but whose power is checked and _____ by the legislature, called _____, all of which carry on their functions in the city of _____.

Advantages and Disadvantages. Supply-completion items have advantages and disadvantages similar to those of the simple-question type. Good completion items usually cannot be made merely by leaving out one or more words from a sentence or passage from the textbook, because such words often make sense only as a result of their context. Without the context the completion item becomes ambiguous. Teachers should write completion items in their own words, make them self-contained, and make sure that they limit possible correct responses to exactly the kind of achievement intended. They should be careful not to leave out too many words, or overly mutilate a passage so that the item becomes nonsensical, e.g., "The _____ is the _____ of the _____."

Constant-Alternative Items (True-False and Others)

Constant-alternative items require the pupil to choose his answer from two or more alternatives *that remain the same for a whole series of items.* They may be in the form of statements concerning whose truth or falsity the pupil is to make a judgment. Examples:

Directions: For each of the following statements encircle T if the statement is true and F if the statement is false.

The Crusades were successful in converting many Mohammedans to the Christian faith .... T F
The head of a newborn baby is about one-fourth of the total body length .... T F

Permitting such answers as "Doubtful" or "Can't say" yields three alternatives. Another three-alternative type requires the student to say whether two variables are positively related, negatively related, or unrelated. Example:

Directions: Below is given a list of variables influencing test reliability. After each variable write:

+, if reliability is positively related to it.
−, if reliability is negatively related to it.
0, if reliability is not related to it.

Number of items .... _____
Range of item difficulty .... _____
Interdependence of items .... _____
Time allowed with fixed number of items .... _____
Reliability of criterion .... _____

The two-alternative form can be further varied to require the pupil to indicate not only whether the item is true or false but also whether the converse is true or false. Example:

Directions: Below are statements for which you are to encircle the two correct answers from among the following:

> T: The statement is true.
> F: The statement is false.
> CT: The converse is true.
> CF: The converse is false.

A cube is always a rectangular parallelepiped. . . . . . . T   F   CT   CF
Two dihedral angles are equal if their plane angles
are equal. . . . . T   F   CT   CF
All vertebrates are mammals. T   F   CT   CF

Another variation of the constant-choice item requires the pupil to make the proper changes in a single word so as to make false statements correct. Example:

Directions: For each of the following statements if the statement is true, underline the word True. If the statement is false, underline the world False, and write the substitute for the underlined word necessary to make it true.

Nitrogen supports combustion. . . . .   True   False   Oxygen
Water is a chemical element. . . . .   True   False   Compound
NaCl is the symbol for common salt. . . . .   True   False   _____

True-false items with qualifications require the pupil to indicate whether the item is true or false or whether it can be made true by adding certain qualifications to be given or selected by him. Example:

Statements

The President has the power to appoint justices of the Su-
preme Court. . . . .   T   F   1
The President can propose taxation measures. . . . .   T   F   2
The President may appoint ambassadors to other countries. .   T   F   3
The President may appoint Senators-at-large. . . . .   T   F

Qualifications

1. With the consent of the Senate

2. With the consent of the House of Representatives
3. No qualification

True-false items with diagrams present a series of diagrams concerning which the pupil is to make one of a small number of possible judgments (see Fig. 33). Diagrams of the Wheatstone bridge for

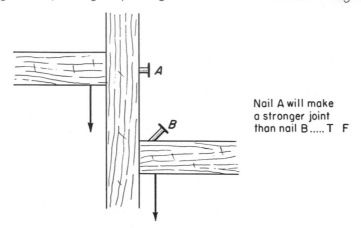

Nail A will make
a stronger joint
than nail B ..... T   F

Fig. 33. True-False Item with Diagram.

measuring electrical resistance have been used in this manner in physics courses, the pupil marking each diagram with a plus sign if it was balanced and with a minus sign if it was unbalanced or incorrectly wired. Diagrams of tools, geometrical figures, housing plans, and similar materials can all be treated in this way.

Advantages and Disadvantages. The limitations of the constant-alternative type of item in its most used form, the true-false test, can easily outweigh its merits unless great care is taken in writing it. It is well adapted to testing the ability to distinguish popular misconceptions and superstitions from scientifically validated truths. For this kind of material the true-false test provides a mode of presentation similar to situations in actual life where the pupil must judge the truth of statements. The true-false item is also particularly well suited to material that does not lend itself to the construction of more than two or three plausible alternatives. For example: Emergency exits from office buildings should open outwardly." Here there are only two possible choices, inwardly or outwardly, so that the construction of a multiple-choice item would lead to absurdities. Phrasing this question as a completion item, "Emergency exits from office buildings should open: _____" would leave the terms of the answer too indefinite.

Perhaps the major advantage is that true-false items enable the teacher to present a large number of items in a short time, because pupils can generally answer more of these items per unit of time than of other types. This fact has led to its major shortcoming in the hands of many teachers. Because teachers have not been careful in constructing true-false items this type of test has perhaps been misused more than any other type. They have often lifted sentences out of textbooks to provide true statements and inserted "not" to secure the required number of false statements. Apart from this, the true-false test of itself tends toward greater ambiguity than do other types. *Only statements that are absolutely true or false should be used.* In subject matter like mathematics or science, such statements can be made readily. In other fields, however, many important materials are matters of judgment, not absolutely true or false. They may be inferences, interpretations, explanations, or generalizations which may be probably true or require qualifications of one sort or another. Such material, often important in education, cannot readily be put into true-false form. Teachers who attempt to do so produce bewildered, confused, cynical, or antagonized students.

The most serious disadvantage of the true-false item and all other constant-alternative forms arises from their tendency to be influenced by response sets, or individual differences in tendencies to respond to all the questions on a test in a constant way unrelated to the purpose of the test. For example, some students tend more than others to answer "true" to true-false items whose answer they are not sure of. Or they may tend to "agree" more often to opinion questionnaire items, or say "like" more often to interest inventory items. Response sets have almost always been found in constant-alternative tests, but hardly at all in changing-alternative types.

Suggestions for Composing True-False Items

1. *Have the number of true statements approximately equal to the number of false statements.* Otherwise pupils may see a prepon-

derance of one type and begin to guess accordingly. Or students with a response set to say "true" when in doubt will have unduly high or low scores.

2. *Avoid "tricking" the pupil by distracting his attention from the crucial part of the item.* Do not put the false part of the statement in a qualifying phrase, for pupils usually assume these phrases to be correct and are misled into concentrating upon the major statement. Example:

Faulty: The President of the United States, a naturalized citizen, holds office for four years in a single term. . . . . T   F
Improved: The President of the United States may be a naturalized citizen and holds office for four years in a single term. . . . T   F

In general, such misdirection of attention can be avoided by putting the crucial element toward the end of the true-false statement.

3. *Avoid "specific determiners," that is, words or modes of expression that are usually associated with a true statement or a false statement.* Analyses of large numbers of teacher-made true-false tests have shown that the vast majority of statements containing the following words were false: only, alone, all, no, none, nothing, always, never, cause, reason. On the other hand, statements containing the following words were usually true: should, may, most, some, often, generally. Furthermore, statements containing enumerations or more than twenty words were usually true. Such words or characteristics as these cease to be specific determiners when they are approximately evenly balanced among true and false statements. Avoid specific determiners because they provide clues which enable pupils to respond correctly without real knowledge or understanding.

4. *Reduce ambiguity by using quantitative rather than qualitative language whenever possible.* Use direct comparisons, for the same reason, whenever a quantitative description is impossible. This means that the teacher should use such terms as the following very little: few, great, many, more, important. Example:

Faulty: Stevenson received a large number of votes in the election of 1956. . . . . T   F
Improved: Stevenson received more than 40 percent of the votes in the election of 1956. . . . . T   F

5. *Avoid involved complex sentence structure with many dependent clauses, double negatives, or unfamiliar language.* Similarly, unless

the intention is to test technical vocabulary, word the questions in simple language. Example:

Faulty: There was marked efflorescence of inventive activity in the nineteenth century. .... T F
Improved: There was a marked increase in inventive activity in the nineteenth century. .... T F

Instructions About "Guessing." Some technicians favor instructions against guessing on true-false or other two-alternative tests; others do not. Such directions are considered desirable on the ground that they decrease the element of chance success which enters into responses on selection-type tests. Consequently it is reasoned that they should result in a more valid measurement of actual achievement. But the important effect of chance is on the reliability of the test, not on how high the scores are. If a test is reliable, chance success is unimportant even if it makes the average score much higher.

Directions against guessing can never achieve their purpose because pupils do not know when they have complete knowledge of the correct response, no knowledge, or partial knowledge. Many guesses are not "pure" in the sense of being based on no knowledge whatsoever. Students may frequently respond correctly on the basis of partial knowledge or "hunches."

Essentially, such directions usually introduce a "personality" or nonintellectual factor into the measurement of achievement. This is the pupil's tendency to gamble, or his willingness to respond on the basis of partial knowledge rather than only when he is completely certain of the correct response. Since pupils differ in this personality trait, instructions against guessing make the test scores depend on both intellectual and personality factors in unknown proportions.

It has been argued that instructions to answer all items may lead pupils to lose respect for tests and to regard them as guessing games. Whatever effect such instructions may have can probably be counteracted by explaining their purpose in simple terms. It is better not to mention the word "guessing," but to instruct pupils to answer every item without omissions, and to put down the answer they feel is the best even though they are not absolutely sure of it.

A further issue in the use of selection-type tests, especially those presenting only two alternatives per item, is the desirability of a scoring formula intended to correct for chance successes, or guessing.

The general and two-choice forms of the scoring formula used for this purpose are as follows:

General Form	Two-Choice Form
(1) $S = T - \dfrac{n}{n-1}W - O$	$S = T - 2W - O$
(2) $S = R - \dfrac{W}{n-1}$	$S = R - W$
(3) $S = R + \dfrac{O}{n}$	$S = R + \dfrac{O}{2}$

where S = score
$\quad T$ = number of items in the test
$\quad R$ = number of right responses
$\quad W$ = number of wrong responses
$\quad O$ = number of omitted responses
$\quad n$ = number of response alternatives presented in each item

These three formulas differ in the kinds of counting required but yield scores that correlate perfectly with one another. The third formula may look more acceptable to pupils because it gives full credit for right responses and an additional fractional credit for items omitted rather than wrong.

These formulas assume that guessed responses in two-choice tests will be right as often as wrong. This assumption is at best justifiable only on the average rather than for any individual pupil. So far as it is not justified, the formulas over- or under-penalize wrong responses. *When every pupil answers every item, the formulas need not be used* because then there is perfect correlation between simple scores (number right) and corrected scores. In general, correction formulas are not worth enough in improved validity to justify the time and effort required to use them.

Changing-Alternative Items (Multiple-Choice)

Changing-alternative items require the pupil to select the best one of a group of several alternatives which change with each item. The most usual form is the multiple-choice item. Example found on the following page.

Why is a fuse placed in an electric circuit? . . . . ————
  (1) To measure the current
  (2) To reduce the current
  (3) To prevent excessive flow of current
  (4) To lower the resistance

Although the pupil can be instructed to select the correct response on almost any basis, only a few are used with any frequency. Among them are the "best" answer, the "correct" answer, the "worst" answer, the "least satisfactory" answer, the "most inclusive" term, the "most dissimilar" term, the "result" from among causes, the "cause" from among results, etc. Examples:

Worst Answer

Directions: Of the four alternatives presented as completions to each statement, choose the worst and write its number in the space at the right.
An isosceles triangle is one in which (1) two sides are equal, (2) two angles are equal, (3) one of the altitudes is perpendicular to its side, (4) the base equals the altitude. . . ————

Most Inclusive Answer

Directions: Following are sets of four words or terms, one of which includes the other three. You are to select the inclusive term from each set and write its number in the space to the right of the set.
(1) Smallpox, (2) tuberculosis, (3) scurvy, (4) disease . . . . ————
(1) tapeworm, (2) typhoid bacillus, (3) parasite, (4) dodder ————

Most Dissimilar Answer

Directions: Following are sets of four words or terms, one of which does not belong with the other three. Select the word or term which does not belong and write its number in the space to the right of the set.
(1) Abraham Lincoln, (2) Ulysses S. Grant, (3) Stephen A. Douglas, (4) Chester A. Arthur . . . . ————
(1) shark, (2) ape, (3) giraffe, (4) kangaroo . . . . ————

Result from Among Causes

Directions: In each group of four events given below there is one result together with three causes which contributed to bringing about this result. Select the result and write its number on the line at the right of the item.

(1) Sinking of the *Lusitania*, (2) unrestricted submarine warfare, (3) declaration of war in 1917, (4) invasion of Belgium .... _____

Cause from Among Results

Directions: From the following groups of four historical events or conditions, select the one that may best be considered to be a cause of the other three.

(1) English religious intolerance, (2) settlement of Jamestown, (3) American freedom of religion, (4) sailing of the *Mayflower* .... _____

The number of alternatives may vary from two to any larger number, but four and five are the most frequently used.

Advantages and Limitations. The changing-alternative type of item is adaptable to testing higher mental processes, such as inferential reasoning and fine discrimination, as well as rote knowledge of isolated facts. It is the most flexible kind of test item available for varying types of mental processes on the basis of subject matter. The multiple-choice item is frequently preferable to the simple question when the correct response is long or involved or can be written in several correct forms. As the number of alternatives becomes greater than two, the possibility of guessing the correct answer is less than in the true-false test; the greater the number and plausibility of these alternatives, the less the chances that a guessed answer will be correct, and the higher the reliability. Finally, multiple-choice tests tend to be free of response sets which may seriously dilute with irrelevant factors what constant-alternative tests measure.

The good multiple-choice test item is difficult to construct. Devising plausible incorrect alternatives places a heavy burden on the ingenuity and psychological insight of the teacher. Constructing a single multiple-choice item with four alternatives may require as much work as constructing four true-false or simple-question items.

Suggestions for Constructing Multiple-Choice Items. Multiple-choice items consist of an introductory part, or stem; the answer; and the false alternatives, or distractors.

1. *The stem may be in the form either of a direct question or of*

an incomplete statement. Pupils prefer the direct question because it defines a specific problem.

2. *If the incomplete-statement form of stem is used it should be meaningful in itself and imply a direct question rather than merely lead into a collection of unrelated true-false statements.* Example:

Faulty: The United States of America (1) has more than 200,000,000 people, (2) grows large amounts of rubber, (3) has few good harbors, (4) produces most of the world's automobiles. .... _____

Improved: The population of the United States is characterized by (1) a stable birth rate, (2) varied nationality backgrounds, (3) its even distribution over the area of the United States, (4) an increasing proportion of young people. .... _____

3. *The distractors should be plausible, so that the pupils who do not possess the achievement being evaluated will tend to select them rather than the correct answer.* The test maker can attain plausibility by making the distractors familiar, reasonable, natural, and related to the same concept as the correct answer. One method of securing plausible distractors is to use the introductory statement as a completion test and then tabulate the incorrect responses of pupils. The incorrect responses that are given more frequently provide suitable distractors.

4. *The length or precision of statement of the alternatives should not vary systematically with their correctness.* Otherwise pupils may come to learn that the long distractors are usually the correct ones, or vice versa.

5. *Have the arrangement of alternatives uniform throughout the test.* The alternatives should come at the end of the statement if the incomplete-statement form of introduction is used. If space permits, they should be listed one under the other rather than placed in a paragraph, because listed alternatives are easier to read and consider separately. Example:

Faulty: The cheapness of land and scarcity of labor in the West created (1) an aristocratic class of landowners, (2) a large class of wage-earning men, (3) a system of servitude, (4) a large class of small freeholders. .... _____

Improved: The cheapness of land and scarcity of labor in the West created
1. an aristocratic class of landowners.
2. a large class of small freeholders.
3. a system of servitude.
4. a large class of wage-earning men. . . . .   _____

6. *Maintain grammatical consistency throughout the item.* You should be able to form a correct sentence by attaching any of the alternatives to the introductory incomplete statement. Example:

Faulty: The best way to employ leisure time is (1) read good books and magazines, (2) movies are usually enjoyable and educational, (3) minding your own business, (4) in playing cards and solving puzzles.   _____
Improved: The best way to employ leisure time is to (1) read good books and magazines, (2) go to the movies, (3) mind your own business, (4) play cards and solve puzzles. . . . .   _____

7. *Have four or five alternatives if possible.* Use fewer if it is impossible to construct others without introducing absurdities. Having the same number of alternatives for every item is unnecessary unless a formula to correct for chance success is used.

8. *Corrections for guessing need not be applied in the usual classroom testing situation.* In standardized multiple-choice tests where there is statistical evidence for the equal plausibility of the distractors, applying the correction for guessing formula may yield worth-while results.

9. *Do not use the multiple-choice form when the simple-question type is more suitable.* Such situations may occur when the answer required by the simple-question item calls for little more writing than does the multiple-choice form, or in computational questions when the response is in numerical form.

10. *The level of mental process required by an item largely depends upon the homogeneity of the alternatives presented by it.* Examples:

Less homogeneous: Which city is nearest to Chicago? (1) Los Angeles, (2) New York, (3) St. Louis, (4) Miami. . .   _____
More homogeneous: Which city is nearest to Chicago? (1) Minneapolis, (2) St. Louis, (3) Cleveland, (4) Milwaukee.   _____

Less homogeneous: Archimedes' Law deals with (1) falling
bodies, (2) liquid-displacing bodies, (3) heated bodies, (4)
light-giving bodies. . . . .   _____

More homogeneous: Archimedes' Law states that a floating
body (1) will seek its own level, (2) will displace a volume
of liquid whose weight equals the body's weight, (3) will
receive pressure from the liquid which is equal in all directions, (4) cannot float midway between the surface of the
liquid and the bottom of the vessel. . . . .   _____

11. *Understanding of definitions is better tested by furnishing
the word and requiring choice between alternative definitions* than
by presenting the definition and requiring choice between alternative
words. Example:

Faulty: Water enters the air by a process called (1) osmosis,
(2) filtration, (3) condensation, (4) evaporation. . . . . . .   _____

Improved: Evaporation is a process by which (1) vapors turn
into liquids, (2) liquids pass between two porous surfaces,
(3) solids dissolve in liquids, (4) liquids turn into vapors.   _____   _

12. *Distractors can often be made attractive and plausible by
expressing them in textbook phraseology,* the correct response being
expressed in original terms. If this device is used too often, however,
it can become an irrelevant cue.

Matching Items

Matching exercises consist of two sets of items to be associated
on some basis furnished by the directions. The variety of bases upon
which the two lists of items can be matched is unlimited. Examples
of bases are events and dates, events and places, events and results,
inventions and inventors, books and authors, processes and products,
usages and rules, names and definitions, causes and effects. Similarly,
the lists may be presented in many varying forms—diagrams, maps,
pictures, chronologically or logically arranged items with numbered
gaps between them. Example:

Directions: After each animal write the number of its gestation and
incubation period.

Gestation and Incubation Period   *Animals*

1. 330–340 days   1. Swine .... _____
2. 280–283 days   2. Chickens .... _____
3. 143–150 days   3. Mares .... _____
4. 112–114 days   4. Sheep .... _____
5. 67–70 days   5. Cattle .... _____
6. 20–21 days

A variation of the matching form is *compound matching,* which requires matching three or more lists with one another on indicated bases. Example:

Directions: After each city write first the number of its state and then the letter of its major industry.

States	*Major Industries*	*Cities*
1. Illinois	a. Autos	1. Detroit ..... _____
2. Indiana	b. Airplanes	2. Akron ...... _____
3. Michigan	c. Flour milling	3. St. Paul ..... _____
4. Minnesota	d. Meat packing	4. Chicago ..... _____
5. New Jersey	e. Electrical equip-	5. Schenectady . _____
	ment	6. Pittsburgh ... _____
6. New York	f. Publishing	
7. Ohio	g. Rubber	
8. Pennsylvania	h. Steel	
9. Texas	i. Telephones	

The matching form is frequently modified in various ways. It is sometimes arranged so that each item in the list of alternatives may be used more than once as a response. This makes it impossible to answer correctly by a process of elimination. It may be arranged so as to require the use of more than one alternative for some test items. This enables the testing of ability to recognize terms which share meanings in common with other items. The alternatives may be arranged so as to make it easy to find the number of the alternative if its meaning has already been decided upon. Such arrangements may be alphabetical, chronological, or logical, or have other meaningful bases.

The *check list* requires the student to go through a list of phrases or statements and mark each one that fulfills certain requirements set up in the directions. Example is found on the following page.

✓	aileron		windbeacon
✓	rudder	✓	strut
	gear shift	✓	propeller
	mast		periscope
✓	stabilizer	✓	stick
	accelerator		helium bag
✓	throttle		ripcord

It is evident that the check list is similar to the true-false item in scoring, advantages, and disadvantages.

The *master list* requires the pupil to select from a constant group of alternatives, usually more than two, the one that best applies to a group of items. Example:

Directions: From the list at the top select the kind of vote required by the phrases below and place its number on the line at the right.

1. Majority
2. Two thirds majority
3. Three-fourths majority
4. Unanimous

Number of jury votes necessary to convict a criminal ...... _____
Number of votes necessary to expel a member of either House of the United States Congress .... _____
Number of members necessary for a quorum of each House .. _____
Number of votes needed to pass a bill over the President's veto _____
Number of votes necessary to propose amendments to the United States Constitution .... _____
Number of state legislatures that must ratify an amendment before it becomes valid .... _____

The master list differs from the matching form in that the numbers of items contained in the two groups of the master list are much more disproportionate, so that the items in the list of choices must be used more than once. The master list differs from the multiple-choice form in that the alternatives remain the same instead of changing for each question.

Advantages and Disadvantages. The matching form is compact because it uses the same response alternatives for a whole group of items. This compactness makes it efficient in terms of space and testing time. It is peculiarly well suited for making a rapid survey of a specific aspect of a field of subject matter, such as its leading personalities, the time orientation of a group of events, or definitions of basic terms.

Perhaps the chief disadvantage of the matching form is that it requires even greater care than other forms if it is not to be rendered invalid by irrelevant clues, implausible alternatives, and awkward arrangement.

Suggestions for Constructing Matching Items

1. *Use only homogeneous or related materials in any one matching exercise.* For example, if the exercise pertains to the human respiratory system, it should not include parts of the body and bones, definitions and distinctions pertaining to the human nervous system, and so on. Example:

Faulty:

1. Auricle	1. Main respiratory organ .... _____
2. Lung	2. Major subdivision of windpipe ...... _____
3. Trachea	3. Windpipe .... _____
4. Vagus	4. Breastbone .... _____
5. Bronchus	5. Cranial nerve for lung .... _____
6. Esophagus	6. Chamber of heart .... _____
7. Sternum	7. Bone of the leg .... _____
8. Tibia	

Improved:

1. Lung	1. Windpipe .... _____
2. Trachea	2. Subdivision of windpipe .... _____
3. Vagus	3. Respiratory nerve .... _____
4. Bronchus	
5. Bronchiole	

The breastbone, chamber of heart, and bone of the leg are not related to the other terms involved in the respiratory system and could easily be answered by elimination.

One way to determine whether a matching set will elicit the type of achievement desired is to examine how the correct answer has to be selected for each question. Must it be selected on the basis of real knowledge? If the selection has to proceed by eliminating correct responses, will this elimination be based upon the obvious unfitness, either logically, grammatically, or generically, of all but the correct alternative? If so, the matching exercise is probably not calling for the desired achievement.

2. *Make the number of response alternatives larger than the number of items to reduce the chance of guessing the correct response.* You can accomplish this also by permitting some of the response alternatives to be used more than once in the same matching set.

3. *Always indicate clearly the basis for the matching, if it is not obvious.* This should be done both in the directions and in the headings of the columns of items to be matched. Example:

Faulty:

1. Brazil	1. rice	_____
2. Iowa	2. corn	_____
3. China	3. rubber	_____
4. Germany	4. silk	_____
5. India		
6. Japan		

Instructing the pupil merely to match these groups of items without giving him some basis for doing so gives the teacher no justification for considering some responses correct and others incorrect. In the improved illustration the basis for matching is clearly indicated, the pupil knows what is expected, and a definite criterion for determining correct responses has been set up.

Improved:

Test to Identify Fibers	*Fibers*
a. Tears easily with a shrill sound and ends of yarn are even and curled.	1. silk _____
b. Tears with difficulty, with dull sound; leaves irregular edge.	2. wool _____
c. Tears with difficulty, with dull sound; leaves ends of yarn straight.	3. rayon _____
d. Tears easily with shrill sound, leaving threads of uneven length.	
e. Tears with shrill sound, with threads long and uneven in length.	

4. *Have one of the lists of items to be matched consist of single words, short phrases, numbers, or other quickly examined material.* It is preferable that this list of short terms be the list of response

alternatives. This, of course, is what makes the matching form less suitable for testing understanding of terms and definitions than the multiple-choice forms, which may require the pupil to select from among definitions rather than from among terms.

5. *Arrange response alternatives chronologically or alphabetically to facilitate the pupil's finding the response once he has decided what he is looking for.*

6. *The number of response alternatives should seldom be greater than ten.* Longer lists require the pupil to spend too much time just finding the correct response. For machine-scoring (IBM) answer sheets, matching sets generally consist of three items to be matched against five response alternatives. Example:

TEST BOOKLET   ANSWER SHEET

Author	Test
56. Thorndike	1. TAT
57. Thurstone	2. CAVD
58. Terman	3. Army Alpha
	4. Primary Mental Abilities
	5. Stanford-Binet

	1	2	3	4	5
56.	‖	█	‖	‖	‖
57.	‖	‖	‖	█	‖
58.	‖	‖	‖	‖	█

7. *Never carry a matching set over from one page to the next.* A student is confused when he has to look for a response on a different page than the one that contains the question or the directions.

Analogies

Analogies are not a distinct form of test item, but rather a way of putting questions to which any of the other forms may be adapted. The pupil is presented with two terms whose relationship he must infer. A third term is then given for which he must either supply or select a fourth term whose relationship to the third is the same as that between the first two. Examples:

Animals : oxygen : : plans :   (carbon dioxide)

Two points are to a straight line as   (two lines)   to a plane.

Verb is to adverb as noun is to   (adjective)

Any of the other forms of short-answer test item may be used with analogies. The pupil may be required to furnish the missing terms as in the completion form. He may select the missing term from a group of changing alternatives for each analogy, as in the multiple-choice form. A list of analogies may be presented with a list of response alternatives, as in the matching form. Complete analogies may also be furnished, the pupil being required to judge them true or false.

Advantages and Disadvantages. Intelligence and mental ability tests have made more use of analogies than achievement tests have, perhaps because the artificiality of the analogies form requires more general mental ability for a correct response than specific achievement of instructional objectives does. Analogies do, however, provide a compact way in which to put a question. If pupils can be made thoroughly familiar with this form so that it loses its artificiality for them, it can become an efficient testing device. The advantage in brevity of the analogies form may be seen in the following examples:

Oxygen : O : : chlorine : _____(Cl)_____
instead of
What is the chemical symbol for chlorine?
Animals : oxygen : . plants · _____(carbon dioxide)_____
instead of
What gas is indispensable in the respiration of plants?

Suggestions for Constructing Analogies Items. The pertinent suggestions are the same as those for constructing the kind of item to which the analogies form is applied. That is, if the analogies are to be items of the supply type, the suggestions for constructing the latter items should be considered. Perhaps the only special rule for analogies is that the directions, especially for younger, less "test-wise" pupils, should be especially clear. Analogies usually require practice exercises and close observation by the teacher to insure that all pupils understand what the analogies form requires of them.

Rearrangement Items

Rearrangement items require the pupil to put into some specified order a series of randomly presented material. Any kind of specified order may be called for, such as chronology, difficulty, importance, length, weight, or logic. Examples:

Chronological Order

Directions: Given below are groups of three events or men whose numbers you are to write in chronological order in the space at the right of the items.
1. (1) Wilson, (2) Lincoln, (3) Washington were Presidents of the United States .... _____
2. (1) Catholics, (2) Quakers, (3) Puritans were religious groups who settled in America .... _____

Logical Order

Directions: A greenhouse catches and holds much of the heat radiation from the sun. Place a cross (x) before the statements below which help to explain this phenomenon. (Some of the statements are false; some of them are true but do not apply.)
_____ 1. The glass transmits the longer heat waves more readily than than the shorter heat waves.
_____ 2. Objects inside the greenhouse, once warmed, radiate very long heat waves.
_____ 3. The heated glass radiates the shorter waves to objects within the greenhouse.
_____ 4. The glass roof reflects the longer heat waves.
_____ 5. The shorter heat waves from the sun are transmitted readily through the glass.
_____ 6. The glass roof absorbs long heat waves.
Now rearrange the pertinent statements above in the proper order to give a thoroughly complete explanation. *Use the numbers.* _____
Answer

The pupil may also be required to rearrange items and statements in outline form with the proper headings, classifications, and subordinations.

Advantages and Limitations. More than is true of most other types, the mental processes used in rearrangement items depend upon how the subject matter has been presented in the classroom. If the proper order has been explicitly presented in class, the test may measure only rote memory. Higher levels of understanding are elicited only if the pupil is required to make the rearrangement originally.

Suggestions for Scoring Rearrangement Items. Apart from scoring, the considerations in designing rearrangement tests are similar to those for other forms.

When the number of parts to be arranged is small, say four or less, it is often sufficient to consider the response correct only if the rearrangement is correct for all parts, and to give one point for the correct answer. When more than four parts are to be arranged, a practical scoring scheme involves adding the *squares of the differences* between the pupil's order and the correct order:

Correct order:		1	2	3	4	5	
Worst possible answer:		5	4	3	2	1	
Differences:		4	2	0	2	4	
Squares of differences:		16	4	0	4	16	Total: 40

The sum of the squared differences between the correct and the worst possible arrangement is 40. If a pupil's arrangement is 3 1 2 4 5, the sum of the squared differences from the correct arrangement is 6. As in golf, the more correct the pupil's response, the lower the score. Subtracting these from the *worst* possible score gives scores such that the higher ones are the better ones.

When each item consists of three elements to be ranked, the pupil needs to indicate only the "most" and "least." It may look as follows for each item:

Directions: Cross out the *m* opposite the activity that would probably have the most attraction for an "extrovert," and *l* opposite the activity that would have the least.
21. listening to classical records .... 21. m ✖
22. going to a prize fight .... 22. ✖ l
23. going fishing .... 23. m l

The scoring key should be punched with holes over the two correct responses. Then the number of cross-out marks showing through (2, 1, or 0) is the score on the item. For added discrimination, another key punched with the opposite of the correct answer (e.g., 21 with *m* and 22 with *l*) can be used; all items showing two cross-out marks through this key will score minus one (−1).

ARRANGING AND ADMINISTERING
SHORT-ANSWER TESTS

After the test items have been constructed, they must be arranged for maximum efficiency of administration and scoring. This entails assembling items into parts, editing the items, determining the order of difficulty within parts, arranging items for efficient scoring, preparing the scoring key, providing directions for the pupil, and providing directions for the test administrator. We now take up each of these.

Assembling Items into Parts

After constructing the test items, the teacher may have a collection of them in varying forms. The number of items will be whatever is sufficient adequately to sample achievement of the instructional objectives at which the test is aimed and to yield a reliable score. The teacher should check all of the items against the course objectives and against the table of specifications for the specific test to insure that all intended objectives are covered and that one objective is not emphasized at the expense of another. He must prepare enough items to make the test sufficiently reliable, since test reliability depends to some extent upon the number of items.

Editing the Items and Arranging Them in Order of
Difficulty Within Parts

These two steps are discussed together because they can be conveniently carried out at the same time. In editing the items, check to see that you have followed the suggestions for constructing that form. If possible, secure the opinions of other teachers by asking them to read each item carefully and attempt to answer it. During or after the editing, try to arrange the items of each type in order of difficulty. Since research has shown that subjective estimates of the difficulty of an item merely approximate the difficulty as measured by the percentage of pupils failing an item, do not try to obtain more than a rough order of difficulty. Rather than ranking them, classify the items into a few categories, such as "very difficult," "fairly difficult," "average," "fairly easy," "very easy."

To make the test maximally efficient in measuring individual differences in achievement, the test items should range fairly widely in difficulty. There should be a few very easy items, a few very difficult items; the rest should be evenly distributed along the range of difficulty. Any item so easy that 100 percent of the pupils succeed with it has no value for discriminating among students. The same is true of any item so difficult that none of the pupils answer it correctly. Since such items do not discriminate between good and poor students, they can serve no purpose except perhaps to emphasize and motivate achievement of certain objectives to be evaluated in future tests, or to reassure the teacher that all students have these knowledges.

For maximum discriminatory value, the average score should be about half the total possible score (when corrected for chance); the range of scores for the group tested will tend to approximate the whole range from near zero to almost perfect. Perfect scores are usually undesirable because they indicate that the good pupil has been denied an opportunity to show the full extent of his achievement. Similarly, zero scores show that the test has failed to reveal what little achievement the poor pupil has made.

The statements in the preceding two paragraphs apply only when test items tap achievement of objectives that are important to the individual and his society. Suppose true achievement in a certain course of instruction is at a uniformly high level in all the pupils tested. Then the items valid to evaluate it will be passed by high percentages, say 80 or 90 percent, of the pupils. To make the items center around the 50 percent level of difficulty in this situation might be possible only by asking "trivial," less valid questions. In short, *in constructing achievement tests the validity of test items is more important than their difficulty.* It is only when achievement is not at such a uniformly high level that test authors can meet both the validity and the difficulty requirements for optimum functioning of the test.

In handwriting, typing, shorthand, computational speed, woodworking, and other areas with objective and external limits on the degree of skill or level of achievement, the test maker is concerned more with having a very large percentage of pupils reach a high standard than in obtaining an average of 50 percent difficulty for a test. In a shorthand test, for example, a speed of more than so many words per minute is an adequate and valid standard regardless of whether it is achieved by 50 or 100 percent of the students in a given group. To raise the standard for the sake of bringing the level of difficulty closer to 50 percent is to sacrifice validity for the power to discriminate.

In each type of test item, the order of presentation should be from "easy" through "moderately difficult" to "most difficult." This order of increasing difficulty may lead to a better distribution of working time and to better morale, as we indicated on page 228 in connection with the essay test.

Arranging Items for Easy Scoring

The spaces for the pupil's responses should usually be arranged in a column running from top to bottom of the page. This arrangement can be followed for all types of test items. In simple-question and completion items, the omitted words or phrases may occur in the middle of sentences or be scattered throughout connected discourse. Here also the answers may be arranged in a column by inserting a number in each blank which corresponds to a numbered answer space at the right side of the page. Example:

Items should be arranged in   1   order of difficulty

                                                    1. *Increasing*

mainly in order to affect pupil   2   in a desirable way.

                                                    2. *Morale*

When tests are to be scored mechanically or electrically by means of the International Test Scoring Machine, it is necessary to use a special answer sheet (see Fig. 20, page 156). Pupils make only a pencil mark between pairs of dotted lines under the headings T or F for true-false items, or letters or numbers corresponding to the alternatives for multiple-choice and other types of items. Teachers can secure a special manual from the IBM Corporation that will help them in arranging the test.[17]

[17] International Business Machines Corporation, Department of Education, *Methods of Adapting Tests for Scoring by the IBM Electric Test Scoring Machine*, 1947.

Preparing the Scoring Key

Fill in the correct responses on one copy of a mimeographed test and use it as a scoring key. Place it next to the pupil's responses and mark them correct or incorrect. Experience has taught that the scoring key should be checked and rechecked before it is used.

One of the most efficient methods for scoring classroom tests calls for a separate answer sheet, as for standardized tests. The answer key may be duplicated by any method—hectograph, ditto, mimeograph, or printing—and a scoring stencil can be made of ordinary tagboard or discarded manila file folders. First write the answers to the test on a copy of the answer sheet and transfer them to the tagboard stencil by means of carbon paper; align the stencil to match the answer sheet. Then punch holes in the scoring stencil so that only the correct answers show when you place the stencil over a marked answer sheet.

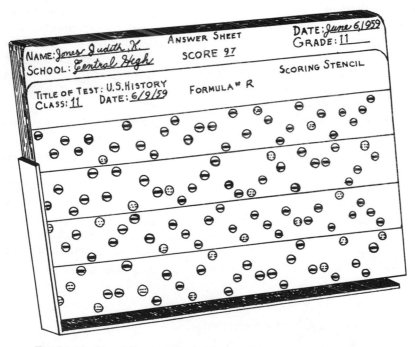

Fig. 34. Cardboard Box for Aligning Scoring Stencil on Answer Sheets.

When a large number of answer sheets are to be scored, you will find helpful a frame made by using two sides and the bottom of a cardboard box with the sides cut down to about 1 inch above the bottom (see Fig. 34). Place the answer sheets in this box frame, with the answer stencil on top. As you score each answer sheet, pull it out from under the scoring stencil and mark the score on it. Tapping the remaining answer sheets and scoring stencil in the box immediately realigns them for scoring the next answer sheet. This reduces the time required to "fit" the scoring stencil over an answer sheet prior to scoring.

Directions to the Pupil

How detailed the directions to pupils should be depends on how mature and experienced with tests they are. General directions for the entire test may appear on the front page; these cover the purpose of the test and (1) writing his name and other identifying data in the proper spaces, (2) when to begin work, (3) amount of time allotted, (4) observing and following specific directions for each part of the test, (5) distributing his time on easy and hard items, (6) whether going back to preceding parts is permitted, (7) stopping work when told, (8) asking questions, and (9) whether or not to answer every item.

Directions for specific parts of the test should tell the pupil what each type of item gives him and what it requires of him. Again, the pupil's age and familiarity with the type of test item being used should mainly determine the form of the directions. Brevity, simplicity, and completeness should be the goals. Sample items already answered may be provided to show the pupil how to proceed. Practice exercises may be provided. If the test involves a time limit, these practice exercises should not be given within the time limit of the test itself. The pupil should gain from the directions a clear idea of what he is to do and of where and how he is to record what he has done.

Directions to the Test Administrator

Whether the teacher gives a test of his own or one made elsewhere, directions for administering it should give him a clear idea of what to do and what *not* to do. He should make the necessary provisions for (1) furnishing pupils with pencils and other equipment such as answer sheets, (2) passing out test booklets, (3) reading directions with the pupils and answering questions concerning them, (4) giving starting and stopping signals, (5) observing total and part-time limits, and (6) collecting test papers and other equipment.

IMPROVEMENT OF OBJECTIVE-TYPE TESTS

Up to this point we have discussed the principles for the construction of good objective-type tests. In applying these rules, however, it is necessary for the teacher to use his own judgment as to how well the items in a test will work. He must make personal judgments as to whether or not the kinds of information being tested (content validity) is relevant to the kinds of evaluations to be made of the students tested. Such judgment is a primary basis for all good teacher-made tests. But there are more objective and empirical techniques that can help to determine whether or not the specific items in the test are really working in the manner they should. We usually want to know that the specific items are such that the better students in a class are more likely to answer them correctly than the poorer students. This section presents a technique for the improvement of such examinations—item analysis.

Item Analysis

In effect, item analysis is a postadministration examination of a test. After a test has been administered and scored, a tabulation is made to determine the level of difficulty and the power of discrimination of each item in the test. Item analysis data have considerable value to the test constructor in revealing, to some extent, faulty items. In this way a teacher will be able to know which items in a test are worth retaining in his file of test items, which ones may be improved, and which ones should be discarded entirely. In addition, since a classroom test should also be used as a teaching-learning experience, item analysis data can have value in class discussions as aids in clarifying the intended meaning of items misunderstood by some students.

Two terms generally used in item analysis are *difficulty* and *discrimination*. The difficulty of an item may be defined as the proportion of the examinees that marked the item correctly. The level of difficulty is indicated by a numerical term, the *difficulty index*, which may range from zero to 100 percent. An item answered *correctly* by 60 percent of the students is said to have a difficulty index of 60. Obviously any item of zero or 100 percent difficulty would not differentiate between good and poor students and, therefore, has no functional value in a test. A general rule of thumb is to consider as worthless for measurement any items whose difficulty index is lower than 10 or higher than 90.

Item discrimination, or the discriminating power of a test item, refers to the degree to which success or failure on an item indicates possession of the ability being measured. In other words, a single test item is regarded as having positive discriminating power if the examinees who rank higher in ability answer it correctly more often than those who rank lower in ability. An item may be considered as having no discriminating power when the good and poor students answer it correctly about equally often. An item may be said to have negative discriminating power when the poor students answer it correctly more often than the good students do. The discriminating power of a test item is indicated by a numerical term, the *discrimination index*, which may range from a minus 1.00 to a plus 1.00. In actual practice, discrimination indexes close to 1.00 or −1.00 will virtually never be obtained. Items with discrimination indexes above .20 are ordinarily regarded as having sufficient discriminating power for use in most tests of academic achievement.

Procedure for Making a Simple Item Analysis

Item analysis is done by tallying the students' answers to each item. For a 50-item four-choice test for a class of 30 students *complete* analysis would mean 50 times 30 or 1500 tallies. But in such a small class the immediate teaching purpose will be served by the following not very laborious method.

1. Select the ten students who scored highest on the test (the High group) and the ten students who scored lowest on the test (the Low group). These groups of ten may or may not be the highest- and lowest-scoring 27 percents which a measurement theorist, T. L. Kelley, once demonstrated analytically as the best proportion for use in item analysis. But for informal classroom tests, it does not matter much; the top 10 and bottom 10 give good round numbers and still give useful information in the typical class of about 30 pupils.

2. For each student in the High group, go through a copy of the test and, next to each response chosen by the student, make a tally mark like this: "1." When you have done this for each student in the High group, you will have a total of ten tally marks opposite the choices of each item in the multiple-choice test. For example, consider the following item from a history test, where the right answer is italicized:

Andrew Jackson secured his followers from
000 1 ⊦⊦⊦⊤ A. *the farmers of the West.*
   00 1 B. the slave owners of the South.
 0000 11 C. the bankers of the East.
    0 1 D. the manufacturers of the East.

Six of the ten students in the High group chose the right answer.

3. Next, for each student in the Low group, tally a different mark, such as a "0," in the same way as was done for the High group. In the example, three of the ten students in the Low group chose the right answer.

Such data, although based on a small number of cases, would be useful to the teacher in judging the difficulty and discrimination values of the item. For the item shown above, the teacher could justifiably infer that the item seemed to fall at about the 50 percent level of difficulty, because 9 of the 20 students tallied answered correctly. Similarly, the teacher could infer that the item discriminated in the right direction, because more students, namely six, in the High group answer it correctly than in the Low group, namely three.

In practice, it has been found that the necessary tallies for a 50-item, 4-choice test can be made in about 40 minutes. (Red and green pencils are often used, instead of tallies of different shape, for the Low and High groups, respectively.) Teachers who have used this procedure report that it yields information that "makes sense" to the students as well as the teacher. That is, the items that seem too hard or too easy according to the item analysis also seem too hard or too easy according to subjective judgment of the items in retrospect. And the items that discriminate well or poorly according to the item analysis often seem to be good or poor items in relation to the content of the whole test, as judged in retrospect.

Obviously, for long tests given to many students, so that the High and Low groups can be much larger than 10, hand-tallying is too laborious. Scoring machines and punch card equipment are used to make item analyses for such tests.

PRODUCT AND PROCEDURE EVALUATION (MANIPULATIVE PERFORMANCE TESTS)

As we noted previously, not all achievement of instructional objectives can be expressed in verbal, mathematical, or other symbols. Tests of the types thus far discussed are often inadequate. There still remains a large sphere of educational activity quite untouched by either short-answer or essay tests. This is the area in which a pupil's achievement is expressed by means of a *product* or a *procedure* —some direct indication of his skill and understanding.

By a product, we mean some material object that the pupil makes. A product is well illustrated in industrial arts and home economics— a piece of woodwork or metalwork, a mechanical drawing, chairs, tables, lamps, funnels, dustpans, bookends, dresses, cooked foods, etc. Products such as these and often the procedures used in producing them must be evaluated.

In other subjects products may similarly constitute an important aspect of achievement. In English—notebooks, compositions, and term papers; in the social studies—maps, tables, notebooks, and term papers; in art—drawings and models; in the natural sciences—laboratory setups, specimen preparations, models, notebooks, and general procedures. In the elementary grades, handwriting must be evaluated as a product. Thus we take up the eighth question listed at the beginning of this chapter: "If a nonlanguage product or procedure device is to be used, how should it be constructed?"

We can evaluate products in terms of their component features, or of their overall "general merit" in which features are not considered separately. We now consider each of these approaches.

In general, product evaluation devices help us systematize judgments concerning the product. This point is perhaps best clarified by an analogy to short-answer tests. In a short-answer test the pupil's "product" is his set of responses to the test items and this "product" is evaluated by means of the scoring key. The products considered here, however, are more complex and detailed than responses to short-answer test items. Hence the evaluation device analogous to the scoring key must be analytical, so as to reduce the single complex product to a series of simpler features analogous to test items. Just as the short answer test forces the analysis of a complex achievement into a number of simpler, more unitary test item responses, so the product evaluation device must yield an analysis of complex, multi-featured products into a number of more unitary features. Each feature can then be separately considered and evaluated. The total evaluation of the product is usually the sum of the evaluations of the separate features. The separate features are sometimes weighted differently.

Furthermore, just as each item on the short answer test must be scored, usually either right or wrong, so each feature of the product must be given a score—usually, as we shall see, along a multivalued continuum. Thus constructing a product evaluation device involves (1) analyzing the product into specific features, and (2) providing various levels of quality for scoring each of the features.

Analyzing the Product into Specific Features

The features into which a product is analyzed should first be *relevant to the instructional objectives* at which the experience in making the product is aimed. Here again, evaluation must proceed in close touch with instructional objectives. For example, a product should not be evaluated on the basis of the feature "neatness" unless neatness has been an objective of instruction.

Second, the features into which a product is analyzed should be *amenable to reliable evaluation*. Features should be sufficiently explicit, definite, and unambiguous that competent judges tend to agree in their evaluations of them. Features that can be evaluated by physical instruments like rulers or thermometers lead to greater agreement among judges than subjective features like "decorative value," grace, or general merit. But before we regard a feature of a product as too intangible for evaluation, we should realize that many such features can be made scorable by techniques like the quality scale, discussed below.

The features into which a product is analyzed should be *grouped* on some basis that increases the efficiency and meaningfulness of the judgment. The features may be arranged in the order in which the product is examined, or in terms of general and specific features. The following is an example of how features of industrial arts projects might be grouped according to the method of judgment:

By inspection: neatness, placement on page, arrowheads, etc.
By physical measurement: dimensions, accuracy, circles, etc.
By rating scale or inspection: lettering, lines, numbers, etc.

Another method of arranging the features, especially valuable when the product evaluation device is used also for instructional purposes, is in the order in which they emerge during the production of the product itself. Some features are best judged before the product is completed because they may be hidden or changed by later operations or parts of the product. Inspecting mortise and tenon joints in woodworking, and measuring dry ingredients for a cake in a home economics course illustrate this problem.

Note that the analyzing process parallels the discussion of instructional objectives and the table of test specifications. Evaluation must depend on the purposes or objectives of the endeavor being evaluated.

Scoring Specific Features

The problem of scoring specific features breaks down into two related problems: (1) how many points or values the feature can have, and

(2) how to describe and define the various points along the scale on which the feature is scored. The simplest answer to both problems is twofold scoring, such as "present or absent," "good or bad." This converts the product evaluation device into a simple check list, each of the features being checked according to whether it is present or absent in the product. The total score for the product is the total number of desirable features it has, as represented by the number of check marks.

Although this method is simple, most features are not completely present or absent, but rather are present in varying degrees between these two extremes. Twofold scoring may lead to considerable loss of refinement and reliability in the evaluation.

Hence a scoring device often presents several degrees of quality of the feature under consideration. The number of degrees (or steps or scale units or alternatives) presented for each feature depends on the fineness of discrimination possible and desirable for that feature. For an objectively measurable feature such as the accuracy of a dimension, a large number of degrees of quality are possible, whereas more subjective features, such as neatness or legibility, necessarily have fewer degrees. In general, the more degrees or the finer the discrimination possible, the more reliable the resulting evaluation or measurement. Hence to maximize reliability the number of degrees should be as large as practical considerations permit.

The reliability of rating human personality traits reaches its maximum when about seven degrees of discrimination are used for each trait. More than seven usually yields no appreciable increase in reliability and less than seven usually results in some sacrifice of reliability. If the various degrees are defined by scaling techniques which assign scores to various products chosen to illustrate different degrees of quality, more degrees may be used. The Thorndike Handwriting Scale has fifteen samples of handwriting, each of which sample defines some point along the range from poorest to best in "general merit."

How should the various degrees for each feature be presented? In twofold scoring, simply by defining the two degrees as "present or absent" or "good or bad." For three or more levels an intermediate term may be inserted: "excellent, average, poor." Each of these terms may be given a numerical value such as 3, 2, 1.

A modification is to furnish a *graphic scale* in the form of a straight line whose ends and intermediate points are properly labeled, as follows:

Very poor	Average	Very good
1	2	3

In making his rating the judge places a check mark on this line at the point which, to his mind, represents the merit of the feature. He gives this mark a score proportional to its distance from the "poor" end of the line, say the number of "half inches" from that end.

Instead of being defined by *general* descriptive adjectives like "good" and "poor," the points along the graphic scale or the levels of quality may be defined in *specific* terms. The Minnesota Score Card for Meat Roast gives the levels for different features:

FOOD SCORE CARDS
(Adapted from Clara M. Brown and others)
Meat Roast

	1	2	3	Score
APPEARANCE	1. Shriveled		Plump and slightly moist	1. _____
COLOR	2. Pale or burned		Well browned	2. _____
MOISTURE CONTENT	3. Dry		Juicy	3. _____
TENDERNESS	4. Tough		Easily cut or pierced with fork	4. _____
TASTE AND FLAVOR	5. Flat or too highly seasoned		Well seasoned	5. _____
	6. Raw, tasteless, or burned		Flavor developed	6. _____

SOURCE. Clara Brown, *Evaluation and Investigation of Home Economics*, New York: F. S. Crofts and Company, 1941. By permission of Appleton-Century-Crofts.

Illustrative Product and Procedure Evaluation Devices

The reader will understand the preceding discussion better if he becomes familiar with some of the rating scales, score cards, check lists, and quality scales developed in different fields. He can apply the ideas and principles used in these illustrations to whatever kinds of products and procedures especially interest him.

Measuring Scale of Handwriting. The Ayres Handwriting Scale[18] measures different qualities of handwriting. Portions of the "Gettysburg Edition" are shown here (Fig. 35). To secure samples of pupils'

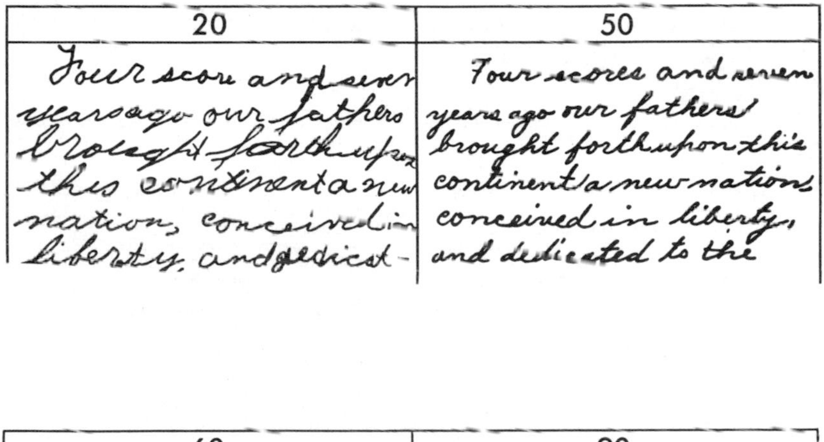

Fig. 35. Measuring Scale for Handwriting.

[18] Published by the Russell Sage Foundation.

handwriting, the teacher writes the first three sentences of Lincoln's Gettysburg Address on the blackboard and has his pupils copy it until they are familiar with it. Then at a given signal the pupils copy it from the beginning; they write exactly two minutes with ink on ruled paper. He scores the samples of handwriting by sliding them along the scale until he finds writing of the same quality. The number at the top of the scale gives the value assigned to the writing he is measuring.

Check List for Use of Microscope. Tyler[19] applied the check list technique to products and procedures in the laboratory sciences by observing students' difficulties in using a microscope. He called one student at a time into a special room in which there was a table with a microscope, yeast culture, slide covers, cloth, and lens papers on it. He then asked the student to find a yeast cell under the microscope. He kept a record of the time and checked the student's actions on the check list shown in Table 12.

Table 12. Check List of Student Reactions in Finding an Object Under the Microscope

STUDENT'S ACTIONS	Sequence of Actions	STUDENT'S ACTIONS (Continued)	Sequence of Actions
a. Takes slide	....1....	ab. Breaks cover glass	...12....
b. Wipes slide with lens paper	....2....	ac. Breaks slide	....
c. Wipes slide with cloth	....	ad. With eye away from eyepiece turns down coarse adjustment	....
d. Wipes slide with finger	....		
e. Moves bottle of culture along the table	....	ae. Turns up coarse adjustment a great distance	..13,22..
f. Places drop or two of culture on slide	....3....	af. With eye at eyepiece turns down fine adjustment a great distance	..14,23..
g. Adds more culture	....		
h. Adds few drops of water	....	ag. With eye away from eyepiece turns down fine adjustment a great distance	...15....
i. Hunts for cover glasses	....4....		
j. Wipes cover glass with lens paper	....5....	ah. Turns up fine adjustment screw a great distance	....
k. Wipes cover with cloth	....	ai. Turns fine adjustment screw a few turns	....
l. Wipes cover with finger	....		
m. Adjusts cover with finger	....	aj. Removes slide from stage	...16....
n. Wipes off surplus fluid	....	ak. Wipes objective with lens paper	....
o. Places slide on stage	....6....		
p. Looks through eyepiece with right eye	....	al. Wipes objective with cloth	....
		am. Wipes objective with finger	...17....
q. Looks through eyepiece with left eye	....7....	an. Wipes eyepiece with lens paper	....
r. Turns to objective of lowest power	....9....	ao. Wipes eyepiece with cloth	....
s. Turns to low-power objective	...21....	ap. Wipes eyepiece with finger	...18....
t. Turns to high-power objective	....	aq. Makes another mount	....
u. Holds one eye closed	....8....	ar. Takes another microscope	....
v. Looks for light	....	as. Finds object	....
w. Adjusts concave mirror	....	at. Pauses for an interval	....
x. Adjusts plane mirror	....	au. Asks, "What do you want me to do?"	....
y. Adjusts diaphragm	....		
z. Does not touch diaphragm	...10....	av. Asks whether to use high power	....
aa. With eye at eyepiece turns down coarse adjustment	...11....	aw. Says, "I'm satisfied"	....

[19] R. W. Tyler, *op. cit.*

Table 12. Check List of Student Reactions in Finding an Object Under the Microscope
(Continued)

STUDENT'S ACTIONS (Continued)	Sequence of Actions
ax. Says that the mount is all right for his eye	....
ay. Says he cannot do it	..19, 24..
az. Told to start new mount	....
aaa. Directed to find object under low power	...20....
aab. Directed to find object under high power	....
NOTICEABLE CHARACTERISTICS OF STUDENT'S BEHAVIOR	
a. Awkward in movements	....
b. Obviously dexterous in movements	
c. Slow and deliberate	....√....
d. Very rapid	....
e. Fingers tremble	....
f. Obviously perturbed	....
g. Obviously angry	....
h. Does not take work seriously	....
i Unable to work without specific directions	...√....
j. Obviously satisfied with his unsuccessful efforts	...√....

SKILLS IN WHICH STUDENT NEEDS FURTHER TRAINING	Sequence of Actions
a. In cleaning objective	....√....
b. In cleaning eyepiece	....√....
c. In focusing low power	....√....
d. In focusing high power	....√....
e. In adjusting mirror	....√....
f. In using diaphragm	....√....
g. In keeping both eyes open	....√....
h. In protecting slide and objective from breaking by careless focusing	....√....

CHARACTERIZATION OF THE STUDENT'S MOUNT	Sequence of Actions
a. Poor light	....√....
b. Poor focus	....
c. Excellent mount	....
d. Good mount	....
e. Fair mount	....
f. Poor mount	....
g. Very poor mount	....
h. Nothing in view but a thread in his eyepiece	....
i. Something on objective	....
j. Smeared lens	....√....
k. Unable to find object	...√....

Any scientific laboratory apparatus and any procedure, such as caring for infants, baking, preparing meals, etc., can be evaluated with check lists like this. The sequential feature, with steps numbered in the order in which they are performed, is especially useful in observing procedures. The technique can be further refined by using rating scales for the quality of each feature of a product or a procedure. When numbering for sequence, the number can be placed at a point along a scale of quality or excellence.

"Setups" for Evaluating Shop Procedures. Paper-and-pencil tests are difficult to use in evaluating shop procedures because these tests have to rely on drawings instead of the actual objects. A highly flexible technique that uses many of the techniques of short-answer testing is illustrated in the machine shop test which appears on the following page.[20]

Each student observes several shop situations or "setups" in succession, reads one or more questions related to each situation, and records the number of his choice of answer on a form like that shown on page 278.

[20] For this illustration we are indebted to Emil W. Ross.

MACHINE SHOP TEST

Name _____ Class period _____

Instructions

You will be assigned a position to start this test at a place in the shop where there is a question typed on a 5 x 8 card, and also several possible answers. Pick out the answer that you think is correct, and note the *number* in front of that answer. Write *this number* in the answer space below, *after* the correct question number. Be sure that the first answer you write is after the correct number. Then the others will follow in order.

You will be given two minutes to answer each question. At the sound of the bell, change to the question with the next higher number, with the exception that from question number "20" you will go to question number "1." Do not go ahead. Do not talk. You may figure on the back of this sheet, but do not write on the question card.

If a question pertains to a setup on a machine, DO NOT CHANGE ANYTHING ON THE SETUP UNLESS THE QUESTION CARD TELLS YOU TO DO SO. Otherwise you may make it impossible for the next student to answer that question.

1. _____	7. _____	14. _____
2. _____	8. _____	15. _____
3. _____	9. _____	16. _____
4. _____	10. _____	17. _____
5. _____	11. _____	18. _____
6. _____	12. _____	19. _____
	13. _____	

20. Write your answer below. You may continue writing on the other side if necessary, but be very brief.

[*Sample questions*: The following questions illustrate either different methods of phrasing questions, or different types of situations appropriate to this particular form of test. For actual use, each of these questions and its alternative answers are typed on a separate card. Note that any one of the starred responses could be made the desired response. Comments on each question are included after the question.]

    1. Which one of the following is a correct statement?

       *(1) The hacksaw blade is in the frame backwards.

       *(2) A finer toothed blade should be used on this job.

       *(3) The piece protrudes too far from the vise.

       (4) One should saw on the other side of the vise.

[The required setup consists of a hacksaw, a vise holding a piece of work, and a saw cut started.]

2. Which one of the following statements tells what is wrong with this shaper setup? You may engage the clutch.
    *(1) The stroke is too long.
    *(2) The stroke position is wrong.
    (3) Paper should not have been left under the work.
    *(4) The vise is turned wrong.
["What is wrong" can apply to a great many shop situations.]

· · · · · ·

4. Which one of the following measurements is nearest the diameter of this piece? Use the micrometers provided.
    *(1) 1.091"
    *(2) 1.116"
    *(3) 1.191"
    *(4) 1.216"
[These are easily confused micrometer readings. The question form is equally well adapted to other methods of measurement.]

5. Which one of the following statements explains why this lathe tool bit cut rough?
    (1) The feed is too high.
    (2) The speed is too fast.
    (3) The work is too loose between centers.
    *(4) The cutting edge is too high.
[The cause of faulty work requires careful observation. The setup should show the actual operation partly finished.]

· · · · · ·

20. Rules are necessary either to prolong the life of equipment or to improve the appearance of a shop. Name five things wrong on this lathe, according to the rules of this particular shop. [Such a question requires more space and so is last on the answer form.]

Situational items can be devised as products or as features of a process in making a more complex product. Such items can be adapted realistically to any laboratory work in which various phases of an ongoing process can be identified and scored.

Note that paper forms and outlines of procedures such as check lists and rating scales do not guarantee reliable and valid evaluation. In a very real sense the judge or rater is the instrument and the paper form merely a convenient and systematically organized aid. Hence the important task is to train the judge or observer.

OPEN-BOOK EXAMINATIONS

To promote examinations that require "thinking" rather than mere recall of textbook information, some writers have suggested examinations in which the students are permitted to use textbooks and notes. These open-book examinations may test the worth of a course, encourage sound preparation on the part of the pupil, present a more natural situation, and necessitate comprehensive thought questions.

The examinations need not be in the form of essay questions. Short-answer questions can readily be put in such a form as to require ability "to see situations as a whole," to "use facts in solving problems," to "draw inferences from known to unknown situations," and in general to achieve broader, more permanent objectives of instruction than mere memorization of the facts and procedures in textbooks and lecture notes.

Questions for open-book examinations must be constructed so that the pupil cannot answer them simply by turning to the proper page in a textbook. They must be arranged so as to require him to understand the large sections or basic principles of a unit, a book, or a course, to draw together under a single heading the scattered instances of a fundamental generalization, or to cite specific examples of a trend.

It is possible to construct open-book examinations for any course that stresses more than the memorization of facts and procedures from textbooks, lectures, or other sources. These examinations force teachers to stress mental processes other than memory. A similar shift in emphasis will occur in the pupil's study habits and methods of preparing for examinations. Open-book examinations appeal to pupils as more "natural" and representative of how they will use their achievement in out-of-school life. In real life, problem solving goes on with the available resources at hand. Consumers, voters, lawyers, engineers, and physicians use "open-book" methods to solve their problems.

The Stalnakers reported their experience with these examinations in the humanities at the University of Chicago.[21] By splitting the

[21] J. M. and Ruth C. Stalnaker, Open-book examinations: Results, *J. Higher Educ.*, 1934, 6:214–216.

final examination into a three-hour morning open-book session and a three-hour afternoon closed-book session they were able to compare the relative standing of the students on the two types of examinations. In general, they found that the relative standing did not change and that the results of both types of examinations were similarly related to the scores on an intelligence test. This means that the open-book gave neither more nor less advantage to the more intelligent student than the closed-book examination did.

ORAL EXAMINATIONS

In the past, teachers gave frequent oral examinations by having pupils stand up by their seats and recite the lessons they had studied. This technique is less often used today because of the development of group discussion techniques and evaluation by means of short-answer tests. However, oral questioning is a good way to discover what thought processes a pupil uses in solving a problem.

In the preschool, kindergarten, and lower primary grades the oral examination is probably the only way to evaluate achievement because the pupils have not yet learned to read. In higher grades oral examinations are often desirable when the teacher wishes to evaluate a pupil's ability to discuss broad types of problems in which integration of knowledge in several areas is important. These examinations also have some value as a diagnostic tool in situations where written tests or product and procedure techniques cannot be used.

On the adverse side, oral examinations have the same limitations as essay examinations—poor sampling of content, great consumption of time, and low reliability. They certainly cannot alone provide a satisfactory basis for determining grades for a pupil's work in a given area of instruction.

LABORATORY EXERCISES AND DISCUSSION QUESTIONS

1. Illustrate in terms of specific pupil behaviors and subject matters what you mean by ability to translate, ability to interpret, ability to

apply, ability to analyze, and ability to evaluate. (A *Taxonomy of Educational Objectives* will help you.)

2. How have your attitudes toward essay and short-answer tests and your methods of preparing for them changed compared with those reported in this chapter? Which kind of test usually had better motivational and instructional effects for you? Did these effects differ in the areas in which you excelled as against those in which you had difficulty?

3. What are some practical procedures for increasing the reliability of a teacher-made short-answer test? Of an essay test?

4. For a specific product, give an illustration of a feature related to instructional objectives and one which is not; similarly, illustrate a feature amenable to evaluation and one relatively not so amenable.

5. In what sense does the improvement of essay questions make them more similar to short-answer test items? What properties are still unique with essay tests?

6. It has been said that most problems of life outside of school in which books are used are open-book examinations. Discuss this statement in school and for making school work more realistic. Is there still a place for closed-book examinations? Explain.

7. Give an example of how very young children can learn to solve problems by using the scientific method. How would you evaluate this activity?

8. Write an essay question in your subject-matter area aimed at each of the following objectives from the *Taxonomy:*
   Extrapolation
   Analysis of relationships
   Synthesis in the form of deriving a set of abstract relations
   Application of principles
   Evaluation in terms of internal evidence

9. Criticize the following as an essay question: "Discuss the current strike at Colossal Motors." Reword it in the light of your criticisms, retaining its good features or revising it entirely.

10. Construct five short-answer items dealing with a specific objective in the subject you plan to teach. Try these out on your fellow students. Do the results bring suggestions for improvement? What?

11. Write directions for a set of matching items. Submit them to the class for criticism. Are they clear and simple enough to be understood by pupils at a grade level below the one being tested?

12. Construct multiple-choice items to measure the following:
    a. Knowledge of the procedures for adding fractions.

b. Knowledge of social forces operating during the Reconstruction Period.

c. Importance of geographic factors in community life.

d. Interpretation of a graph showing relationship between height of husbands and of their wives.

e. Ability to understand and apply criteria for selecting a test.

Suggested References

Ahmann, J. S., and M. D. Glock, *Evaluating Pupil Growth*, Boston: Allyn and Bacon, 1959.

See Chapter 7, Informal Objective Achievement Tests; Chapter 8, Measuring Understanding Objectively; Chapter 9, Informal Essay Achievement Tests; and Chapter 11, Evaluating Procedures and Products.

Brownell, W. A., The measurement of understanding, *45th Yearb. Natl. Soc. Stud. Educ.*, Part I.

A comprehensive and, in the earlier chapters at least, theoretical presentation of methods intended for all levels of education and most school subjects.

Downie, N. M., and R. W. Heath, *Basic Statistical Methods*, New York: Harper & Row, 2nd ed., 1965.

The student interested in reviewing statistics or extending his statistical insight concerning test theory and technology will find this a very useful book.

Educational Testing Service, Judges Disagree on Qualities that Characterize Good Writing, *ETS Developments*, February 1961, 9:2.

This article should be read by all those who believe that essay tests can be used effectively for all educational evaluation.

Ebel, R. L., *Measuring Educational Achievement*, New York: Prentice-Hall, 1965.

This text emphasizes techniques of test development and analysis especially pertinent to the classroom teacher.

Gerberich, J. R., *Specimen Objective Test Items*, New York: Longmans, Green, 1956.

This volume presents a brief orientation on the nature and methods of constructing achievement tests, steps in the process of constructing tests, a detailed treatment of the instructional outcomes of what should be the primary determiners of the types of pupil behavior to be measured, and extensive test samples to indicate some of the ways by which these outcomes can be measured.

Green, John A., *Teacher-Made Tests*, New York: Harper & Row, 1963. Chapters 2 through 6 include planning of measuring instruments, construction and use of informal objective tests, performance tests, essay tests, and oral examinations.

Greene, H. A., A. N. Jorgensen, and J. R. Gerberich, *Measurement and Evaluation in the Elementary School*, 2nd ed., 1953; *Measurement and Evaluation in the Secondary School*, 2nd ed., 1954, New York: Longmans, Green.

These two books have several chapters on the development, construction, and improvement of objective test items in specific subject-matter fields in secondary education, and for the different grade levels in the instructional fields of elementary schools. Contains examples of test items for different outcomes of education.

Lindquist, E. F. (ed.), *Educational Measurement*, Washington: American Council on Education, 1951.

Robert L. Ebel presents in Chapter 7 (pp. 185–189) definitive treatment of the planning of short-answer tests and the art of writing test items; illustrative examples. Chapter 6 by K. W. Vaughn is a comprehensive review of the problems and techniques for planning objective tests. In Chapter 11, G. Spaulding provides useful assistance in reproducing objective tests. Chapter 12, by D. G. Ryans and N. Frederiksen, reviews the principles and procedures for developing performance tests of educational achievement. In Chapter 13, J. M. Stalnaker gives an excellent discussion of the essay examination procedure and the techniques for improving it.

Micheels, W. J., and M. R. Karnes, *Measuring Educational Achievement*, New York: McGraw-Hill, 1950.

These authors provide an excellent reference for teachers of industrial arts education. They make suggestions for the construction of different types of tests for evaluating achievement in shop courses. Considerable emphasis is given to the manipulative-performance type of evaluation.

Stanley, Julian C., *Measurement in Today's Schools*, Englewood Cliffs: Prentice-Hall, 4th ed., 1964.

Chapters 7 and 8 discuss, respectively, constructing specific types of objective tests and constructing and using essay tests.

Stodola, Quentin, *Making the Classroom Test: A Guide for Teachers*, Evaluation and Advisory Service Series, No. 4, Princeton: Educational Testing Service, 1959.

Practical suggestions for test construction. Includes plans and procedures used by four teachers in making good tests. This pamphlet may be obtained from ETS upon request.

Travers, Robert M. W., *How To Make Achievement Tests*, New York: Odyssey, 1950.

The author describes briefly but succinctly, and in a straightforward, understandable manner, the steps in planning evaluation instruments and constructing objective tests.

Wood, Dorothy Adkins, *Test Construction*, Columbus: Merrill, 1960.

This 135-page paperback book provides many excellent guides to test construction, with many illustrations of good test items in several instructional fields.

CHAPTER 9

Assigning marks and reporting pupil progress

Nature of School Marks and Appraisal
  Differences Between Test Scores and Marks
  Reasons for Marking Systems
  Kinds of Marking Systems
  Criticism of Marks

Bases of Marking Systems
  Factors in a Mark on a Single Test
  Factors in a Mark on a Course of Instruction

Assigning Marks from Test Scores
  Grading "on the Curve"
  Combining Test Scores Prior to Grading

Combining Marks for Final Grades

Types of Reporting Practices

One of the most persistent and perplexing problems teachers face is assigning marks—making value judgments of the status and progress of students at periodical intervals. One function of school marks, grades, and reports is to maintain communication between teachers and pupils and parents. Communicating with parents effectively and improving their understanding of pupil problems help schools enlist their support in developing realistic and constructive educational programs. In this chapter we shall consider the kinds of questions that arise among teachers. (For some of these questions no satisfactory, generally applicable answers have been found.)

What are the best evaluation techniques?
What is the best way to give marks?
Is it best to mark pupils in relation to their own apparent ability? Or in relation to the progress of their classmates? Or in relation to both themselves and their classmates?
Is it best to mark pupils according to a standard previously decided upon for their particular grade or educational level?
What is the best technique for reporting pupil progress to parents?
Is the report card as good as letters to parents or interviews when the amount of time and effort expended is taken into consideration? How often and at what times should report cards be sent to parents?

NATURE OF SCHOOL MARKS AND APPRAISAL

In this section we discuss the differences between test scores and school marks, reasons for having marking systems, various kinds of marking systems, and some of the criticisms of marks and grades.

Differences Between Test Scores and Marks

As we noted in Chapter 3, a raw score on a test has practically no significance without additional data for interpreting it. Even if the teacher transforms raw scores into percentile ranks, grade placement scores, or various norms they merely compare the performance of one pupil with that of others. Test scores are only indexes of measurement, and measurement in itself has no particular meaning. Marks or grades, on the other hand, are indexes of evaluation; they imply that value judgments have been made with the assistance of other criteria and in terms of some type of value, objective, goal, or standard. For example, a score may be 69 on a test having 125 items, but a pupil's grade or mark may be either "C" or "A," "55%" or

"80%," "passed" or "failed," depending on the nature of the objective or standard used in making the value judgment.

Reasons for Marking Systems

Among the purposes of marking systems, the more common are to provide a basis for (1) information for parents on pupil status or progress, (2) promotion and graduation, (3) motivation of school work, (4) guidance of learning, (5) guidance of educational and vocational planning, (6) guidance of personal development, (7) honors, (8) participation in many school activities, (9) reports and recommendations to future employers, (10) data for curriculum studies, (11) reports to a school the pupil may attend later.

Kinds of Marking Systems

Many kinds of marking systems have been devised. With so many reasons for using marks, no one system could be expected to be satisfactory for all purposes. Early systems usually reported marks on a 100-point scale or percentage system, in which all grades of 70 or higher were considered to indicate satisfactory or "passing" work, and marks lower than 70 to indicate "failure." In a typical classroom there would be grade reports for a particular subject with marks at almost any level and pupils would be differentiated by grades of 81, 82, 83, 84, etc. Such a system implied a precision and refinement of evaluation not justified by available measurement instruments and techniques.

Some educators have suggested using just two categories of grading: pass or fail (P-F), satisfactory or unsatisfactory (S-U), plus or minus. This practice tends to have the opposite effect of the preceding one in that it implies that all students who receive a "pass" grade are alike in their abilities or achievement in whatever is being marked. This system has not been widely accepted, and where it has been used many teachers have begun reporting P+, P, and P−, so that they actually are using a four-point system.

The marking system most frequently used is based on five points, with four marks indicating passing or satisfactory work and one mark indicating failure or unsatisfactory work. These points are usually given in letter grades from high to low (A, B, C, D, and F) or numbers (1, 2, 3, 4, 5, or in reverse order). Although some teachers use only the five categories, others use plus and minus signs to indicate performance slightly above or below a given mark.

The major shortcoming of grades or marks is that few of them are defined meaningfully. The same marks often mean different things to different teachers even in the same school system. In every school system it is important that some definition be given for each mark to facilitate uniformity in understanding. The following definitions of grades are helpful, but they are still questionable regarding what is meant by the "goals" stated in them, or the term "achieved."

Grade	Significance of Grade
A	Excellent. This student is outstanding. He has achieved all the major and minor goals of the class. His level of achievement is considerably above the minimum required for doing more advanced work in the same field. Usually 5 to 10 percent of the pupils in a typical class receive this grade.
B	Highly satisfactory. The work of this student is generally better than average. He has achieved all the major goals and many of the minor goals of the class. His level is somewhat above the minimum required for doing advanced work in the same field. Usually about 20 to 30 percent of the pupils in a typical class receive this grade.
C	Satisfactory. This student's work is quite acceptable but not outstanding. He has achieved all the major goals, but not many of the minor goals. His level of achievement barely meets the minimum required for more advanced work in the same field, but he has no major handicaps to overcome. Usually about 35 to 40 percent of the students in a typical class receive this grade.
D	Poor. The work of this student is noticeably weak. He has achieved only a few of the major goals of the class. His level of achievement is so limited that he is not prepared to work on a more advanced level in the same field without considerable remedial work and individual assistance. Usually about 20 to 30 percent of the pupils in a typical class receive this grade.

Grade   *Significance of Grade*

F   Unsatisfactory. This student does not meet the minimum requirements of the class. He has achieved none of the major goals. He has failed to accomplish the minimum essential for continued progress in the same field. Usually less than 5 percent of the pupils in a typical class receive this grade.

The "more advanced work in the same field" in the above may not be pertinent for students in such classes as eighth-grade geography or ninth-grade world history.

Furthermore, these definitions are based upon the extent to which pupils have accomplished some general goals or the objectives of instruction in the class. Students may be assigned the same mark, according to these definitions, when their different abilities vary considerably, depending upon the teacher's goals. For example, teachers often mark on the basis of "individual goals," "ability goals," "goals of effort," or some combination of these and other goals. *Individual goals* may indicate the extent of individual progress (difference between achievement at beginning and end) regardless of the level of the student's achievement at the beginning and end of the reporting period. *Ability goals* may indicate the extent to which students are working up to their "capacity" as measured by some test of capacity or intelligence. *Goals of effort* may indicate the extent to which they are working at something regardless of whether they have accomplished anything or not. Thus, two pupils may receive B's in history. For one pupil the mark represents an A knowledge of history and a C effort; for the other, it represents a C knowledge of history and an A effort.

A better system of marking might include a number of letter marks: one for knowledge of history, one for the amount of effort the pupil has expended, another for the extent to which he is working up to his "capacity," and so on. But can a teacher judge "knowledge," "effort," and "capacity" accurately for all pupils?

Grading "on the curve" is another type of marking system. This is a system whereby sometimes predetermined percentages of students are awarded each of five letter or number grades and sometimes the grades are awarded on the basis of the relative status of pupils. The accompanying table shows three of the more common percentages of pupils for each grade or mark. This system derived its name from the proportions of cases found within given standard deviation distances on a normal curve (see Glossary, and p. 295). Techniques for deriving these grades are discussed later in this chapter.

Mark	Percentage of Students per Mark		
	I	II	III
A	7	10	5
B	24	20	20
C	38	40	50
D	24	20	20
F	7	10	5

Regardless of the marking system used, teachers do not adhere to it rigidly. In grading "on the curve" most distributions of marks are decidedly skewed, with more good than poor marks given. This skewness is even more pronounced with advanced students, perhaps because they are a more select group. Obviously progress in school is marked by continuous selection. If we assume that educability is "normally" distributed at birth, there is already considerable selection in the first grade.

Criticism of Marks

As typically used, marks have several shortcomings. Whereas the stated purposes for any marking system may be very worth while, the actual effects of it may not serve these purposes. For some pupils, marks often become the end and aim of education, for their primary goal is a "good" mark regardless of how much they have learned or how they have gone about getting the mark. Marks often lead pupils to concentrate on whatever the teacher uses as the basis for assigning them. In some cases, they tend to make pupils overemphasize the acquisition of subject matter, with little consideration given to any other objectives of education. This is not an inherent defect of marks, but rather an outcome of the way they are often used.

Teachers often use marks for disciplinary and motivational purposes, especially when other methods fail. Pupils may be forced to conform by the threat of poor marks, or motivated to do more work by the promise of better marks. Frequently, low marks unduly discourage pupils at the low end of the class achievement scale, although it is they who most need encouragement; such pupils often feel, "It doesn't do any good to work harder because I can't get a good grade anyway." On the other hand, brighter students are not encouraged to do as well as they can because they get satisfactory marks with little effort. In this respect, marks tend to encourage mediocrity in superior children.

BASES FOR MARKING SYSTEMS

A teacher should consider a number of questions in deciding on the bases for a marking system. What should the marking scale mean? What is the meaning of an "A"? Is it the highest grade given by a teacher? In any year? In this particular class? In this particular school? Or in some other school where he taught previously? Is it a typical grade, indicating satisfactory work, or is it never achieved by anyone because no one is "perfect"?

Is there a place for ability marking in school? Should top grades be given to all students who are working up to their full "capacities"? Should "level of the course" enter into grade distributions? Is it permissible to give top grades to all students who take an advanced elective course? If students in ninth-grade general mathematics have grades ranging from A to F, should the grades for those who survived algebra and geometry and are now taking trigonometry also range from A to F or should they be limited to A and B?

Is it advisable to give excellent marks abundantly for encouragement? Is it advisable to give poor marks for "driving" purposes? In other words, should grading scales and grading standards be altered at times for specific purposes?

What courses or types of performance requiring grading in school do not lend themselves to a multipoint scale, such as A to F? Are there courses or objectives that can only be evaluated as "acceptable" or "not acceptable"? How may these grades be combined with other grading systems? What factors should be combined to obtain the grade or mark? How should they be weighted in the combined mark?

No general rules can apply in answering all these questions. Individual school systems need to make their own decisions concerning the bases for their marking systems. Above all, an effort should be made to define a marking system so that it will produce some degree of uniformity in grading among teachers and some uniformity in understanding the system among pupils and their parents. Some educators believe an ideal situation would prevail if this type of uniformity were attained in all levels of education in all parts of the country. But the wide differences in specific purposes among schools today make it unlikely that this ideal will be reached. The questions raised in this section, however, provide a number of topics for class discussion and for in-service training of faculties.

Factors in a Mark on a Single Test

If a mark is to be given for a short-answer test in arithmetic, it should represent accomplishment in arithmetic. It should not be affected by other factors, such as handwriting, neatness, conduct, or others that do not represent the pupil's ability in arithmetic. If the test includes arithmetic computation, arithmetic reasoning, and the vocabulary of arithmetic, the grade should reflect all three aspects of arithmetic. On the other hand, if a student misspells words that are not part of the specific arithmetic vocabulary being tested, the misspellings should not be counted in his mark for arithmetic ability.

In essay tests, the grade should represent an evaluation of the pupil's accomplishments in the specific factors being tested. If the test is designed to sample knowledge of the "steps in the enactment of a law in Congress," for example, the grade should reflect only the factors pertaining to that knowledge, not ability in spelling, language, grammar, handwriting, etc.

It is often difficult, however, to distinguish between the content of an answer and the style of writing and the grammar used. Often the answer "looks right" but is written so poorly that the teacher cannot be sure. How teachers resolve such problems is hard to control; it may depend more on their temperament and values than on any principles of measurement they can accept intellectually.

Factors in a Mark on a Course of Instruction

The mark for a course of instruction over an extended period of time, such as a quarter or semester, is usually a composite of the marks on tests on units of instruction given at intervals and other evidences of pupil achievement in the course. In determining the final mark for a course, the teacher should give the same consideration to making it a measure of what it is intended to measure as he does in assigning a mark to a single test. If he is marking other objectives—such as development of responsibility, cooperation among students, improvement of written expression, speaking ability, neatness, promptness—in addition to the cognitive objectives of the course of instruction—history, for example—should he give them separate marks? Or include them in the mark for history itself? Whatever the answer, teachers should try to arrive at it openly, with full awareness of what they are doing, rather than unconsciously or unintentionally.

In combining marks for units within a course to arrive at the course grade, the teacher should consider the method of weighting each subgrade. In some courses he can obtain the final grade by simply averaging the unit grades. In others he may base the course grade only upon the final evaluation. For example, in a course in history the class may have covered four units in the term, each relatively independent of the others. That is, he could have presented any one of them at any time because the content does not depend upon what has been learned in other units. In this case, averaging unit grades is satisfactory for deriving a course grade. But in another case, such as algebra, the hierarchy of knowledge is such that each unit of instruction depends upon a previous one. Here the final unit of instruction gives a more adequate measure of a student's accomplishment than an average of his marks on all units. Suppose two pupils have the same abilities in algebra at the end of a semester. Pupil A did very poorly on the first unit and received a low grade. He worked hard and improved in each of the succeeding units. Pupil B did very well on the first unit, but progressively poorer on the succeeding ones. If all units grades are averaged for these pupils, Pupil B will have a higher grade at the end of the term than Pupil A, even though they completed the term with the same abilities.

ASSIGNING MARKS FROM TEST SCORES

Theoretically, the best method of assigning marks from test scores is on the basis of some *absolute standard* whereby a teacher could administer a test and know in advance just what score will be required for a given letter grade. Unfortunately, this is impossible in most situations because usually there is no absolute standard. If the teacher sets an a priori absolute standard, such as a given percentage of items answered correctly for a given grade, a test that happens to be too easy will result in all the students receiving the top grade. Similarly, a test that is too difficult will result in all the pupils failing. Both results are unrealistic, for it is unlikely that any public-school class will have all superior students or all failures.

Assuming that most classes are not too far from the average with respect to age, number of years in school, previous experience in a given subject, motivation, and many other factors, teachers often conclude that the performance of the middle half of the class on the test should be given an average grade regardless of the scores made on the test. Then, if the average score on the test seems low in relation to the total possible score it indicates that more instruction is needed for the entire class or that the test was too difficult.

Grading "on the Curve"

Grading "on the curve" means that grades are assigned according to the relative status of the pupils taking a test, all of whom have been exposed to similar instruction. It means that the large group who receive scores in the middle of the distribution will get the average mark for the class. The relatively few pupils at the extremes of the distribution will get the top and bottom marks, respectively, and the pupils between the middle and extreme groups will get the above- and below-average grades. One common procedure is to determine the cutting scores for the various grade distributions according to the divisions of the test-score scale shown in the accompanying tabulation. If these standard deviation distances were based on a normal distribution of scores, the percentages of pupils in each group would be approximately 7, 24, 38, 24, and 7, respectively, as shown in Fig. 36.

Grade	Division of Test Score Scale	Percent Normal Distribution
A	$+1.5s$ and up	7
B	$+.5s$ to $+1.49s$	24
C	$-.5s$ to $+.49s$	38
D	$-1.5s$ to $-.51s$	24
F	$-1.51s$ and down	7

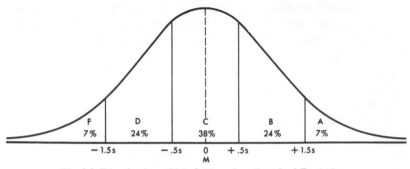

Fig. 36. Distribution of Marks Based on Standard Deviations.

Let us see how this procedure would apply to a *typical* group of twenty-five pupils in general mathematics at the ninth-grade level, who have the following raw scores on a test:

65, 64, 63, 58, 57, 56, 55, 55, 54, 50, 48, 48,
46, 45, 45, 44, 43, 42, 41, 36, 35, 32, 30, 28, 20

We round off the arithmetic mean of this group of scores at 46, and the standard deviation at 12. Using the above procedure, we determine the cutting scores for grades as follows:

Grade	Lower Limits		Scores	Number of Pupils	Percent of Pupils
A	M +1.5s or 46 + 18 = 64		64 and up	2	8
B	M + .5s or 46 + 6 = 52		52 to 63	7	28
C	M − .5s or 46 − 6 = 40		40 to 51	10	40
D	M −1.5s or 46 − 18 = 28		28 to 39	5	20
F	Below 1.5s or	Below 28	27 and down	1	4

This procedure yields percentages of pupils with grades from A to F of 8, 28, 40, 20, and 4, respectively. The difference between these percentages and those in Fig. 36 is due to the fact that the scores in this particular class are not normally distributed.

This procedure may allocate marks to a typical class more fairly than using the percentage of items answered correctly on a test or deciding arbitrarily that a certain percentage of pupils are to be assigned at each grade level. But the teacher should use it with discretion. In the example, the three pupils at the top of the distribution have scores of 65, 64, and 63. If he used the procedure strictly, the teacher would give A's only to the two with scores of 65 and 64. In view of the considerable gap in the score distribution between 63 and 58, the next highest score, it would seem that the pupil with the score of 63 is more like the two above than like the group given B's. Thus, it is perhaps better to include the score of 63 in the A group. When there are gaps in a distribution of scores, it is often desirable to shift the cutting scores upward to the lowest score at any grade level. Thus, in the example, the teacher would report the cutting scores to the class as: A—63 and up; B—54 to 62; C—41 to 53; D—28 to 40; F—below 28. In this way a teacher can prevent the somewhat warranted resentment on the part of students who had scores that "just missed getting a higher mark."

When a class or group is *not considered typical*, or if the course of instruction is an advanced one in which no pupil will be considered a failure, the grading scale may be moved to the left so that there will be a higher proportion of A's and B's, very few D's, and perhaps no F's. In graduate courses at the university level, for example, marks are often distributed as follows: A for scores $+.5s$ and up; B for scores $+.5s$ to $-.5s$; C for scores $-.5s$ to $-2.0s$; and D for scores below $-2.0s$. In graduate courses it is expected that there will be a much larger percentage of superior than of inferior students. The weaker students usually drop out during the undergraduate program; hence a graduate class should be composed primarily of A and B students, with very few D students, and, extremely rarely, an F student.

Combining Test Scores Prior to Grading

Sometimes a teacher gives a series of tests during a course and wants to combine the test scores for the course grade. If only the tests themselves enter into the course grade this procedure is readily justified. However, if other criteria are also used, the procedure discussed in the next section should receive particular attention. When combining test scores it is not often desirable to combine raw scores because they make the weights given the various tests depend too much on the number of questions, the difficulty of the test, and similar, possibly irrelevant, factors.

If a teacher wants all his test scores to have equal value in the composite grade, he should change each score to some type of standard score. One of the better procedures is to convert the raw scores to T-scores, as discussed in Chapter 3. If he wishes to give more weight to some of his tests than to others, he can multiply the standard scores by that weight and combine them for a total score. This procedure is explained in the next section.

COMBINING MARKS FOR FINAL GRADES

Course or unit grades are not usually based upon test results alone. Teachers often use other criteria as part of the basis for course grades. These criteria may include such items as a term paper or special project, class contributions, daily "homework," and unit tests. If the teacher grades each unit, he should take all determiners into consideration and weight them according to their relative importance. For example, he gives a student the following marks on various determiners for a given unit on instruction; Daily Class Work—C; Unit Project—C; Unit Examination—B. He can weight these determiners and obtain the unit grade by converting each determiner grade to grade points, using the equivalent of 4 points for A, 3 for B, 2 for C, 1 for D, and 0 for F. The Unit Examination may be considered worth twice as much as either of the other two determiners. Fig. 37

UNITS	I						II						III		
Pupil Names	Daily Class Work	Unit Project	Unit Examination	Total Grade Points	Grade Point Average	Unit Grade	Daily Class Work	Unit Project	Unit Examination	Total Grade Points	Grade Point Average	Unit Grade	Daily Class Work	Unit Project	Unit Examination
Weights	1	1	2	T	T/4		1	1	2	T	T/4				
James Brown	2 C	2 C	6 B	10	2.5	C⁺									
Mildred Cary	4 A	2 C	6 B	12	3.0	B									
Pat Cronen	2 C	2 C	4 C	8	2.0	C									
Wayne English	1 D	2 C	0 F	3	.8	D⁻									
Bert Johns	4 A	2 C	1 D	7	2.0	C									
Rachel Apps	3 B	2 C	8 A	13	2.8	B⁻									

Fig. 37. Teacher's Class Record and Grading Process.

shows this example as part of a teacher's class record. In this record the teacher has indicated the grade and equivalent grade points assigned for each determiner. He has a column for recording the total grade points for the unit, another column for the grade point average, and a third column for the final unit grade. This final grade is determined from the average grade points for the unit.

The same procedure will serve in combining several units of instruction in a course for the final course grade. If there are three units in a semester, the teacher can determine the semester mark by averaging the three unit grade point averages, just as the three determiners were combined for the unit grade in Fig. 37.

TYPES OF REPORTING PRACTICES

In Chapter 4 we discussed ways of using test results, especially through norms and profiles. These techniques are also useful in reporting pupil status and progress for specific classes or units of instruction. Other types of reports include cumulative records, class analysis charts, letters to parents, conferences between teachers and parents, home visits, and report cards. Cumulative records and class analysis charts are usually kept in a central file of a school; the other types are used primarily for reporting to parents. Regardless of the types of reports a teacher is called upon to make, they should provide specific information about pupils regarding all the major objectives of the educational program.

As far as possible, the reports should have separate marks for the achievement of specific objectives or outcomes of instruction rather than a single omnibus mark. Reports to parents are often made on report cards that provide for marks on such factors as the following, among others:

Days absent	Language
Times tardy	Arithmetic
Deportment	Social studies
Reading	Science
Writing	Music
Spelling	Art

When teachers are required to give a mark for each of the above, the mark can only represent a global or omnibus appraisal that does not provide for specific differentiation among the pupil's accomplishments in each of the areas of instruction. The mark for social studies, for example, may represent a composite of his mastery of the subject-matter content of social studies, his skill in locating sources of information, his research activities, his study skills and habits, his ability to work with other pupils in group activities, the correctness and effectiveness of his oral and written expression, and many other factors.

The complexity of marks, as they are often reported, is further increased by their being influenced, in varying degree, by the pupil's status, improvement, effort, "capacity," etc. Pupils may have a uniform standing in all these factors, or they may be outstanding in some and mediocre or poor in others.

A single mark for social studies, then, must be the overall resultant of complex interaction among many considerations, many of which are necessarily subjective. Yet it is not meaningless. Many judgments in life—those involved in appraising the overall desirability of a house, a car, or even a prospective spouse, for example—are based on many interacting considerations. Single omnibus judgments such as "accept" or "reject" must be made, and they have some value in reports to parents.

It would be nice if reports could include a detailed statement concerning specific objectives of each course of instruction. Such reports would include subject-matter achievement, character outcomes, social adjustment, and other factors, each of them evaluated independently. Subject-matter achievement would represent accomplishment in more than one type of achievement, and each would have a separate mark. Preferably descriptive words or phrases rather than letter grades would be used for reporting the separate evaluation of less tangible pupil qualities like effort, citizenship, personal traits, and the like.

Such reporting is not feasible at present, and perhaps it never will be. Teachers simply do not have available the tools (tests, etc.) with which to make such detailed appraisals with the necessary validity. Even if these tools were available, their use would probably not be feasible in terms of time and money. It is questionable, furthermore, whether most parents will understand and use such detailed information.

Instead of such a program, conferences between parents and

teachers provide a safe and workable method of improving on the communication provided by the typical report card. The conferences can be tailored to the individual pupil and his parents. The variables important for understanding one pupil may not be the same for another. What one parent is interested in may differ from another parent's concern. Such conferences can remedy the shortcomings of single omnibus grades for each part of the curriculum about as well as present-day educational measurement allows.

Since no universally acceptable practice has yet been devised, each local school system must plan its own reporting system. This should involve the cooperation of pupils, parents, teachers, and administrators. Through cooperative effort and consideration of the principles of objectivity and specificity in determining the marking and reporting system, a procedure can be worked out which will not only make marking and reporting more meaningful, but result in better educational practices.

LABORATORY EXERCISES AND DISCUSSION QUESTIONS

1. Examine your own experience for instances when your learning was evaluated on a superficial or otherwise inadequate basis. How would improved evaluation have affected your education?
2. Assume that you and the other members of this class are teaching in a 12-grade school. You are meeting to determine the marking and grading policies of the school. What is the school's viewpoint on the purposes of marking? How should the bases for marking differ in the primary, elementary, and secondary levels? What weight should be given various factors in determining marks? Can this weighting be made objective? Is it practicable to do so? If not, how will it be determined? What type of progress reports are to be made to parents? How much of the pupil appraisals is to be recorded on their permanent cumulative records?
3. Collect samples of report cards and reporting practices used in several schools. Discuss the advantages and limitations of each. As a class, establish an "ideal" reporting procedure and the type of reports to be made.
4. Obtain the scores given on an examination in your teaching area (or level). Determine the marks to be assigned to each score. Describe

to the class for discussion and criticism the bases upon which you determined these marks.

SUGGESTED REFERENCES

Ahmann, J. S., and M. D. Glock, *Evaluating Pupil Growth*, Boston: Allyn and Bacon, 1959.
   In Chapter 17 authors analyze reporting problems and support a many-sided approach emphasizing cooperative participation. Promotion practices and problems are also considered.
Green, John A., *Teacher-Made Tests*, New York: Harper & Row, 1963.
   There is a good discussion of scoring, grading, and assignment of course marks in Chapter 8.
Noll, V. H., *Introduction to Educational Measurement*, 2nd ed., Boston: Houghton Mifflin, 1965, pp. 380–454.
   Noll discusses the purposes and procedures for using the results of measurement in classification, grouping, diagnosis and remedial work, counseling and guidance, marking and motivation. He also introduces the problems involved in identifying exceptional children, interpreting schools to the community, and improving the school staff.
"Reporting Pupil Progress," *The National Elementary Principal*, 1952, 31, No. 6.
Stanley, Julian C., *Measurement in Today's Schools*, Englewood Cliffs: Prentice-Hall, 4th ed., 1964.
   Chapter 11 is concerned with grading, reporting, and promoting.
Strang, Ruth, *How to Report Pupil Progress*, Chicago: Science Research Associates, 1955.
   A brief but abundantly illustrated nontechnical discussion.
Thomas, R. M., *Judging Student Progress*, New York: Longmans, Green, 1954.
   In Chapter 13 the author explains the advantages and disadvantages of various procedures for reporting student progress, the types of specific and accurate letters and comments to be written to parents, the principles and techniques of assigning grades, and the development of report cards and other reports. Includes many examples.
Wrinkle, W. L., *Improving Marking and Reporting Practices*, New York: Holt, Rinehart and Winston, 1947.
   A report on a program for revising practices in an elementary and secondary school.

PART FOUR
Appraisal of Personality Aspects

CHAPTER ~ *10*

Determining attitudes and interests

305

For the moment, let us consider attitudes as being "feelings for or against something." Curriculum builders, school administrators, and teachers are aware that educational procedures and curricula can and do change attitudes. And even when attitudes are not subject to the influence, conscious or unconscious, of the school but are shaped by out-of-school experiences, the school cannot avoid being concerned with these aspects of pupils. Education cannot proceed as if human beings were intellectual machines governed by pure reason. From the standpoint of both society and the individual, the importance of attitudes needs only to be mentioned to be appreciated. A society is stable to the extent that attitude patterns function in the lives of individuals in society without creating undue stresses and strains. Education must therefore be concerned with whether it is producing types of attitude patterns that serve as integrating forces in society.

Does concern with attitudes imply a system of indoctrination rather than of education? Educators have upheld the slogan that children must be taught *how* to think but not *what* to think. Yet this slogan contains a fundamental psychological self-contradiction. Thinking does not occur in the abstract or in a vacuum but employs the individual's attitude patterns and experience. Hence, in the process of teaching *how* to think the school will inevitably also to a considerable extent be teaching *what* to think.

From the standpoint of the individual, attitudes are important to mental hygiene. A person's own evaluation of his conduct and desires in relation to social values *as he understands them* constitutes the basis for his social-emotional adjustment. His attitudes toward his environment—playmates, teachers, institutions, customs—all have a basic effect on his mental ease or dis-ease. His attitudes also affect what he perceives, remembers, and thinks. The integration of the intellectual-emotional life of pupils is as much a matter of attitude as is social integration, the problem of holding society together.

More specifically, attitudes are a vital concern of guidance, and consequently of educational evaluation, because they affect:

1. *The pupil's fitness for various curricula.* Unless a pupil has a favorable attitude toward a series of instructional objectives and sets them up as desirable goals for himself, the educative process will be relatively ineffective.

2. *The pupil's fitness for various occupational goals.* Bingham[1] summarized the connection between attitudes and occupational fitness in terms of whether (a) the individual will like the actual work of an occupation; (b) he will find himself among congenial associates, with interests similar to his own; (c) indications of his future abilities may be uncovered; (d) alternative fields of occupation, not yet seriously considered, may be brought to light.

3. *The pupil's fitness for participation in a democratic social order.* Attitudes toward social groups, institutions, practices, and policies are all attitudes in which society and the schools have a real stake. Most important of all, perhaps, are the pupil's attitudes toward the acceptance of social responsibility. Guidance concerned with individual and social progress requires the evaluation of the pupil's respect for his right to vote and his sensitivity to social problems.

DEFINITION OF ATTITUDES

As we stated above, attitudes may be informally defined as feelings for or against something. This definition provides the framework for a more careful definition. The term "feeling" points to the differences between attitudes and detailed, rational, intellectual, cognitive mental processes. Attitudes are linked to the emotions, for pleasant and unpleasant associations—fear, rage, love, and all the learned variations in them—play a part in attitudes.

The phrase "for or against" expresses the directionality of attitudes, the fact that they are characterized by approaches or withdrawals, likes or dislikes, avoidant or adient tendencies, favorable or unfavorable reactions, loves or hates, as responses to stimuli.

The word "something" signifies that attitudes are not merely mental images or verbalized ideas, but take on meaning only when considered in relation to some specific or generalized object, situation, or stimulus.

A further characteristic of attitudes is that they often have so great an effect on behavior that the attitude enables the prediction of other behavior. Or behavior may be so influenced by other forces

[1] W. V. Bingham, *Aptitudes and Aptitude Testing,* New York: Harper & Row, 1937, p. 82.

that it will not follow the expressed attitude; e.g., a pupil who expresses opposition to cheating proceeds to cheat on an examination. Another characteristic of attitudes, which is sometimes overlooked, is that they are learned.

In summary, an attitude may be defined as an emotionalized tendency, organized through experience, to react positively or negatively toward a psychological object.

Attitudes and Allied Concepts

Certain concepts allied to attitudes, some of them essentially synonyms or near-synonyms, are considered here since they are frequently used in popular discussion and technical literature. Such concepts are *interests, motives, values, appreciation, morale, ideals,* and *character*. Although there are additional concepts, these show how such concepts refer basically to attitudes.

Interests, as observed, are presumably the reflection of attractions and aversions in behavior, of feelings of pleasantness and unpleasantness, likes and dislikes. A distinction may be made between attitudes and interests in that interests merely indicate the degree to which an individual prefers to hold an object before his consciousness whether he reacts approvingly or disapprovingly toward it, whereas attitudes indicate his reaction in terms of its direction, pleasantness or unpleasantness, agreement or disagreement. An individual often does not prefer to hold an object before his consciousness unless he values it positively or finds it pleasurable. But this is not always so. An atheist may be deeply interested in religion, although he is against it and assigns negative value to it.

Motives, to an important extent, are constituted of attitudes. A highly favorable attitude toward a particular teacher may motivate a pupil to emulate that teacher. Attitudes have even been defined as predispositions to motivate arousal.[2] Motives are in this sense more specific and temporary. When goals are reached, motives are satisfied; but the attitude, or tendency to have the motive, persists from one occasion to the next.

[2] T. M. Newcomb, *Social Psychology,* New York: Holt, Rinehart and Winston, 1950.

Values are the things of life considered important or worth while. These values may be positive (freedom, education, the family, law observance, justice) or negative (cruelty, crime, injustice, intolerance, ignorance, poverty). The saint and the racketeer differ chiefly in their value systems. Values are thus essentially attitude objects; they usually refer to the objects of pervasive systems of attitudes.

Appreciation as used here refers to aesthetic appreciation and connotes an emotional reaction and perception of the aesthetic meaning or goodness of some object or event. It involves also the acceptance-rejection notion, and hence is largely an attitude. *Taste* in a sense is practically synonymous with appreciation.

Morale refers to the *esprit de corps*, the emotional integration of a group. It is the integrating pattern of attitudes with reference to attitude objects judged to be of vital concern to the group. These attitude objects may be threats or goals whose achievement is endangered by the absence of morale. There is the morale of an army or of the civilian population in wartime, the morale of the classroom or of an industrial organization or of a teaching staff.

Ideals are the conscious aspects of the social ritual in which we all participate. Conscious striving toward "ways of doing things" most acceptably is the essence of ideals. They are the individual's conscious adjustment to the demands of society, the public, as he conceives and understands them. The public, however, may be a "phantom" public and have no counterpart in reality; this is seen, for example, in the attempted control of a small child's behavior by means of Santa Claus or the "bogy man."

Character has ethical connotations; the person of character is the moral person defined in terms of attitudes. He behaves in accordance with socially approved individual ideals.

This sketchy exploration of the meanings of related terms may suffice to show the central nature of the concept of attitudes. Further elaboration of the concept is contained in the classic works of John Dewey[3] and Gordon Allport.[4]

[3] John Dewey, *Human Nature and Conduct*, New York: Holt, Rinehart and Winston, 1922.
[4] G. W. Allport, Attitudes, in Carl Murchison (ed.), *Handbook of Social Psychology*, Worcester: Clark Univ. Press, 1935.

DIMENSIONS OF ATTITUDES

It is helpful to think of attitudes as having various dimensions. Having these dimensions in mind can lead teachers to more adequate ways of thinking about the attitudes of their pupils.

Favorableness

Favorableness is the dimension most often considered and measured. It is the degree to which a person is for or against a given attitude object. When people speak of someone's attitude toward the United Nations, federal aid to education, or the core curriculum, they usually have in mind that person's favorableness toward these things. Those who believe that capital punishment should be continued are favorable toward this practice; those who believe it should be abolished are less favorable.

Intensity

Intensity is the strength of the feeling. Two people can have equally intense attitudes but be at opposite extremes as far as favorableness is concerned. The more favorable or unfavorable the attitude, the more intense it is; people who are neutral have the least intense attitude. An example of this is seen in attitudes toward so-called "progressive" education. People who are ardently in favor of or opposed to progressive education will be found on any large university campus, along with a neutral group whose attitudes show little intensity on the matter, and still another group that is actively unfavorable.

Salience

Salience is the readiness with which an attitude can be aroused—its "closeness to the surface" in a person's mind. Some people, when asked what they consider the most important problem facing humanity today, immediately think of preventing war; others, the "curse of drink"; still others, juvenile delinquency. Salience is best discovered by asking questions that allow the respondent's attitudes to appear freely. Among first-graders, attitudes toward age groups are highly salient. When they meet a new child they are immediately impressed with whether or not he is older than they are. Among adults, attitudes toward occupations are more salient. When they meet a stranger, they are more interested in what kind of work he does. Their attitudes toward occupations are more likely to determine their respect for or interest in him.

Generality

The number and variety of attitude objects toward which a person has a single, internally consistent, overall attitude are a reflection of the generality of his attitude. Some people can be labeled "liberals" or "conservatives" because they have consistent attitudes toward a wide range of objects, such as racial and nationality groups, government planning, socialized medicine, world government, federal aid to education, civil liberties, and the like. Knowing whether a person is "liberal" or "conservative" makes possible fairly accurate predictions of his attitudes toward a wide variety of topics. This fact means that, by and large, many attitudes tend to be highly generalized, with a wide range and substantial internal consistency.

Public vs. Private Attitudes

This is not a sharp twofold distinction, but a continuum. Public attitudes are those that people talk about freely in almost any social situation; a simple example is attitude toward different kinds of weather. A less public attitude is probably that toward the major political parties. Kinsey required his elaborate interviewing techniques because attitudes toward sex behavior are private in American society. The more a person thinks his attitudes are likely to be disapproved or punished, the more private he is likely to keep them. This is one reason why attitude questionnaires are sometimes administered anonymously.

Common vs. Individual Attitudes

When many people have attitudes toward a given attitude object, we speak of common attitudes. Individuals may, however, have attitudes toward things that no one else is aware of or cares about. A man's attitude toward one of his neckties, and a teacher's attitude toward a given pupil's reading habits are individual attitudes; the man's attitude toward the Republican party or the teacher's attitude toward his principal are common attitudes.

MEASURING ATTITUDES AND INTERESTS

We first point out a distinction between two functions of attitude measurement in schools. (1) The attitudes of pupils may be evaluated as educational outcomes, as indications of the degree to which pupils have acquired certain attitudes set up as objectives of instruction. Attitudes have been set up as objectives of instruction in all areas of the curriculum—social studies, mathematics, natural science, art, language studies, and the like. (2) Attitude may be evaluated as part of the attempt to predict the interest and hence adjustment of pupils in various curricula and occupations.

This distinction between the two functions of attitude measurement arises from the difference in the degree to which attitudes are set up as instructional objectives. Attitudes toward curricula and vocations are not established as goals. It may be considered desirable, for example, for all pupils to acquire certain attitudes toward democratic principles; but for all pupils to acquire certain attitudes toward and interest in a medical or mechanical career is not set up as a goal.

Techniques for measuring and evaluating attitudes vary widely. Although attitudes may be inferred from nonverbal, overt behavior (effort expended for a cause, relative amounts of money spent for goods and services, and the like), most of the systematic work has dealt with verbal indexes of attitudes.

Single-Question Technique

The simplest method of measuring attitudes is the ballot or single-response counting, as exemplified in various public opinion polls. These polling devices are in effect two-point "scales." For example, in measuring attitude toward capital punishment, the item in question might be "Capital punishment is necessary." The percentage of "agree" votes would be taken as an index of the attitude of a group of persons.

Reliability and Validity. What do answers obtained with questions like this mean? Several types of meanings, or validity, can be distinguished.

1. If the only interest is in knowing the present attitude of a group of students toward capital punishment, it can be argued that their anonymously recorded opinions are reliable and valid, since by definition the sole interest concerns these opinions, with no implications for further student behavior.

2. "Real-life voting" criteria are often available as bases for validating responses to single questions of this kind. Illustrations of such validation are the predictions of election opinion polls.

3. Another type of criterion is the agreement of the answers with known social commitments. Clearly, membership in the Temperance League or the Prohibition party would validate answers to questions on the desirability of the sale and use of alcoholic beverages.

4. Expert opinions frequently serve as criteria of validity. Questions designed to get at citizenship attitudes were used in surveys of a sample of college graduates by *Time,*[5] and of high-school and college students by Drucker and Remmers.[6] The questions were validated by submitting them to political scientists, psychologists, sociologists, and educators. The questions that produced substantial agreement as to the best answer of three alternatives—"agree," "disagree," or "doubtful"—were used in the surveys.

5. Nonverbal, usually future, behavior is still another kind of criterion. Soldiers' responses to opinion questions made it possible to predict what proportion of veterans of World War II would take advantage of the educational provisions of the G.I. Bill of Rights (8.0 percent predicted, 8.1 percent did). Consumer and market research also uses this type of criterion. Manufacturers validate surveys of consumer acceptance of their product against actual sales.

One major problem of opinion research is how to word a question

[5] E. Havemann and Patricia S. West, *They Went to College,* New York: Harcourt, Brace & World, 1952.

[6] A. J. Drucker and H. H. Remmers, Citizenship attitudes of graduated seniors at Purdue University, U.S. college graduates, and high school pupils, *J. Educ. Psychol.,* 1951, 42:231–235.

so that it means the same thing to everyone concerned. The errors arising from wording cannot be eliminated completely. Since meanings are built up in the individual through experience, and since no two individuals have identical experience, it follows that in strictest logic no word can have exactly the same meaning for any two individuals.

Payne has written a useful volume devoted solely to the ways of phrasing questions so as to achieve maximum validity.[7]

For the single question, it is obvious that only the test-retest method of estimating reliability is feasible. In this method the time interval must be long enough to minimize the memory factor. This interval is indeterminate—how can one tell when the first answer has been forgotten? Moreover, it is possible that real changes in attitude will have taken place. Stating questions in alternate form is a possibility, but making questions equivalent is difficult.

Attitude Scales

Attitudes have been measured by several types of scales. We shall discuss here the types developed by Thurstone, Remmers, and Likert. Two volumes by Remmers[8] and Edwards[9] discuss these methods further.

Thurstone-Type Scales. Thurstone's technique requires asking thirty or more judges to sort into eleven categories a large number of statements expressing opinions concerning an attitude object. At one extreme is the most favorable attitude, at the other the least favorable; the neutral position is at the center. The judges are to perceive these categories as separated by equal steps on a continuum of favorability. Hence the method is called the *equal-appearing-intervals* technique. The median scale value assigned by the judges to each of the statements in the collection is then determined. Only the unambiguous and relevant statements as determined by analysis

[7] Stanley L. Payne, *The Art of Asking Questions*, Princeton: Princeton Univ. Press, 1951.

[8] H. H. Remmers, *Introduction to Opinion and Attitude Measurement*, New York: Harper & Row, 1954.

[9] A. L. Edwards, *Techniques of Attitude Scale Construction*, New York: Appleton-Century-Crofts, 1957.

of the sortings are retained. From these are chosen the statements that represent approximately equal steps along the entire continuum of favorability. The scale is administered by asking subjects to place a check mark after all the statements they endorse as expressing their own sentiment, opinion, or attitude. The subject's score on the scale is the mean or the median scale value of the opinions he has endorsed.

Because this method of constructing a scale to measure attitude toward any psychological object requires a great deal of labor, it is obviously impossible to build scales measuring all possible significant attitude objects. Hence other types of scales have been developed.

Remmers' Master-Type Scales. Remmers developed generalized or master attitude scales to measure attitudes toward any one of a *class* of attitude objects such as school subjects or vocations. The statements in the general attitude scale are not related specifically to any single attitude object; but if the name of the appropriate object is written in at the head of the scale, the statements can be interpreted meaningfully for any representative of the class of objects for which the scale is intended. The scale values of Remmers' scales are determined by Thurstone's equal-appearing-intervals technique.

The Remmers' master scales are illustrated by the excerpt of the Kelley-Remmers' Scale for Measuring Attitude Toward Any Institution, shown in Fig. 38. Whereas in the Thurstone scales the statements are arranged in random order, in the Remmers' scales they appear in order of decreasing favorableness. This arrangement greatly decreases the time and labor required for scoring without affecting the accuracy of the measurement.

Likert-Type Scales. Compared to either the Thurstone or the Remmers' scales, the Likert-type scales are fairly easy to construct. First are listed statements that reflect favorable and unfavorable attitudes about an attitude object. Then the subjects are asked to respond to them on a five-point scale: "strongly agree," "agree," "undecided," "disagree," and "strongly disagree." The scales are usually scored by assigning values from 1 to 5 to these alternatives, the 5 being at the favorable end of the response continuum. A subject's score is the total of the values indicated. Likert-type scales

A SCALE FOR MEASURING ATTITUDE TOWARD ANY INSTITUTION

Ida B. Kelley   Edited by H. H. Remmers

Form A

Please fill in the blanks below.   (You may leave the space for your name blank if you wish.)

Name_____

Male   Female (encircle one)   Date_____

Age_____.   Class if in School_____

Directions:

Following is a list of statements about institutions. Place a plus sign (+) before each statement with which you agree with reference to the institution or institutions listed at the left of the statements.   The person in charge will tell you the institution or institutions to write in at the head of the columns to the left of the statements.   Your score will in no way affect your grade in any course.

Institution					
					1. Is perfect in every way.
					2. Is the most admirable of institutions.
					3. Is necessary to the very existence of civilization.
					4. Is the most beloved of institutions.
					5. Represents the best thought in modern life.
					6. Grew up in answer to a felt need and is serving that need perfectly.
					7. Exerts a strong influence for good government and right living.
					8. Has more pleasant things connected with it than any other institution.
					9. Is a strong influence for right living.
					10. Gives real help in meeting moral problems.
					11. Gives real help in meeting social problems.
					12. Is valuable in creating ideals.
					13. Is necessary to the very existence of society.
					14. Encourages social improvement.
					15. Serves society as a whole well.
					16. Aids the individual in wise use of leisure time.

Fig. 38. Excerpt from Remmers-Type Attitude Scale.

can be constructed in a relatively short time, require no judges, and can be scored rapidly. The results obtained with this type of scale, as far as reliability and validity are concerned, are quite comparable to those obtained by Thurstone and Remmers.

MEASURING ATTITUDES AS EDUCATIONAL–VOCATIONAL INTERESTS

School offerings should be adapted to the abilities, needs, and interests of pupils. Attention should accordingly be given to the interests of pupils, procedures for identifying those interests, and ways and means of capitalizing upon them for instructional and vocational guidance. Because interests motivate learning, they are one of the major aspects of the learning situation. When pupils are interested they work harder, longer, and more effectively. Counselors have found that an informal discussion of pupil interests or the use of an interest inventory frequently starts pupils thinking about future plans and contributes to the rapport needed in the counseling situation. But effective concern with interests depends upon the approach used in identifying them.

Approaches to the Identification and Evaluation of Interests

Interests may be classified into four groups depending upon how information about them is obtained. Super[10] has identified these groups as (1) expressed interests, (2) manifested interests, (3) interests inferred from tests, and (4) inventoried interests. The first three can be identified by informal techniques such as student writings, check lists, and questionnaires; the fourth is usually identified by means of standardized inventories.

Expressed interests can be identified by asking a pupil to tell or write about the activities, vocational and avocational, which he most and least enjoys. These accounts are often quite unreliable, depending upon his background of experiences, his passing fancies, or his desire to be interested in some activity merely because it is the socially acceptable thing to do. He may not know how to tell the truth

[10] D. E. Super and John O. Crites, *Appraising Vocational Fitness*, New York: Harper & Row, 2nd ed., 1962.

about his feelings. He may be unwilling to be frank about liking a certain occupation because he considers its socioeconomic status too low. The boy who glories in working with automobile engines as a "grease monkey" or a "hot-rodder," but whose parents have taught him to disrespect working with his hands, may not report his interests frankly. Again a pupil may report interest on the basis of information which is inadequate in range and content. Thus a boy may claim to be interested in engineering because he considers it to be outdoor masculine work, but he has no appreciation of its mathematical basis. The boy who reports an aversion to selling because of a childhood failure in selling magazines may be generalizing unjustifiably for all selling occupations. Despite these sources of error, teachers have found expressed interests useful in helping pupils find topics for English compositions, in selecting appropriate instructional materials, and in stimulating group discussion.

Manifested interests may be identified by directly observing the pupil or by finding out about his hobbies and other activities. A person who builds bird houses, collects stamps or coins, assembles model airplanes or cars, is manifesting an interest in such activities. However, this type of interest may be transitory, moving from one thing to another as relationships among pupils change.

Interests are often *inferred from achievement tests.* High scores on tests in various subject-matter fields are often assumed to accompany strong interest in those areas. However, ability in school subjects is by no means an adequate indicator of interest either in them or in the occupations related to them. Many researchers have found low correlations between measured interests and abilities or achievements as measured by tests or school grades. On the other hand, if the teacher rank orders a pupil's scores on an interest inventory and compares it with his ranking on comparable achievement tests, he may indeed find that the pupil's stronger interests tend to coincide with his stronger areas of achievement.

Inventoried interests are interests that are measured with standardized instruments which require a pupil to choose from a large number of activities those that he likes and dislikes. Some interest inventories make use of the fact that (1) persons successful in the same occupation or field of work have similar patterns of interests, and (2) the interest patterns of persons successful in one field of work differ from those of people in another field of work. At the present time the major emphasis in interest measurement is directed toward vocational guidance. Relatively few inventories have been devised for classroom or educational guidance at either the elementary- or secondary-school level.

Interest Inventories

We now turn to illustrations of standardized interest evaluation devices. Of the six interest inventories described below, the first is designed primarily for the elementary-school level, four are for secondary-school students and adults, and the last is for college students. Buros' *Mental Measurements Yearbooks* contain descriptions of other inventories.

What I Like To Do—An Inventory of Children's Interests.[11] The principal purposes of this inventory are to provide (1) a workable means of identifying pupil interests so they may be used effectively in guidance and instruction, and (2) a research instrument for a psychological study of children's interests. The inventory is designed for use in Grades 4 through 7 and measures interests in the following eight areas:

Art: preference for arts and crafts activities and appreciation of the fine arts

Music: appreciation for all kinds of music and liking for musical activities

Social Studies: social awareness and curiosity, ranging from the pupil's own group to the world—past and present

Active Play: preference for independent physical activities and for competitive and non-competitive group sports

Quiet Play: preference for independent and group "things to do" of a less active nature

Manual Arts: preference for creative and mechanical activities—both boys and girls

Home Arts: liking for "around the house" activities—both boys and girls

Science: curiosity about and interest in the natural world

[11] Louis P. Thorpe, Charles E. Meyers, and Marcella R. Sea, *What I Like To Do: An Inventory of Children's Interests*, Chicago: Science Research Associates, Inc., 1954.

The inventory asks pupils to answer 294 questions of the following types by marking an X in answer spaces under No, ?, or Yes.

Would you like to	No	?	Yes
Paint pictures of people	____	____	____
Learn to play the piano	____	____	____
Visit the White House	____	____	____
Swim under water	____	____	____
Collect snapshots	____	____	____
Make jewelry out of shells	____	____	____
Learn why we need sleep	____	____	____

For Grades 5, 6, and 7 the inventory can be easily administered in a 50-minute class period. For Grade 4 two periods of about 30 minutes each are recommended. A published leaflet contains tables of percentile norms for boys and girls at each grade level. These norms are based on a carefully selected national sample of pupils in Grades 4 through 6.

Vocational Interest Inventory.[12] This inventory is designed to identify vocational interests in Grades 9 through 12 in nine areas: commercial, mechanical, aesthetic, manual, agricultural, academic (professional), scientific (professional), general service, and domestic. A pupil indicates his liking or distaste for 35 activities in each of the nine areas by placing a plus sign (+) or zero (0), respectively, before each statement, such as those below:

( ) Assorting and filing recipes, cards, clippings, and papers.
( ) Reparing bicycles, lawnmowers, clocks, and doorbells.
( ) Designing flower vase, book ends, plaques.
( ) Working with heavy tools or machinery.
( ) Following directions for doing or making something.
( ) Being chairman of homeroom, class, or program.
( ) Studying diseases of plants in the laboratory.
( ) Being responsible for school equipment or supplies.
( ) Preparing meals for guests or sick people.

The norms on this inventory are based on pupils in fifty Missouri high schools, and are published in *Personnel Work in High Schools,* the book by the authors of the inventory. The book contains the

[12] C. E. and E. G. Germane, *Personnel Work in High Schools,* New York: Silver Burdett, 1941.

following statement by the publisher: "We have granted the pur-chasers of this book the right to reproduce and utilize these tests in his or her own school system without charge. We do not provide and offer for sale printed copies of these tests." No time limits are suggested for administering the inventory.

Occupational Interest Inventory.[13]   This inventory has two forms, Intermediate for Grades 7 through 12, and Advanced for Grades 9 to adulthood. The inventory yields three groups of scores arranged as follows:

Fields of interests: personal-social, natural, mechanical, business, the arts, and the sciences
Types of interests: verbal, manipulative, and computational
Level of interests: in routine tasks, with tasks requiring considerable skill, with tasks requiring expert knowledge, skill, and judgment

The publishers suggest a time allotment of approximately 30 to 40 minutes. The first part asks the pupil to indicate his preferences for 240 paired activities such as the following:

Take care of children and assist in their education.
Buy and sell used cars, radios, or other articles for profit.

Grade, sort, or pack fruit or vegetables.
Guard property or help children cross streets.

In the second part, designed to evaluate levels of interests, the pupil chooses the one activity he prefers most out of three in each of 30 groups, as in the following:

Develop new ideas for drawings, paintings, or color designs.
Draw cartoons, comics, or caricatures of people.
Copy posters, signs, or campaign slogans.

The pupil may make his answers to the pairs and triads of items directly in the inventory booklet, on separate machine-scorable answer sheets, or on Scoreze answer sheets. The back of the answer sheets contains profile blanks for (1) fields of interests, (2) types of interests, and (3) level of interests. Major fields are identified by scores above the 70th percentile, rejected fields by scores below the

[13] Edwin A. Lee and Louis P. Thorpe, *Occupational Interest Inventory*, Monterey, Calif.: California Test Bureau, 1956.

30th percentile. Norms are provided for the composite population in both standard score and percentile ranks for each subarea of the inventory.

Kuder Preference Records.[14] This inventory is one of the most widely used. It appears in two forms, vocational and personal, which differ in emphasis and purpose. The vocational form (C) is most useful for junior and senior high-school pupils because it is not directed solely at the professional level. Occupational interests are classified in ten areas as follows:

Outdoor: working with animals and growing things
Mechanical: working with machines and tools
Computational: working with numbers
Scientific: discovering new facts and solving problems
Persuasive: meeting and dealing with people; promoting projects or selling
Artistic: doing creative work with one's hands—usually work that has "eye" appeal, involving design, color, and materials
Literary: reading and writing
Musical: reading about music and musicians, going to concerts, playing instruments, and singing
Social Service: helping other people
Clerical: office work requiring precision and accuracy

The personal form (A) measures types of preferences independent of and supplementary to those covered by the vocational form. It measures preferences for five different types of personal and social activities:

Preference for being active in groups
Preference for familiar and stable situations
Preference for dealing with ideas
Preference for avoiding conflicts
Preference for directing others

The inventory uses a forced-choice technique in which a pupil checks the most and least liked of three possibilities presented in triads as those found on the following page.

[14] Frederic Kuder, *Kuder Preference Records*, Chicago: Science Research Associates, Inc., 1948.

Read a story to a sick person.
Teach tricks to a dog.
Take apart a toy that won't work to see how to repair it.

Compile a dictionary of slang.
Discover a cure for hay fever.
Install improved office procedures in a big business.

Talk to a person who acts as if he feels very superior to you.
Talk to a person who slaps you on the back in a familiar manner.
Talk to a person who tries to flatter you.

The administration of either form requires approximately 40 to 50 minutes. Instructions to pupils are so simple that the inventory can be self-administered and the profiles filled in by the pupil. (An example of the profile is shown in Fig. 30.) In the profiles provided for either form for various occupational groups, the high and low scores indicate to a striking degree that different occupational groups are differentiated by the Kuder Preference Records. The Inventory Manual has suggestions for interpreting the scores for vocational guidance.

Vocational Interest Blanks.[15] These consist of approximately 400 items dealing with the following:

Likes and dislikes for occupations
Likes and dislikes for school subjects
Likes and dislikes for amusements
Likes and dislikes for activities
Likes and dislikes for peculiarities of people
Order of preference of activities
Order of importance of factors affecting one's work
Order of preference of men one would most and least like to have been
Positions one would most and least prefer to hold in a club or society
Comparison of interests between two items
Self-rating of present abilities and characteristics

Likes and dislikes are indicated by circling L, I, or D—like, indifference, and dislike, respectively—as shown in the illustrative items found on page 324.

[15] E. K. Strong, Jr., *Vocational Interest Blank* (a form for men and one for women), Stanford, Calif.: Stanford University Press.

1. Actor (not movie)	L	I	D
7. Athletic director	L	I	D
111. Economics	L	I	D
123. Military drill	L	I	D
141. Driving an automobile	L	I	D
261. People with gold teeth	L	I	D
377. Get "rattled" easily	Yes	?	No (rating abilities)
385. Win confidence and loyalty .	Yes	?	No

The blank is scored by means of 50 separate scoring keys which provide scores indicative of (1) masculinity-femininity, (2) maturity of interests, (3) occupational level, (4–44) interest in 41 specific occupations and (45–50) in six occupational groups. The scoring must be done separately for each score desired. Obviously, scoring would be a laborious procedure except that the blanks may be machine scored by Engineers Northwest[16] for a nominal fee. Although the reliability of the scores of high-school students has, in general, been somewhat lower than that for college students, the blanks are considered useful for high-school juniors and seniors.

Study of Values.[17]   The Study of Values is designed primarily to yield measures of the attitudes of college students or college-educated adults. The instrument contains 30 two-alternative items and 15 four-alternative items. The two-alternative items are illustrated by the following:

The main object of scientific research should be the discovery   (a)   (b) of pure truth rather than its practical applications.
  (a) Yes; (b) No .... □   □

If the pupil agrees with alternative (a) and disagrees with (b), he writes 3 under (a) and 0 under (b). If he has a slight preference for (a) over (b), he writes 2 under (a) and 1 under (b). He similarly indicates agreement with (b) or slight preference for (b). Illustrative of the four-alternative items is the following:

Do you think that a good government should aim chiefly at—
  ———— a. more aid for the poor, sick, and old?

[16] 100 Metropolitan Life Building, Minneapolis, Minnesota.
[17] G. W. Allport, P. E. Vernon, and G. Lindzey, A Study of Values, Boston: Houghton Mifflin, rev. ed., 1951.

_____ b. the development of manufacturing and trade?

_____ c. introducing more ethical principles into its policies and diplomacy?

_____ d. establishing a position of prestige and respect among nations?

The student ranks these alternatives 1, 2, 3, or 4 to indicate his relative preference for them. The scores on the Study of Values have been shown to be related to various educational and occupational groupings. The six scores yielded by the inventory may thus prove valuable for acquiring self-understanding and providing a basis for educational and vocational guidance.

General Significance of Interest Inventories

Interest inventories have been criticized as being subject to "faking," in that a student can make his score come out much as he wants it. Considerable experimental evidence has supported this criticism. This does not mean, however, that such inventories are not valid for guidance. An interest inventory is essentially a means whereby the student can communicate with himself and his counselor. It is better than unorganized introspection and conversation because it is systematically organized and makes possible comparisons with other people of known occupational status. The student is free to tell himself anything he wants to. But if he is motivated to learn his own interests accurately, he can do so more efficiently and thoroughly with an interest inventory than without one. Teachers should make clear to students that the purpose of the inventory is to help *them* know more about *themselves*, that the instrument is not a "test," and that there are no right or wrong responses. With such instructions, students genuinely enjoy taking the inventory, are eager to learn the results, and usually gain some self-understanding from it.

Good follow-up procedures, after a student has identified the areas in which he has strong interests, include the use of many types of bulletins and materials describing in detail the types of occupations related to these areas, the kinds of abilities needed in them, the type and amount of training necessary, job opportunities, and other essential information for finding, getting, and holding a job. Many publishers provide occupational information materials, such as the Career Information Kit.[18] This particular set of materials lists over 500 vocational publications plus 35 educational and vocational guidance publications with factual occupational information describing jobs held by over 90 percent of today's work force.

LABORATORY EXERCISES AND DISCUSSION QUESTIONS

1. Does the fact that adolescent interests are relatively not stabilized make the use of interest inventories inadvisable? What are some ways in which these inventories can be used to advantage with junior and senior high-school pupils?
2. List some of the attitudes that should be educational outcomes for all pupils, and other attitudes in which pupils may differ among themselves without conflicting with the aims of the educative process.
3. Sketch the differences in attitudes and interests which might lead one boy to become a scientist and another to become a professional bridge player.
4. Attitudes toward vocations or vocational interests have been shown to be markedly affected by information concerning vocations acquired when pupils make workbooks dealing with them. Plan an experiment to show this effect and discuss its implications for vocational guidance.
5. Examine the *Mental Measurements Yearbooks* reviews of three interest evaluation devices. Abstract statements from the reviews and descriptions of the devices. Then examine specimen sets of the tests and complete the test evaluation form in Chapter 5.
6. What are some of the issues and problems in high school for which scales or inventories of attitudes should be devised?

SUGGESTED REFERENCES

Anastasi, Anne, *Psychological Testing*, New York: Macmillan, 2nd ed., 1961.
  Chapter 19 discusses various measures of interests and attitudes and the place of interests in personality theory.
Edwards, A. L., *Techniques of Attitude Scale Construction*, New York: Appleton-Century-Crofts, 1957.

[18] SRA *Career Information Kit*, Chicago: Science Research Associates, Inc.

Intended to assist those who wish to develop their own attitude scales; presents most of the better-established methods and also the author's scale-discrimination technique which combines several of the others in a workable scheme.

Freeman, Frank S., *Theory and Practice of Psychological Testing,* New York: Holt, Rinehart and Winston, 3rd ed., 1962.

Chapter 24 contains an excellent discussion of interest inventories, attitudes, values, and opinion polling.

Krathwohl, David R., *et al., Taxonomy of Educational Objectives, Handbook II: Affective Domain,* New York: McKay, 1964.

A breakthrough in the classification of affective educational objectives.

Remmers, H. H. *Introduction to Opinion and Attitude Measurement,* New York: Harper & Row, 1954.

A comprehensive discussion of the techniques used in measuring opinions and attitudes and applications of these techniques. Deals with sampling and indirect methods and also with applications in business, industry, community interrelations, and education.

Thomas, R. M., *Judging Student Progress,* New York: Longmans, Green, 1954.

A relatively nontechnical account of rating scales and check lists is given in Chapter 11. The discussion centers particularly around school use of the instruments.

Thorndike, R. L., and Elizabeth Hagen, *Measurement and Evaluation in Psychology and Education,* New York: Wiley, 2nd ed., 1961.

Assessing emotional
and social adjustment

Communicating Impressions of Personality to Others:
  Rating Methods
  Types of Rating Scales
  Suggestions for Constructing Graphic Rating Scales
    Alternation of Scale Directionality. Explicit Trait Questions. Continuous
    Lines. Diction of Phrases. Phrasing Extreme Levels. Phrasing Inter-
    mediate Levels
  Errors in Rating Methods
  Available Rating Devices

Projective Techniques

The importance of feeling well, of not being continually stirred up, and of getting along well with people is second only to the importance of living. But the number of possible points of view, of ways of analyzing emotional and social adjustment, seems to be exasperatingly large. In considering these aspects of pupils, we shall try to meet the teacher's practical needs for evaluation data for guidance purposes.

THE NATURE OF ADJUSTMENT

Adjustment may be defined as the process whereby a living organism varies its activities or changes its environment to satisfy its needs. An organism's needs can be fulfilled only by behavior effectively adapted to its opportunities. When external circumstances change, the organism must modify its behavior and adopt new ways of satisfying its wants. The three fundamental ways in which the adjustment process can take place are new forms of response, a change in the environment, and the modification of the needs themselves. Conceived thus generally, adjustment may be identified with living itself.

The common usage of the term "adjustment," however, refers to more fundamental, continuous, and pervasive levels of activity, not to narrow functions like the eye's reaction to light, the finger's reaction to pain, and the "mind's" reaction to such a problem as $2 + 2 = ?$. Adjustment here means the satisfaction of drives, needs, or motives involving the whole organism.

Important Motives

Many lists of needs or motives have been made—self-preservation, race preservation, inquisitiveness, combativeness, fear, gregariousness, sociability, maternal love, sex, constructiveness, sympathy, rivalry, secretiveness, feeding, curiosity, self-assertion, questioning, imitation, jealousy, repulsion, submissiveness, shyness, modesty, playing, walking, friendliness, cooperation, and so on. It is impossible scientifically to choose among these various lists.

No matter how vague and inadequate the words or symbols may be, however, it *is* possible to list the fundamental needs of human beings in American society briefly but meaningfully. For our present purpose, we shall not be concerned with the so-called "unlearned" organic drives such as air getting, temperature regulation, hunger, thirst, rest and sleep, and elimination. We are concerned with the form drives take when they have been molded by interaction with the social world in which they must be satisfied. Here is a list of important needs or desires or motives of pupils useful to classroom teachers.

1. *The desire for social approval.* Favorable attention, sympathy, companionship, conformity to the mores, customs, and fashions of one social group are all basic needs of pupils. Social approval is one of the most powerful forces directing personality and behavior.

2. *The desire for mastery.* The urges to excel, to succeed, to overcome obstructions, to defeat a rival, to achieve a goal, to solve a problem, to dominate a situation are all manifestations of this type of motive. Success and mastery along some line of endeavor are essential to the emotional well-being of everyone.

3. *The desire for new experience.* Exploratory patterns, curiosity, inventiveness, concern with the fresh, the strange, and the unfamiliar, all of these seem to be basic needs of human beings.

4. *The desire for security.* The feeling of being wanted, of being assured that one's presence and contribution are welcome, the need for stable affection from family and personal relationships, all constitute another important category of human motivation. The origin of this desire, in the physiological needs and the love responses of

the infant, is strongly related to but not identical with the origin of the desire for social approval.

5. *The desire for individuality.* The need to assume adult responsibility, to take up obligations and become independent of the family's material and emotional support, to attain adult individuality or self-integration, is a motive derived largely from the needs of society. The continuously recurring truth that today's children must soon run the world has caused this desire for independence and responsibility to become an integral part of human make-up.

These five kinds of motivation interact and are interdependent. In all but the most elementary situations, combinations of motives determine an individual's behavior. Frequently all the strong motives of an individual determine a single action. Our categories, neither definitive nor complete, are merely a convenient descriptive device.

The Adjustment Process

How is this discussion of motivation related to the teacher's understanding of what aspects of emotional and social adjustment of pupils should be evaluated? The answer comes from an analysis of the process of adjustment which will show how motivation and adjustment are related.

The adjustment process can be analyzed into four principal steps:

1. *The operation of a motive.*

2. *The presence of some obstacle to the immediate satisfaction of the motive.* Such obstacles or thwarting factors may be divided into three general classes: *environmental obstacles,* such as walls around a prison, or an oversolicitous mother, or the customs of society, or the activities of other persons; *personal defects*—lameness, mental defects, social defects such as lack of position or education, emotional instability; *conflict between antagonistic motives,* which, unlike physical forces, do not cancel each other but rather result in increased tension, vacillation, and nonspecific activity.

3. *Responses, often trial-and-error reactions, guided in varying degree by past experience.* At this stage emotional and social maladjustments usually arise. If the responses are not immediately successful in bringing about the satisfaction of the desire, an emotional

response may arise leading to a persistent nonadjustive reaction, that is, excessive persistence in an unadaptive mode of activity. Failure to adjust continues, with thwarting and lack of satisfaction of the desire; this in turn produces another attempt to overcome the obstacles, another thwarting, and another heightening of the emotional response—a vicious circle.

4. *Solution, satisfaction, adjustment of the problem, desire, or motive.* This is the goal of the adjustment process, the point at which it should result in personal happiness and social utility.

This conception, shown schematically in Fig. 39[1] should lead to the "mental hygiene" point of view which substitutes understanding for censure and opens the way to objective evaluation and guidance.

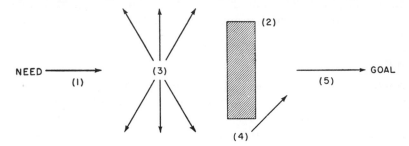

The organism (1) upon encountering an obstacle or difficulty (2) shows excess and varied activity (3) until one of the variant ways of reacting (4) resolves the difficulty and results in attainment of the goal.

Fig. 39. *Schematic Representation of a Problem Situation and the Process of Adjustment.*

Maladjustment and undesirable behavior are "caused" by the interaction of the person with his environment. Moralistic hostile reactions to people who exhibit maladjustment are incompatible with such an analysis.

SYMPTOMS OF MALADJUSTMENT

How do children behave when they are in the third stage of the the adjustment process mentioned above—when they are being

[1] J. F. Dashiell, *Fundamentals of General Psychology*, Boston: Houghton Mifflin, 1936.

satisfied or thwarted? What signs of poor mental health are most frequently displayed by children in school?

Teachers may regard as most serious children's behavior problems which attack the teacher's moral sensitivities, personal integrity, authority, or immediate teaching purposes. In contrast, the quiet, compliant, submissive, obedient child whose behavior is agreeable to teachers and who respects their authority is not considered a maladjusted child. But the amount of trouble a child gives a teacher is not a valid measure of his mental health. Clinical psychologists believe that the withdrawing modes of behavior are more serious and dangerous than the aggressive types. Withdrawn children are more likely to escape detection and develop serious mental disorder.

What is the teacher to evaluate in this area? What are the symptoms that a teacher should note in evaluating a pupil's emotional and social adjustment? Myers has provided a useful classification of the specific types of mentally unhealthy pupils most frequently encountered in school:[2]

1. The "unsociable" child
2. The "model" child
3. The "defensive" child
4. The "nervous" child
5. The "emotional" child

The "unsociable" child is always wandering off by himself, prefers to play alone, shows lack of interest in joining other children in their activities, is bookish, and usually likes nothing better than to stay in and do little chores for the teacher. Such a child is developing a habit of social withdrawal—not a good foundation for later mental health.

The "model" child displays characteristics commonly regarded as virtues but he carries them to such an extreme that they become symptomatic of poor mental health. Neatness, conscientiousness, courtesy, honesty, ambition, caution, and thrift become excessive and are undesirable when they constitute a means of evading difficulties. The child who manifests any of them in excess is often inadequate in more important things; he tries to get the approval he craves by being a paragon in some respect.

The "defensive" child rationalizes, that is, gives elaborate and logical-sounding reasons to explain an act he really performs for purely emotional reasons. Carried to excess, this useful method of self-justification and fact-dodging, and its allied mechanisms, alibis and bragging, become harmful and symptomatic of ill health.

The "nervous" child—timid, fearful, anxious, shy, awkward, and socially ill at ease—feels insecure and uncertain, and believes he is different. Tics, such as grimacing, twitching, jerking, nail biting, lip pulling, shrugging, nodding, blinking, twisting, picking, or scratching, are symptoms of the condition. He often uses the neurotic device of exaggerating minor pains and illnesses to secure sympathy and attention.

The "emotional" child has unstable uncontrolled habits of emotional expression. Inability or unwillingness to repress an emotion is incompatible with group living. But mere repression is not enough; for emotion, repressed or not, arouses widespread organic disturbances of the digestive activities, gastric secretions, circulation, blood chemistry, and so on, with important effects on physical and mental health. Not merely emotional control but not so much emotion itself is desirable. Among other things, this means that teachers should be extremely sparing in using fear as an incentive. Less emotionalizing will help lessen the fear of the child who has developed so many fears that he is almost always afraid, has no confidence in himself or others, and shows great anxiety about trying anything new or strange. He has digestive disturbances, night terrors, inability to go to sleep, restlessness, lack of appetite, food fussiness, and a general appearance of malnutrition. The children's behavior problems in Fig. 40 make more specific the aspects of emotional and social adjustment with which teachers should be concerned. This list from Wickman's study[3] lists the fifty behavior problems most frequently reported by teachers, ranked according to the seriousness thirty clinical psychologists attached to them.

[3] E. K. Wickman, *Children's Behavior and Teacher's Attitude*, New York: Commonwealth Fund, 1928.

Type of Problem	Average Score	Rated Seriousness of Problem Rating Scale		
		Of Only Slight Importance 4.5	Of Considerable Importance 12.5	Of Extremely Great Importance 20.5
Unsocialness	17.3			
Suspiciousness	16.4			
Unhappy, depressed	16.2			
Resentfulness	14.1			
Fearfulness	14.0			
Cruelty, bullying	13.5			
Easily discouraged	13.4			
Suggestible	13.3			
Overcritical of others	13.2			
Sensitiveness	13.1			
Domineering	13.0			
Sullenness	12.6			
Stealing	12.5			
Shyness	12.5			
Physical coward	12.0			
Selfishness	11.8			
Temper tantrums	11.7			
Dreaminess	11.3			
Nervousness	11.3			
Stubbornness	10.9			
Unreliableness	10.4			
Truancy	10.3			
Untruthfulness	10.3			
Cheating	10.3			
Heterosexual activity	9.9			
Lack of interest in work	9.6			
Enuresis (bed-wetting)	9.2			
Obscene notes, talk	8.8			
Tattling	8.8			
Attracting attention	8.5			
Quarrelsomeness	8.3			
Impudence, rudeness	7.6			
Imaginative lying	7.5			
Inattention	7.3			
Slovenly in appearance	7.2			
Laziness	7.2			
Impertinence, defiance	7.1			
Carelessness in work	7.1			
Thoughtlessness	6.8			
Restlessness	6.4			
Masturbation	6.4			
Disobedience	6.4			
Tardiness	5.6			
Inquisitiveness	5.3			
Destroying school materials	5.1			
Disorderliness in class	3.4			
Profanity	2.9			
Interrupting	2.8			
Smoking	2.3			
Whispering	0.8			

Fig. 40. Ratings by Mental Hygienists on the Relative Seriousness of Behavior Problems in Children. (Ratings of 30 Clinicians.)

ADJUSTMENT MECHANISMS

Adjustment mechanisms are ways of responding that help the individual either to protect himself from threats and discomforts or to improve his self concept. They are activated as overt behavior when the individual does something about tension. They may also, however, involve no observable activity, as when he builds "castles in Spain." Some of the adjustment mechanisms are rationalization, projection, repression, compensation, fantasy, regression, identification, and sublimation.

Rationalization is a mechanism which the individual uses to give plausible, socially acceptable reasons for his behavior rather than the "real" reasons that are often too painful to acknowledge. The failing college freshman, who asserted, when interviewed by one of the authors, that he could easily get all A's but proposed to get a "well-rounded" education, was rationalizing.

Projection consists of attributing to another person one's own unacknowledged thoughts or feelings, thus relieving oneself of guilt or anxiety. "That teacher certainly doesn't like me," spoken by a hostile pupil, is an example. Like rationalization, projection leads to self-deception.

In *repression* perceptions and ideas painful to consciousness are buried in the unconscious system although they are still dynamic. Anger and hatred toward parents and suffering at their hands may be repressed in the unconscious, i.e., excluded from normal recall. Thus the individual may have feelings of guilt or hostility, although the experiences which originally caused these feelings are not subject to voluntary recall.

In *compensation* an individual covers up or disguises an undesirable trait by exaggerating a different one. In a world dominated by adults, children use this mechanism frequently to relieve the disappointments, frustrations, and anxieties they develop. It may underlie youthful delinquency such as stealing, vandalism, fighting, and defiance of authority. Similarly, the unathletic boy may compensate by becoming an honor student.

Fantasy or daydreaming represents desires in the person's imagination as already fulfilled. The youngster who "can't keep his mind on his studies" but instead stares vacantly out of the window is fleeing from the uninteresting and—to him—meaningless study assignment to a pleasurable imaginative experience. In its extreme form this mechanism results in schizophrenia, in which the individual is completely cut off from reality and lives only in his imagination.

Regression is a return to a mode of behavior possibly appropriate at an earlier stage of development. To say that an individual is "acting childishly" is a popular way of describing this mechanism.

Identification is an unconscious mental process in which the individual behaves as if he were the other person. The six-year-old who wears a cowboy outfit and behaves in accordance with his notion of the hypothetical cowboy is identifying with the cowboy. Children almost always identify with the parent of the same sex and sometimes with their teacher. Such identification accounts for much of the learning of attitudes that takes place in life.

Sublimation is the unconscious redirection of one's energies into socially acceptable and useful modes of behavior. The little boy's sadistic pleasure in mistreating a small animal may be sublimated into his becoming a surgeon. The unmarried woman teacher becomes the mother substitute for the whole roomful of children.

This sketch describes some of the more important adjustment mechanisms. The concepts are not too precisely defined, and clear distinctions among mechanisms are not always possible. Nonetheless, the teacher will find such concepts useful in understanding pupil behavior.

GENERAL PROCEDURES FOR EVALUATING EMOTIONAL AND SOCIAL ADJUSTMENT

What can teachers do to evaluate the emotional and social adjustment of their pupils? The answer depends in part on whether the purpose is (1) to *screen*, out of a large number, the pupils whose maladjustments are serious enough to require special attention or (2) to *understand* the adjustment patterns of individual pupils. The techniques we shall consider do not fall sharply into these two categories. Yet some are definitely more appropriate for one than the other.

Suppose a school superintendent, principal, or group of teachers have decided to do something about the maladjusted children in their schools. They all know a few individual pupils who are "odd" or have "got into trouble" with school or community authorities. These individuals almost select themselves for special attention. But the suspicion is well warranted that there are other pupils, less conspicuous in the everyday course of school affairs, who are at least as much, if not more, in need of special attention as far as their adjustment is concerned.

Some kind of relatively large-scale survey or screening program is called for. Large-scale programs for identifying maladjusted pupils must be feasible administratively. This means that they must not require large amounts of time, money, and professional skill. The techniques that clinical psychologists and psychiatrists use in diagnosing an individual child or adult do not apply in this situation. Schools cannot have each pupil subjected to a time-consuming battery of diagnostic techniques that must be applied individually by skilled professionals and interpreted with much subtlety and insight.

Three sources of evidence usable in relatively large-scale surveys of pupil adjustment are (1) the pupil, (2) his peers, and (3) the teacher. Using the pupil as a source of evidence concerning his adjustment means that his own opinions and descriptions of himself apply. In *some* ways, no one knows better than the pupil what his problems are, how he feels about himself, and how he gets along with other people. We can in a sense "talk" with him and "hear" his answers—in the survey situation—by means of the kind of standardized, printed "interview" that is known as the questionnaire or inventory.

The second source of evidence, the student's peers, refers to the attitudes, evaluations, and reactions to the pupil of those with whom he studies, works, and plays in school. Some aspects of his adjustment depend by definition on how his fellow pupils feel about him. When we ask pupils about their preferences among their fellow pupils, we are using them as sources of evidence concerning pupil adjustment.

The teacher can serve as a source of evidence because he has a direct opportunity to observe the pupil in and out of the classroom. Here we refer to the informal, unarranged, everyday evidence that comes to teachers and results in their perceptions of how pupils behave—feel, think, perceive, and act—in a variety of situations. We will discuss each of these sources of evidence.

INVENTORIES: TECHNIQUES THAT USE THE PUPIL AS A SOURCE OF EVIDENCE

Inventories, surveys, schedules, or questionnaires are used to obtain evidence from the pupil himself concerning his adjustment. The term "test" is often avoided in referring to these devices because they do not call upon a pupil to perform at his best or maximum level. Rather, they depend upon his willingness and ability to describe what is *typical*, or generally true, of himself.

We shall describe the inventory technique by giving an account of the SRA Youth Inventory.[4] This inventory consists of 296 statements of problems in eight areas. The pupil is instructed as follows:

Read each statement in the questionnaire carefully. If it expresses something that has been a problem to you, mark one of the boxes corresponding to that statement. If the statement does not express one of your difficulties, or does not apply to you, do not make any mark on the answer sheet, but go on to the next statement.

Each of the statements in Fig. 41 is taken from one of the eight areas.

The inventory provides percentile norms for boys and girls by grades separately for each of the areas. It was standardized on a nationally representative sample of 3000 students. Reliabilities of the eight areas range from .90 to .97. For the total score the reliability is .98.

The inventory is of value for surveying students' problems because it can provide a relatively nonthreatening means of communication between the student and his teachers and counselors. The mere act of administering it can establish a social atmosphere in which consideration of emotional and social adjustment problems becomes

---

[4] H. H. Remmers and B. Shimberg, *The SRA Youth Inventory*, Chicago: Science Research Associates, 1956. (Form S, Grades 7–12.)

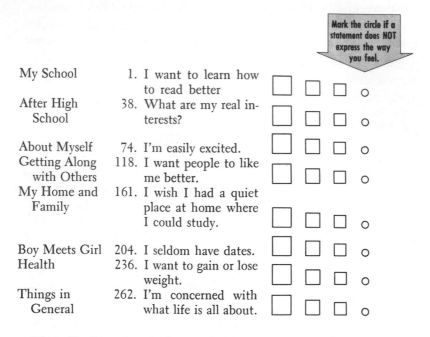

			Mark the circle if a statement does NOT express the way you feel.
My School	1.	I want to learn how to read better	□ □ □ ○
After High School	38.	What are my real interests?	□ □ □ ○
About Myself	74.	I'm easily excited.	□ □ □ ○
Getting Along with Others	118.	I want people to like me better.	□ □ □ ○
My Home and Family	161.	I wish I had a quiet place at home where I could study.	□ □ □ ○
Boy Meets Girl	204.	I seldom have dates.	□ □ □ ○
Health	236.	I want to gain or lose weight.	□ □ □ ○
Things in General	262.	I'm concerned with what life is all about.	□ □ □ ○

(Note: Pupils are instructed to mark the largest square if a given statement represents a serious problem, the medium-sized square if the problem is less serious, the smallest square if the problem is recognizable but not serious, or the circle if the statement does *not* represent a problem.)

Fig. 41. Sample from SRA Youth Inventory.

acceptable. Students may sense this atmosphere, realizing that other students may also have problems. The specific information that his scores give the student can lay the basis for constructive activity toward the solution of problems.

The inventory and its results are primarily a beginning step. What the student does about his problems from that point on, how the teacher adjusts his own activities and behavior to promote the adjustment of his students, how the administrator reexamines his curriculum with the aid of inventory results are all essentially outside the scope of this book. The manual provides suggestions as to possible next steps for students, teachers, counselors, and administrators in realizing the potential values of the inventory.

Problems of Appraising Adjustment with Self-Inventories

The foregoing should make clear the general procedure followed in using inventories. Inventories have been criticized on various grounds. Their validity and usefulness depend, of course, on the purposes for which they are used. Many of the objections to them have been aimed against their use in situations for which they neither were designed nor are suitable. We shall consider three of the more common problems.

1. One of the major problems with inventories is *obtaining frank responses*. Since adjustment is by definition an emotional and social matter, it is something that people are generally unable to consider without being influenced by their desire for social acceptance. Frankness of response will largely depend on the rapport established between the pupil and those he expects to examine his responses. The greater his trust in and acceptance of his teachers, the more he will try to give truthful answers to adjustment inventories.

In developing the SRA Youth Inventory, the authors had half of their large national sample of pupils sign their answer sheets; the other half were allowed to remain anonymous. The authors found very little difference between the percentages of signers and of nonsigners who checked given items as problems for themselves. The greatest difference (6 percent) was on the item "My teachers play favorites." When a pupil is convinced that the inventory is aimed at improving his own adjustment, frankness apparently is not a serious problem.

2. A second problem is that, even if pupils want to be frank, they may *lack sufficient insight into themselves* to be able to give objectively true responses. This becomes important when the objective truth of a given response must be assumed. For example, pupils may simply not know the truth about themselves concerning such questions as "Do you frequently have spells of the blues?" and "Does your ambition need occasional stimulation through contact with successful people?" People are prone to use the kinds of adjustment mechanisms described previously in answering questions like these. When objective truth need not be counted on, however, this difficulty is less relevant. It may not be the truth of an answer that determines whether a pupil is adjusted, but rather the way he feels

about the question. It is educationally and psychologically significant that a pupil *thinks* he has a problem even if, on objective grounds, he does not. So again the validity and usefulness of the inventory approach depend on the kinds of interpretation to be made. When an outside criterion of adjustment, such as counselors' ratings, is used, this difficulty may become unimportant. If inventory results tend to agree with such criteria, it does not matter whether responses are "true" to fact.

3. A third problem in using self-inventories for the measurement of adjustment is *developing acceptable external criteria* against which to validate these instruments. This difficulty is not, of course, unique to self-inventories. Inventories used in screening pupils are seldom "disguised" and can therefore readily be "faked" by anyone wanting to do so. It follows that inventories should not be expected to yield valid results against external criteria of adjustment when administered under conditions unfavorable to frank and insightful responses. Furthermore, on logical grounds alone, these inventories should not be expected to yield results that correlate perfectly with appraisals of adjustment by other persons. An individual's report of his own adjustment cannot be expected to have the same content and significance as the adjustment someone else perceives in him, however complete and extensive the other person's opportunity to observe has been. It is reasonable, however, to expect self-descriptions to be of some use in appraising adjustment when they are collected under conditions that make for a reasonable degree of frankness and insightfulness.

Validity of Inventories

When self-inventories have been validated against external criteria of adjustment, such as ratings by psychiatrists and clinical psychologists, or against "success" in school as defined by grades, their statistical and empirical validity has seldom been high. Coefficients of validity tend to range from nearly zero to .70 in various studies.

Suppose, however, that an inventory is used to give pupils in a school system an opportunity, under nonthreatening conditions, to tell teachers and counselors that they think they have certain problems and to compare themselves with other pupils of the same age, grade, and cultural background as to the kinds and numbers of problems they say they have. For such purposes personality inventories and problem check lists can be considered valid.

As in all educational and psychological measurement, the validity of inventories is specific to their purpose. Personality inventories may have substantial validity when used not as indexes of adjustment objectively defined, but as indexes of self-reported adjustment.

Are Adjustment Inventories Useful?

A major question still remains: "Are valid indexes of self-reported adjustment useful in the work of the schools?" The answer must always depend on the particular school situation. Judged from the widespread use of such inventories by teachers and counselors in school situations and by some research studies, inventories fill a need. No better alternative seems to be available for large-scale, feasible, useful surveys of pupil adjustment. Insistence on clinically sophisticated depth techniques means that schools will fail to do as adequate a job as is now possible. Although other techniques for appraising adjustment in the schools are available, none allow such a useful, large-scale program at so little cost.

Kinds of Errors in Screening

Any device for appraising adjustment, including adjustment inventories, can lead to two kinds of errors: (1) "misses," i.e., errors by which maladjusted individuals go undetected, and (2) "false positives," i.e., errors by which individuals are identified as maladjusted by the inventory although, on the basis of other valid evidence, they are not. The latter kind of error is relatively easy to correct in the normal, everyday procedures of teaching and counseling in the schools. A pupil thus falsely identified as maladjusted may receive special attention from his teachers and counselors for some time, but the error of self-perception may soon become apparent as his normal adjustment manifests itself. Errors of the first kind, "misses," are more serious. If the inventories alone were used, such errors would mean that pupils who need special attention from teachers, counselors, and perhaps clinical psychologists or psychiatrists would not be so identified.

Personality inventories often have relatively low validity. (Validity of inventories is often defined as agreement with clinicians' ratings of adjustment.) Nonetheless, such inventories can succeed to a greater than chance extent in correctly classifying individuals as to their adjustment. Can the kinds and numbers of errors such inventories entail be tolerated? This depends on the kinds of human and financial cost that the school system can stand. To minimize the amount of undetected and unacted-upon maladjustment among children and youth means greatly increasing the financial outlay for skilled professional workers in mental health problems. In such a program the number of "misses" may be minimized. In less expensive programs, where resources are available only for the few children who are most in need, inventories can be used with relatively high cutting scores so that only the most serious cases are identified for special attention.

In summary, the inventory approach to appraising emotional and social adjustment often does good and seldom does harm in the school program. The special attention that "false positives" receive may be desirable in any case, as part of the program of individualized attention that modern education advocates. For the pupils correctly identified as maladjusted by this relatively inexpensive procedure, the special attention may make an important difference. Personality inventories certainly are not sufficient, and may perhaps not even be necessary to mental health programs in the school; nevertheless, they can be helpful in many schools and in the present state of psychological technique.

Available Adjustment Inventories

A large number of nonprojective character, personality, and adjustment inventories are commercially available. Some have been developed primarily for research purposes and have not proved satisfactory for use in typical school situations. For many, a sizeable literature has been accumulated and reviews are given in one or more of the

Mental Measurements Yearbooks. The following are illustrative of over 200 such inventories listed in *Tests in Print,* but a prospective user should make his own selection of those listed on the basis of the principles already discussed in this volume and according to his specific purposes.

California Psychological Inventory, for ages 13 and over, has 18 scores: dominance, capacity for status, sociability, social presence, self-acceptance, sense of well-being, responsibility, socialization, self-control, tolerance, good impression, communality, achievement via conformance, achievement via independence, intellectual efficiency, psychological-mindedness, flexibility, femininity.[5]

IPAT High School Personality Questionnaire, for ages 12–18; (formerly called *The Junior Personality Quiz*) has 14 scores: schizothymia vs. cyclothymia, mental defect vs. general intelligence, general neuroticism vs. ego strength, phlegmatic temperament vs. excitability, submissiveness vs. dominance, desurgency vs. surgency, lack of rigid internal standards vs. super-ego strength, threctia vs. parmia, harria vs. premisia, dynamic simplicity vs. neurasthenic self-critical tendency, confident adequacy vs. guilt proneness, group dependency vs. self-sufficiency, poor self sentiment formation vs. high strength of self sentiment, low ergic tension vs. high ergic tension.[6]

SOCIOMETRY AND RELATED TECHNIQUES: METHODS THAT USE FELLOW PUPILS AS SOURCES OF EVIDENCE

Social adjustment refers to how an individual gets along with other people. For school children this means how well a pupil gets along

[5] Harrison G. Gough, *California Psychological Inventory,* Consulting Psychologists Press, Inc. For additional information and reviews by Lee J. Cronbach and Robert L. Thorndike, see *Fifth Mental Measurements Yearbook,* 5:37, test number 37 (33 references, 1 excerpt).

[6] R. B. Cattell, H. Beloff, and R. W. Coan, *IPAT High School Personality Questionnaire,* Institute for Personality and Ability Testing, 1953–1960. Also published, with a manual revised for school use, under the title *Jr.–Sr. High School Personality Questionnaire* (Indianapolis: Bobbs-Merrill). For additional information, see 5:72 (4 references).

with his fellow pupils. Whether an individual "deserves" social approval, whether in objective terms he should be approved by his peers, is beside the point. Regardless of how meritorious, how "good" he may be in absolute terms, what matters here is how others perceive him.

Whether a student is accepted by his fellows, whether they "want him around" for different kinds of activities, is important to the student himself. His own perception of his standing among his peers is almost sure to make a great deal of difference to him. If his perception of it is correct, he will behave in appropriate ways. If it is incorrect, either it will be corrected by his fellows' reactions to him or he will continue to behave inappropriately and in one way or another alienate himself from them. Apart from the accuracy of his own perception of his standing among his peers, his actual standing is also important. An individual will be less likely to develop socially desirable habits of interacting with other persons if they continually reject him. If the school is to be concerned with the pupil's social development—this is importantly related to his intellectual development—it must identify the students who need help in improving their social relationships.

The "Guess-Who" Method

To study social adjustment in this sense, variations of the commonsense approach are used. "If you want to know how other pupils feel about a given pupil, ask them." The members of a small, closely knit group, such as a classroom of pupils, are asked to react to one another. One of these techniques is the "Guess-Who" test, the directions for which follow:

Here are some little word-pictures of some children you may know. Read each statement carefully and see if you can guess who it is about. It might be about yourself. There may be more than one picture for the same person. Several boys and girls may fit one picture. Read each statement. Think over your classmates, and write after each statement the names of any boys or girls who may fit it. If the picture does not seem to fit anyone in your class, put down no name, but go on to the next statement. Work carefully, and use your judgment.

1. Here is the class athlete. He (or she) can play baseball, basketball, and tennis, can swim as well as any, and is a good sport.

----

2. This one is always picking on others and annoying them.

In scoring the "Guess-Who" test, many methods have been tried, but adequate results have been obtained simply by totaling the number of times a pupil's name appears, a positive value being given to "desirable" items and a negative value to "undesirable" ones. In practice many pupils in the group are mentioned for a given item and each pupil is mentioned for a fairly large number of items. Thus a rating is usually derived for many pupils over a fairly large number of items, and the results are quite reliable. Obviously, the method provides evidence that the teacher can use in perceiving a pupil's personality through the eyes of his fellow pupils. Results often surprise teachers. The pupil whom the teacher considered to be lonesome and ignored may turn out to be liked and respected, whereas the one the teacher particularly liked because of his good manners and quick learning may be despised by his peers for his snobbishness.

A by-product of such a rating scheme may be better understanding of pupils' values—what they consider important in persons. Inspection of "Guess-Who" rating results may prove such characteristics as neatness, courtesy, and quick obedience to be negatively related to what pupils value in one another. Similarly, positiveness, prankishness, or simply a high level of activity, scorned or ignored by teachers, may prove to be what makes a pupil attractive to his classmates. Insight into pupils' values thus gained provides a basis for evaluating the social learning that inevitably goes on in school. It can give the teacher leads as to how to improve the standing of a pupil rejected by his peers. To make him more accepted, the teacher can either give him an opportunity to acquire the characteristics and skills his fellow pupils value, or undertake to change their values.

Sociometry

Another much-used procedure is called *sociometry*. A "sociometric test" requires each member of a group, such as a classroom group, to choose one or more members for a given purpose. Jennings offers the following illustration of how a sociometric questionnaire may be worded:[7]

We are going to need committees to work on such-and-such problems. Each of you knows with whom you enjoy working most. These may be the same persons with whom you work in other classes, or they may be different, so remember that we are talking about social studies. Put your name at the top of the page, and numbers 1, 2, and 3 on lines below. Opposite "1" put the name of a boy or girl with whom you would most like to work, after "2" your second choice, and after "3" your third. I will keep all of the choices in mind and arrange the committees so that everyone will be with one or more of the three people named. Remember, you may choose a boy or girl who is absent today if you want to. Write down the last name as well as the first name so that I will be sure to know whom you mean. As usual, we shall probably be working in these committees for about eight weeks, or until the Christmas holidays.

It may be assumed that the pupils who are frequently chosen by other pupils for close association show a high degree of social acceptability by their fellow pupils. Requiring the pupils to choose their associates for other purposes can identify different dimensions of acceptability.

What are the advantages of this technique over the ordinary popularity contest or class election? Sociometric techniques have other uses than furnishing estimates of popularity. To achieve the additional purposes requires not merely tallying the number of choices each pupil receives from other pupils for a given purpose, but constructing a sociogram, beginning with the summary sheet shown in Fig. 42.[8]

Enter the names of the group members in alphabetical order along the side and across the top of a large sheet of squared paper. If subgroups such as boys, girls, fifth graders, and the like are to be studied as such, alphabetize the names in each subgroup. Arrange the children's answer sheets in alphabetical order. From each answer sheet, make entries on the summary sheet to indicate who chose

[7] Helen H. Jennings, *Sociometry in Group Relations*, Washington: American Council on Education, rev. ed., 1959, pp. 15–16.

[8] Adapted from Mary L. Northway, *A Primer of Sociometry*, Toronto: Univ. of Toronto Press, 1952, p. 9.

Chosen

Chooser Boys	Boys					Girls					Number Chosen
	Arnold	Ben	Charles	David	⋮	Alice	Betty	Cora	Doris	⋮	
Arnold		ABO	AOO								2
Ben	OOC			OBO		OBO					3
Charles	OBC										1
David	AOC		OBO								2
Girls											
Alice							ABC	OOC			2
Betty							ABC		OBO		2
Cora								OBC		OOC	2
Doris							AOO				1
Total A's	1	1	1	0		2	1	0	0		
Total B's	1	0	1	1		2	2	0	1		
Total C's	3	1	0	0		1	2	1	1		
Combined	5	2	2	1		5	5	1	2		
Number Choosing	3	1	2	1		3	2	1	2		

Fig. 42. An Illustrative Sociometric Summary Sheet.

whom for each sociometric question. Thus, if Arnold chooses Ben on Question A, enter an "A" on the row opposite Arnold in the column under Ben. If he chooses him on Question B, enter a "B." If he did not choose him on Question C, enter a zero. The entries under Ben and opposite Arnold then read "AB0." The total entries in each column give the social acceptance score of the given pupils.

As the teacher fills in this tally he may think of such questions as: "How many mutual or reciprocated choices are there? Which individuals and what proportion of the class are very much in demand? What proportion is ignored? Do girls and boys choose each other? Are there any reciprocated choices across sex lines?[9] Fig. 43[10] shows

[9] Helen H. Jennings, *op. cit.*, pp. 21–22.
[10] Quoted by permission from *ibid.*, p. 23.

TALLY OF SOCIOMETRIC POSITIONS

No. of Boys ....; No. of Girls ....
          Class/Grade ....
          School ....
          City ....
          Date Given ....

Test Question: ....
How many choices were asked for? .... Total no. of choices made by all students? .... Maximum no. of choices possible (multiply size of group by number of choices allowed) ....
Enter in the spaces below the no. of pupils holding each position listed.

Frequency of Choice	Chosen	Number of Pupils Chosen Mutually	Rejected[a]	Rejected Mutually[a]
Not at all	....	....	....	....
Once	....	....	....	....
Twice	....	....	....	....
Three times	....	....	....	....
Four times	....	....	....	....
Five times	....	....	....	....
More than 5 times	....	....	....	....
Total no. of pupils[b]	....	....	....	....

Sample Breakdowns of Tally of Positions Along Group Factor Lines[c]

Frequency of Choice	No. of Choices Received Boys	No. of Choices Received Girls	No. of Choices Received Negro	No. of Choices Received White	No. of Choices Received Live in Housing Project	No. of Choices Received Do Not Live in Housing Project
None	....	....	....	....	....	....
One	....	....	....	....	....	....
Two	....	....	....	....	....	....
Three	....	....	....	....	....	....
Four	....	....	....	....	....	....
Five	....	....	....	....	....	....
Total by category	....	....	....	....	....	....
Total no. of pupils	....	....	....	....	....	....

Further Questions

How many boys chose girls and were not reciprocated? ....
[Or how many white children chose Negro children and were not reciprocated?]
How many girls chose boys and were not reciprocated? ....
Number of mutual choices between boys and girls ....

Special Features

Note here any pattern which is of special interest to you, e.g., "Three of the unchosen pupils chose the same much-chosen pupil."

[a] Enter only if a rejection question was used.
[b] Totals of each column should equal the number of children in the group.
[c] Positions may be broken down into whatever categories for analysis will disclose whether particular group factors are operating to affect its structures.

Fig. 43. Tally of Sociometric Positions. In preparing his own forms, the teacher may substitute whatever categories are appropriate for breaking down the tally of positions and whatever other questions he may be particularly interested in.

the form designed to facilitate the teacher's work in answering such questions. Beyond this kind of tally, he can present the social structure of the class as a whole in a sociogram such as that in Fig. 44.

The positions near the center of the sociogram should be used for children who receive many choices. As the sociometric status of the child decreases, distance from the center increases. It is often helpful, as is done in Fig. 44, to put the girls' symbols on one side and the boys' on the other.

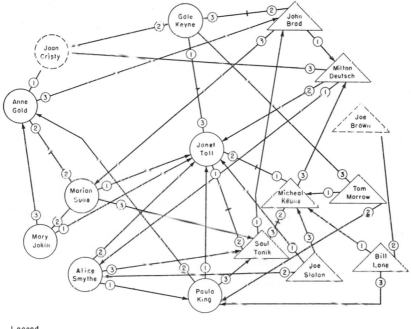

Note: For an absent boy or girl, use the respective symbol dashed, leaving any choice line open-ended (see Joe Brown above).

If rejections are obtained, the choice line may be made in dashes or in a different color.

Whenever a direct line from chooser to chosen cannot be drawn without going through the symbol for another individual, the line should be drawn with an elbow, as in the case of Bill Lane to Paula King.

Fig. 44. A Filled-In Sociogram, Presenting the Choice Patterns Graphically. Blank forms with empty circles and triangles may be mimeographed so that the teacher can fill in the names and draw in the choice lines after the test has been given.

Sociometric data make possible many kinds of interpretation and analysis. The interpretations can be enhanced by supplementary interview data, open questions, themes written by children, diaries, teachers' interviews with parents, and the like. The following from Jennings[11] illustrates merely the beginning of such an interpretation:

To a person looking at a sociogram for the first time, the whole thing may seem to be a meaningless jumble of circles, lines, and triangles. The first problem, then, is to trace the pattern and then gradually see its significance. After a little practice, sociograms can be read for major outlines of characteristic shape at a glance, and study is called for only in connection with details of the interaction of individual children. Once the picture is firmly in mind, or, indeed, while it is actually taking shape, all sorts of questions will suggest themselves for further study.

A good way to begin reading a sociogram is to concentrate on one person and follow all lines that lead from and to him. In the sample sociogram [Fig. 44], the circle marked "Mary Jokin" in the lower left corner has three arrows (unreciprocated choices) running from it to Janet Toll (first), Marian Soue (second), and Anne Gold (third). There are no arrows pointing at Mary. She has not received a single choice. Looking at Janet, we find her first choice is a boy, Saul Tonik, and it is reciprocated as Saul's second possibility; her second choice is another boy, Michael Keane, and is also reciprocated—she is first on Michael's list; her third choice is again reciprocated—by a girl this time, Gale Keyne, and represents another first choice. In addition, there are six arrows pointing at Janet, coming from two boys and four girls; moreover, four of these are first choices and the others second ones. Everyday life in the classroom must obviously be very different for Janet and Mary![12]

How sociometric data should be used in improving children's and youths' social adjustment is beyond the scope of this book. Such data are only part of the information on which educational practice should be grounded.[13]

INFORMAL OBSERVATION: THE TEACHER AS A SOURCE OF EVIDENCE

So far we have taken up the kinds of evidence that teachers can obtain from the pupil himself and from his fellow pupils. These

[11] Quoted by permission from *ibid.*, p. 26.
[12] *Ibid.*, pp. 23–24.
[13] See N. E. Gronlund, *Sociometry in the Classroom*, New York: Harper & Row, 1959, for a discussion of the reliability, validity, and uses of sociometry.

kinds of information must of course be assimilated and interpreted before they can be used. But another type of evidence—what he can observe for himself—the teacher can obtain without working through pupils. As he interacts with learners in and out of the classroom, there is much for him to see and hear. This refers particularly to "expressive" behavior—the unique "style" that characterizes every one of us. A pupil's tone of voice, his rate of speaking, the kinds of words he chooses, his fluency or hesitancy, how much he talks in the presence of his fellows or the opposite sex, whether he initiates conversations and topics of conversation, how often he agrees and disagrees with others, how often his opinion is ignored or sought by others, how often others agree or disagree with him, how often he displays humor as against grim seriousness, how much he seems to be enjoying himself, how constructively he works and plays, how much he avoids his tasks—all these and myriad other cues present themselves continuously to teachers.

Obviously, no teacher can pay attention to all these items all the time. Nor can he be expected to "add" all these items of behavior together in any conscious and systematic way. The teacher must impose some organizing scheme on all this seeming chaos of behavior —indeed, he cannot keep himself from doing so. He uses "stereotypes" that are more or less correct, that is, norms and expectations as to how the typical student will behave. He refines these stereotypes in various ways. He has stereotypes concerning pupils of a given sex, a given age level, a given social class, a given body build, a given type of rural or urban residence, a given skin color or nationality, and the like. Much of what he observes in pupils he immediately and unconsciously compares with these expectations. The comparison results in revising the stereotype more or less, depending both on how well the pupil fits the teacher's expectations and on how "flexible" the teacher is.

Ideally, the teacher comes to his pupils and his observations of their behavior with accurate general expectations. As he observes and collects information about specific pupils and groups, his understanding of their characteristics is modified and comes closer to reality. The teacher who understands pupils best is least rigidly bound by a small number of preconceptions concerning personality. The teacher who is himself insecure in his relationships with others, whose picture of himself is out of focus with the way others perceive him, develops "blind spots" that keep him from understanding his pupils. Needless to say, the teacher who has hostile attitudes toward— prejudices against—members of any racial, religious, social, or nationality group cannot be expected to understand the emotional and social adjustment patterns of pupils who belong to those groups. He will misperceive the motives and behaviors of such pupils. His prejudices will keep him from using his perceptions in accord with social and psychological reality.

The foregoing does not mean that teachers should or can be free of stereotypes, in the sense of expectations and hypotheses. It is only incorrect and rigid stereotypes that interfere with understanding pupils accurately. "Correct" stereotypes as defined by social norms— such as those concerning the proper roles for boys and girls in adolescent society—are indispensable to understanding adolescent boys and girls.

Thus the teacher's mental health, his own emotional and social adjustment, affect the process of evaluating the emotional and social adjustment of pupils. The most important work the teacher does in evaluating emotional and social adjustment is the informal, everyday observation and interpretation whose validity depends on his own psychological security, social understanding, inner complexity, and wisdom. Training programs of the kinds described in *Helping Teachers Understand Children*[14] can contribute much to the teacher's equipment for this purpose.

Anecdotal Records

Anecdotal records—which are often used as supplementary materials for understanding sociometric data—are brief reports of incidents judged to be significant for a pupil's emotional and social adjustment. The choice of incidents recorded is based on some conception of the nature of adjustment and of what is significant. Anecdotes should include both an objective description of behavior and an interpretation of it. Traxler has shown how a report that

[14] Staff of the Division on Child Development and Teacher Personnel, American Council on Education, *Helping Teachers Understand Children*, Washington, 1945.

combines interpretation and recommendation can be broken down so as to be less confusing.[15]

Combined report, interpretation, and recommendation. In a meeting of her club today, Alice showed her jealousy of the new president by firing questions at her whenever there was an opportunity. She tried to create difficulties by constant interruption throughout the period. The other students showed their resentment by calling for her to sit down. It is apparent that she is a natural trouble-maker, and I think her counselor should have her in for a serious talk.

The following presentation of this incident is more objective and less confusing:

Incident. In a meeting of her club today Alice fired questions at the new president at every opportunity. She interrupted many times during the period. On several occasions the other students called for her to sit down.

Interpretation. Alice seemed to be jealous of the new president and desirous of creating difficulty. The other students appeared to resent her action. The girl seemed to enjoy making trouble for others.

Recommendation. It would be advisable for the counselor to lead the girl tactfully into a discussion of her relations with the other students in an effort to bring about better adjustment.

The chief value of anecdotal records is in providing concrete realistic information that goes beyond the use of ambiguous trait names or test scores such as "courteous," "considerate," "cooperative," and the like. A description of actual behavior can tell much about the living reality of a student's adjustment pattern.

Attempts have been made in schools and colleges to set up a system of anecdotal record keeping on a standard, routine basis. Such a system requires that the teacher try to keep a record of all his pupils, making at least a few such records every day and attempting to cover all his pupils over a period of time. Administrative devices such as dictaphones, typist pools, filing systems, and summarizing techniques have been tried. Despite these aids, anecdotal behavior records can make exorbitant demands on the time and energy of

[15] A. E. Traxler, The nature and use of anecdotal records, *Supplementary Bulletin D*, New York: Educational Records Bureau, 1939.

teachers. Also, because of differences in points of view, teachers tend to select incidents for recording that are more or less irrelevant to each other. Observers, such as teachers, tend to overgeneralize on the basis of striking rather than typical incidents.

This experience has raised doubts as to the feasibility of keeping anecdotal records for all the pupils. Practice in writing and analyzing such records for one or two children, however, may provide important training values for the teacher.

COMMUNICATING IMPRESSIONS OF PERSONALITY TO OTHERS: RATING METHODS

When a teacher has observed a pupil in the classroom, in extracurricular activities, and elsewhere, he generally has some confidence in his impressions concerning the pupil. To communicate these impressions to other people, he can use one of the many kinds of rating methods. Such methods make it possible to express in standard, brief, and quantitative form one person's description and evaluation of another.

The general ideas underlying rating methods for describing and evaluating adjustment are the same as those stated in Chapter 8 in connection with product and procedure evaluation. That is, we need (1) to analyze the pupil's adjustment or behavior patterns into various "traits" or other characteristics and (2) to provide a method of scoring each characteristic. Here we point out only the aspects of the procedure that are specific to adjustment evaluation.

A theory of adjustment and the purpose of the ratings determine the traits or dimensions into which the teacher analyzes the pupil's adjustment. The traits should be amenable to reliable evaluation. Research has indicated that judges agree better with one another— that is, are more reliable—in rating traits that show up frequently. The trait should be clearly defined and have the same meaning for all the judges.

Types of Rating Scales

Various schemes have been devised for obtaining a rating on each trait; among them are descriptive, numerical, and graphic rating scales. These may be combined in various ways. *Descriptive rating scales* provide lists of words or phrases, usually from three to seven, from which the rater selects the one most applicable to the person being rated. Example:

Directions: Place a check mark in the square before the phrase which represents your evaluation of the pupil.

Is this pupil at ease and re-   ☐ At ease in all situations.
laxed?   ☐ Usually at ease. Rarely tense.
☐ At ease often but occasionally tense.
☐ Usually tense.
☐ Tense in all situations.

Numerical rating scales assign numbers for the various levels of each trait, from least to most. Example:

Directions: Give the pupil a number from 0 to 10 to represent the degree to which he possesses the traits listed. 0 represents none of the trait, 5 an average amount, and 10 a maximum amount of the trait.

Is this pupil at ease and relaxed? Can he be expected not to get tense and "nervous" in various school and out-of-school situations? .... _____

Graphic rating scales have horizontal lines, defined at each end and perhaps at intermediate points, on which the rater checks the subject's standing with respect to each trait. Example:

	Constant Alternatives				
Is this pupil at ease?					
Is this pupil shy?	Extremely	Rather	Somewhat	Hardly	Not at all
	Extremely	Rather	Somewhat	Hardly	Not at all
		Changing Alternatives			
Is this pupil at ease?					
Is this pupil shy?	At ease in all situations.	Usually at ease. Rarely tense.	At ease often but occasionally tense.	Usually tense.	Tense in all situations.
	Always shy and withdrawn.	Usually shy, occasionally forward.	Shy and withdrawn about half the time.	Usually forward and unreserved.	Invariably forward and self-assertive.

The graphic rating scale embodies features of both the others. In general, all three can be put in either the constant-alternative or the changing-alternative form described in Chapter 8. When each trait is put in the constant-alternative form, the description of each level of the trait is the same for all traits and consequently must be in general terms. In the changing-alternative form, separate descriptions are provided for each level of each trait, as in the preceding example.

Suggestions for Constructing Graphic Rating Scales

In developing graphic rating scales, the following suggestions have sometimes been helpful. Remember, however, that they are mostly based not on experimental findings but on common sense, which has frequently been refuted in the field of testing by experimental facts.

Alternation of Scale Directionality. Vary the desirable end of the rating line at random. In this way response set and halo effect (see below) may be reduced.

Explicit Trait Questions. Introduce each trait by a question phrased so as to describe the trait in objective, observable terms. For example, rather than merely labeling a trait "Emotional stability," it is better to ask such questions as "How well poised is he emotionally? Is he touchy, sensitive to criticism, easily upset? Is he irritated or impatient when things go wrong? Or does he keep on an even keel?"

Continuous Lines. Mark either a great many or no segments on the line. This emphasizes the continuity of the trait better and the rater can place his check mark at any point on the line. In scoring the rating scale, mark off a strip of paper into as many divisions as is desirable and place it along the line to express the number of divisions from the undesirable end of the line numerically.

Diction of Phrases. Fit the words used to describe each level to the understanding of the persons who will make the ratings. Slang and colloquial expressions sometimes help.

Phrasing Extreme Levels. Avoid phrases at the ends of the line that express levels of the trait so rare or extreme that raters will never check them.

Phrasing Intermediate Levels. To induce raters to use a wider range of the line, make the *meaning* of the intermediate levels closer to the average or neutral phrase than to the extreme phrases. This may help counteract the tendency to concentrate ratings around the middle of the line.

Errors in Rating Methods

Various errors may occur in obtaining an opinion about one person from another. These are due primarily to lack of information, bias, and the halo effect.

The person expressing an opinion may not know whereof he speaks. Unless he has had an opportunity to become acquainted with the subject and to observe him along lines pertinent to the trait he is rating, he cannot give valid evidence.

Like the pupil who answers questions on a self-inventory, the rater must be both able and willing to give an "unbiased" judgment. The teacher's insight into a pupil's adjustment is, of course, less than the pupil's, especially concerning the latter's "inner" life. But the teacher is more likely to be frank about a pupil than about himself. When the teacher or other rater is *very* well acquainted with the pupil through long association or intimate friendship, however, ratings often show leniency and favoritism.

The halo effect in rating is the effect of the rater's overall impression of a pupil on his ratings of specific aspects of that pupil. If the teacher thinks well of a pupil in general, he may rate him better in at least some aspects than he would were it not for the halo effect. The opposite tendency may appear when he ranks the pupil low in general. A particular trait is subject to the halo effect when it is not commonly observed or thought about, is not clearly defined, involves relationship to other people rather than being "self-contained," or is highly loaded with emotional significance. To reduce the halo effect, the rater must constantly keep in mind the necessity of considering each trait separately, of not letting one rating be influenced by his other ratings of the pupil. For example, if a pupil is rated highly on his "freedom from tension" his "popularity" must still be considered separately.

The reliability of the average of the ratings obtained from equally well-trained and well-instructed raters increases with the number of raters. But generally the increase is not worth the trouble after about ten ratings have been averaged, except in cases in which larger numbers of raters are easily available and a high reliability is desired, as, for example, in student ratings of teachers.

Available Rating Devices

While there are a number of commercially available rating devices for the nonprojective type of personality appraisal, some of them have been developed primarily for research purposes and have not yet been proven satisfactory for use in typical school situations. For some, a sizeable literature has been accumulated and reviews are given in one or more of the *Mental Measurements Yearbooks*. The following are illustrative of such rating devices listed in *Tests in Print*, but a prospective user should make his own selection of those listed on the basis of the principles already discussed in this volume and according to his specific purposes.

Personality Record (Revised), for grades 7 to 12, has 7 ratings by teachers: seriousness of purpose, industry, initiative, influence, concern for others, responsibility, emotional stability. It is also available in combination with either the *Secondary-School Record, Revised* or the *Junior High School Record*.[16]

Pupil Adjustment Inventory, for kindergarten through grade 12, has ratings in 7 areas: academic, social, emotional, physical, activities and interests, school's influence on pupil, home background.[17]

PROJECTIVE TECHNIQUES

Sometimes a teacher wishes he could get to know his pupils as unique individuals. He wishes he could know what one of them has "on his mind." The inventories discussed earlier in this chapter are "structured"; that is, they tend to fix the lines along which a pupil

[16] Published by the National Association of Secondary-School Principals. For additional information and a review by Verner M. Sims, see *Fourth Mental Measurements Yearbook*, 1941–1958, 4:78, test number 78.

[17] Houghton Mifflin, 1957. For additional information and reviews by Robert H. Bauernfeind and John Pierce-Jones, see *Fifth Mental Measurements Yearbook*, 5:100, test number 100.

can respond and allow him to tell only the kinds of things that the authors of an inventory have built into it. For any individual pupil, such an inventory may miss ideas of particular significance simply because it does not anticipate the unique ways in which that pupil sees himself and the world. Sometimes the questions on such inventories arouse resistance, perhaps unconscious, that prevents valid responses. This is particularly true when the pupil lacks a feeling of freedom and rapport.

By depending on what an individual is conscious of in himself, structured inventories also fail to get at the deeper, underlying parts of his personality that he is largely unaware of. The mechanisms of adjustment, especially repression, make it unlikely that any of us is able to tell about himself in straightforward fashion. Our unique "styles of life," ways of thinking, experiencing, and seeing ourselves in relation to the world are too deep within us to be called up at will and reported to someone else.

Projective techniques have been developed to overcome these limitations of structured approaches to personality. In general, projective techniques present to the subject an ambiguous and unstructured stimulus which calls for a response that can be interpreted by the psychologist so as to reveal much about the personality of the subject. Since their use requires highly specialized professional training, they are not for the classroom teacher. For special studies of learners, they attempt to unravel particularly difficult adjustment problems. The teacher may sometimes expect to have psychologists refer to evidence obtained with such instruments as the Rorschach Inkblot Test or the Thematic Apperception Test.

One classroom technique, the sentence completion test, has also been used as a projective approach to personality; and it is conceivable that rough applications of this approach can be made to yield useful information for the classroom teacher. Any teacher who wants to obtain pupil reactions to the classroom situation and to himself in a relatively unstructured fashion can draw up his own set of incomplete sentences, administer them to his students, and apply his own insight in interpreting the responses. The incomplete sentences found on page 362 illustrate some that might be useful to a teacher.

1. My teacher _____.
2. The kids in this class _____.
3. The things we have to study _____.
4. Homework _____.
5. The books we read _____.
6. The things about school that bother me _____.
7. Boys _____.
8. Girls _____.
9. I don't understand _____.
10. My parents think that school _____.

No teacher without advanced psychological training can expect to interpret the responses with as much insight as clinical psychologists experienced in the development and use of projective techniques. Nevertheless, teachers can secure valuable information with home-made sentence completion techniques. They can use these devices to learn things about their own behavior and characteristics, as seen by pupils, that can help them improve their teaching processes.

When used in the way sketched above, the incomplete sentence technique has the advantage of being unstructured, but it is probably not so disguised as to prevent some pupils from giving what they consider acceptable responses. To minimize their tendency to say only the "right" things, it is probably preferable to allow the pupils to remain anonymous.

LABORATORY EXERCISES AND DISCUSSION QUESTIONS

1. From your experience, cite one or more examples of emotional or social maladjustment. Analyze the case in terms of the motive not satisfied, the nature of the thwarting obstacle, and the reasons for the inadequacy of attempts to overcome the obstacle. If possible, suggest a desirable solution or treatment.
2. Examine three representative devices for appraising emotional and social adjustment and read reviews of them in the *Mental Measurements Yearbook*. Complete the test evaluation form for them in Chapter 5.
3. Construct a sociometric device to determine how a group of thirty

will work best together in committees of five in developing a guidance program in a public school. (Use members of your class, for example.)

4. Develop a rating scale, with changing alternatives, that you could use to rate the behavior of a pupil, in a way pertinent to his emotional and social adjustment, on the playground, in the classroom, in adolescent social life, etc.

5. Write an anecdote about a significant incident in a pupil's behavior as recalled from your own days as a child or adolescent.

SUGGESTED REFERENCES

Anastasi, Anne, *Psychological Testing,* New York: Macmillan, 2nd ed., 1961.

Chapters 20 and 21 discuss techniques for personality assessment.

Anderson, H. H., and G. L. Anderson, *An Introduction to Projective Techniques,* Englewood Cliffs: Prentice-Hall, 1951.

A good survey of the large variety of projective techniques for diagnosing and evaluating personality, including the Rorschach, Thematic Apperception Test, word association, sentence completion, Szondi Test, psychodrama, graphology, finger painting, and drawings of the human form.

Bernard, H. W., *Mental Hygiene for Classroom Teachers,* New York: McGraw-Hill, 1952, pp. 297–362.

Three chapters deal with the role of writing in the release of tensions and the interpretation of personality, with art as an approach to understanding personality, and with play and drama as classroom techniques in understanding pupils.

Froelich, C. P., and J. G. Darley, *Studying Students: Guidance Methods for Individual Analysis.* Chicago: Science Research Associates, 1952. Survey of techniques for gathering data about students and using the data, especially in individual counseling.

Gronlund, N. E., *Sociometry in the Classroom,* New York: Harper & Row, 1959.

A detailed description of how to construct and administer a sociometric test in classroom settings, and how to interpret and apply the results to educational problems.

Institute of School Experimentation, *How to Construct a Sociogram,* New York: Teachers College, Columbia University, 1947.

A step-by-step analysis of the process of constructing a sociogram.

This volume should be very helpful to beginners.

Krathwohl, David R. *et al.*, *Taxonomy of Educational Objectives, Handbook II: Affective Domain*, New York: McKay, 1964.

Highly relevant to assessing emotional and social adjustments viewed as educational objectives.

Northway, M. L., *A Primer of Sociometry*, Toronto: Univ. of Toronto Press, 1952.

An excellent introduction to the entire field of sociometric techniques, by one of the leaders in the field.

Rabin, A. I., and M. R. Haworth (eds.), *Projective Techniques with Children*, Grune, and Stratton, 1960.

Stanley, Julian C., *Measurement in Today's Schools*, Englewood Cliffs: Prentice-Hall, 4th ed., 1964.

Chapter 9 deals with measuring devices and techniques relevant to vocational, emotional, and social adjustments.

or ideas used in judging the content of a test, in estimating its content or logical validity.

Culture-free test. A test devised to rule out the effects of an individual's previous environment on his score. No such test is actually possible. A "culture-free" test does not rule out such effects but merely makes them cquivalent for the persons to be compared.

Cumulative frequency (cf). A column in a frequency distribution table that shows for any given interval how many scores in the distribution lie below the upper limit of that interval.

Curvilinear relationship. A relationship of two variable quantities portrayed by some curve other than a straight line.

Decile. One of the nine points that divide a ranked distribution of scores into ten equal parts.

Decile rank. The rank order, counting from the bottom, of the 10 groups of scores separated by decile points. The first decile rank is the rank of all scores below the 1st decile point. The 10th decile rank is the rank of all scores above the 9th decile point. There is no 10th decile point.

Deviation. The amount by which a score differs from some reference value, such as the mean, the norm, or the score on some other test.

Deviation IQ. A form of standard score that has a mean of 100 and a standard deviation of about 15, as compared with the conventional IQ, which is the ratio of mental age to chronological age.

Diagnostic test. A test used to diagnose, or to show an individual's strengths and weaknesses in a specific area of study. It yields measures of the components, or subparts, of some larger body of information or skill.

Difficulty value. The percentage of some specified group, such as students of a given age or grade, who answer an item correctly. The easier the item, or the higher the percentage of pupils who answer it correctly, the greater is its difficulty value.

Discriminating power. The ability of a test item to differentiate between persons having much of some trait and those having little.

Distractor. Any of the incorrect choices presented in a multiple-choice or matching item. Also called alternative, decoy, foil, mislead.

Distribution, see Frequency distribution.

Educational age (EA), see Achievement age.

Educational quotient (EQ). The ratio of the educational age to the chronological age, i.e., (EA ÷ CA) 100.

Equivalent form. Any of two or more forms of a test that are closely parallel in content and in difficulty of items, and that yield very

Central tendency, index of. A point in a distribution about which a majority of the cases tend to fall; it is intended to typify those measures. Also referred to as the representative value; indicated frequently as the mean, median, or mode.

Chronological age (CA). The time elapsed since birth.

Class analysis chart. A chart that shows the relative performance of members of a class on the several parts of a test battery.

Class interval (i). The range of scores, or the number of score units, between the upper and lower limits of a section, or interval, of test scores in a frequency distribution. Also called step interval, interval, class, class size.

Coefficient of correlation. A measure of the degree of relationship between two sets of measures either for the same group of individuals or for paired individuals (e.g., twins). The Pearson product-moment coefficient is r; the Spearman rank coefficient is rho (ρ).

Coefficient of equivalence. The type of reliability coefficient obtained when parallel, or equivalent, forms of the same test are administered to the same individuals.

Coefficient of internal consistency. The type of reliability coefficient obtained when either the split-halves of Kuder-Richardson formulas are used in computing it.

Coefficient of stability. The type of reliability coefficient obtained when the same test is administered twice to the same individuals.

Completion item. A test question calling for the completion, or filling in, of a word, phrase, sentence, etc., in a sentence or paragraph from which one or more parts have been omitted.

Continuum. A line along which a trait, or set of scores, is conceived as being continuously distributed. A variable such that, no matter how close together any two values may be, it is always possible to have a third value between them. Also called a continuous variable.

Correction for guessing. A reduction in score for wrong answers in order to adjust scores on objective tests to counteract the effects of students' presumably guessing the correct answer. The procedure rests on the false assumption that guessing and chance are the same. May be useful in evaluating a score to determine whether it is above the which chance alone could produce, as in a test of accuracy in predicting another's responses.

Correlation, *see* Coefficient of correlation.

Criterion. A standard by which a test may be judged or evaluated; a set of scores, measures, ratings, products, etc., that a test is designed to predict, or correlate with, as a test of its validity. A set of concepts

370 APPENDIXES

it is based on the false assumption that EA and MA should be perfectly correlated in normal or average pupils.

Achievement test. A measure of the degree to which a person has attained objectives of instruction or education.

Age equivalent. The chronological age for which a given score is the real or estimated average score.

Age-grade table. A table showing the number or percentage of pupils of each age in each school grade.

Age norms. Values representing typical or average performance for persons of any given chronological age level in any measured characteristic.

Age scale. A scale in which the units of measurement are the differences between successive age equivalents, each such difference being taken as if equal to any other.

Aptitude. The capacity to acquire proficiency with a given training. It is not necessarily inborn. An aptitude test is a measure of present characteristics (abilities, achievements, interests, temperament, etc.) predictive of capacity to learn.

Arbitrary reference point. Any arbitrary value in a series, usually one near the middle, from which *deviations* are calculated in a short-cut computation of the mean. Also called assumed mean.

Arithmetic mean. The sum of a set of scores divided by the number of scores. Commonly called average or mean and indicated by the symbol M or $\overline{X}$.

Attitude. One of many terms that refer to an aspect of personality inferred to account for persistent and consistent behavior toward or away from a family of related situations or objects.

Average. A general term applied to measures of central tendency. The three averages most widely used in education are the arithmetic mean, the median, and the mode.

Battery. A group of tests standardized on the same persons, so that the norms of the tests are comparable. Sometimes refers to any two or more tests given to the same persons, whether or not standardized together.

Centile. Any one of the 100 groups or divisions separated by percentile scores. For example, the 1st centile includes all scores below the 1st percentile point; the 31st centile includes all scores between the 30th and 31st percentile points; the 100th centile includes all scores above the 99th percentile point. Note: Centile ranks run from 1 to 100, whereas percentiles (points) run from 1 to 99.

Glossary of common measurement terms[1]

Ability test. A test of maximum performance designed to reveal the level of present status or present ability to function. *See also* General ability, Special ability.

Academic aptitude. The personal characteristics, native and acquired, that make likely a given degree of success in academic pursuits. Also called scholastic aptitude.

Achievement age. The age for which a given achievement test score is the real or estimated average. Also called educational age or subject age.

Achievement quotient (AQ). The ratio between actual level of scholastic performance and that which is expected; determined by the ratio of educational age to mental age, i.e., $(EA \div MA)$ 100. Also called accomplishment quotient. This concept still appears in the literature although it is dangerously misleading; it should be abandoned since

[1] This glossary includes the more common terms in test manuals and the literature of measurement. It has been taken, with some revision, from *A Glossary of 100 Measurement Terms*, by Roger T. Lennon (Test Service Notebook, No. 13, New York: Harcourt, Brace & World), and *A Comprehensive Dictionary of Psychological and Psychoanalytical Terms*, by H. B. English and A. C. English (New York: Longmans, Green, 1958). The reader should consult these and other sources for additional terms and meanings too extensive to be included in this glossary.

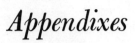

Appendixes

List of test publishers

1. Acorn Publishing Co., Rockville Centre, Long Island, N.Y.
2. American Council on Education, 1785 Massachusetts Ave., Washington 6, D.C.
3. Bureau of Educational Measurements, Kansas State Teachers College, Emporia, Kan.
4. Bureau of Educational Research and Service, State University of Iowa, Iowa City, Iowa.
5. Bureau of Publications, Teachers College, Columbia University, New York 27, N.Y.
6. California Test Bureau, Del Monte Research Park, Monterey, Calif.
7. Committee on Publications, Harvard Graduate School of Education, Cambridge, Mass.
8. Consulting Psychologists Press, Inc., 577 College Ave., Monterey, Calif.
9. Cooperative Test Division, Educational Testing Service, Princeton, N.J.
10. Division of Educational Reference, Purdue University, Lafayette, Ind.
11. Educational Records Bureau, 21 Audubon Ave., New York 32, N.Y.
12. Educational Test Bureau, 720 Washington Ave., S.E., Minneapolis, Minn.
13. Gregory (C. A.) Co., Test Division of Bobbs-Merrill Co., 1720 East 38th St., Indianapolis 6, Ind.
14. Harcourt, Brace & World, Inc., Tarrytown, N.Y.
15. Harvard University Press, Cambridge 38, Mass.
16. Houghton Mifflin Co., 2 Park St., Boston, Mass.

17. Industrial Psychology, 515 Madison Ave., New York 22, N.Y.
18. Marietta Apparatus Co., Marietta, Ohio.
19. Ohio Scholarship Tests, State Department of Education, 751 Northwest Blvd., Columbus 15, Ohio.
20. Psychological Corporation, 304 East 45th St., New York 17, N.Y.
21. Psychological Institute, Box 1118, Lake Alfred, Fla.
22. Psychometric Affiliates, Box 1625, Chicago 90, Ill.
23. Public School Publishing Co., Test Division of Bobbs-Merrill Co., 1720 East 38th St., Indianapolis 6, Ind.
24. Scholastic Testing Service, 3774 West Devon Ave., Chicago 45, Ill.
25. Science Research Associates, 259 East Erie St., Chicago 11, Ill.
26. Sheridan Supply Co., Box 837, Beverly Hills, Calif.
27. Silver Burdett Co., 45 East 17th St., New York, N.Y.
28. Stanford University Press, Stanford, Calif.
29. Stoelting (C. H.) Co., 424 North Homan Ave., Chicago 24, Ill.
30. University of Minnesota Press, Minneapolis 14, Minn.
31. Western Psychological Services, Box 775, Beverly Hills, Calif.
32. Williams and Wilkins Co., Baltimore, Md.

similar average scores, measures of variability, and reliability estimates for a given group.

Error of measurement, *see* Standard error.

Extrapolation. In general, any process of estimating values of a variable beyond the range of available data.

Face validity. The apparent validity of a test that seems fair to and appropriate for the individual being measured. The extent to which a test is made up of items that seem related to the variable being tested. *See* Validity.

Factor. A hypothetical trait derived by factor analysis.

Factor analysis. A method of computing for determining factors from the intercorrelations among a set of variables, usually tests.

Forced-choice item. Any test item in which the individual is *required* to select one or more of the given choices. Usually, however, refers to a multiple-choice item whose choices are of equal preferential value but of different discriminating ability.

Free-response test. A test on which the items require the individual to respond in his own words rather than select among alternatives.

Frequency distribution. A tabulation of scores from high to low, or low to high, showing the number of individuals that obtain each score or fall into each score interval.

General ability. A loose expression for ability to cope with a wide range of problems. Used synonymously with intelligence. Also referred to as scholastic ability.

General education. A term used to refer to a common core of learning for all high-school and college students regardless of the curriculum or course of study in which they are enrolled.

Grade equivalent. The grade level for which a given score is the real or estimated average.

Grade norm. The average score obtained by pupils of a given grade placement. Also referred to as the modal grade age.

Graphic rating scale. A form for recording a rating, according to the strength of some quality or trait, along a straight line (continuum), descriptive phrases of the trait being written below the line.

Group test. A test that can be administered to a number of individuals at the same time by one examiner.

Halo effect. The tendency in rating an individual to let one of his traits influence ratings on other traits.

Heterogeneity. The tendency of a group to show marked dissimilarity.

Homogeneity. The tendency of a group to be alike.

Individual test. A test that can be administered to only one individual at a time.

Intelligence quotient (IQ). The ratio obtained by dividing mental age by chronological age, i.e., (MA ÷ CA) 100. A measure of brightness that takes into consideration both score on an intelligence test and age.

Interpolation. A process of estimating intermediate values between two known points.

Interval, *see* Class interval.

Inventory. An instrument used for cataloguing or listing all or a sample of behaviors, interests, attitudes, etc., regarded as useful or relevant for a given purpose. It is not a "test" or a measure in the usual sense and has no right or wrong answers.

Item analysis. The process of evaluating single test items by any of several methods. It usually involves determining the difficulty value and the discriminating power of an item, and often its correlation with some criterion.

Kuder-Richardson formulas. Formulas for estimating the reliability of a test from information about the individual items in the test, or from the mean score, standard deviation, and number of items in the test. Indicate the internal consistency of the test.

Linear relationship. A relationship between two or more variables that can be represented by a straight line; thus, as one variable increases or decreases, the other moves likewise or inversely.

Local norms. Norms that have been made by collecting data in a certain school or school system and using them, instead of national or regional norms, to evaluate student performance.

Low ceiling. A term applied to a test that is too easy for many individuals, so that many tend to score at or near the top of the possible score scale.

Machine-scorable (machine-scored) test. A test that can be scored by means of a machine.

Mastery test. A test whose primary purpose is to determine the extent to which individuals in a group have learned or mastered a given unit of instruction. This type of test is intended not to differentiate widely among individuals, but to determine whether or not a group of students have achieved a certain level of proficiency. It is used primarily to determine whether or not the group is ready to advance to another unit of instruction.

Matching item. A test item calling for the correct association of each entry in one list with an entry in a second list.

Mean, *see* Arithmetic mean.

Median (Mdn). The middle score in a distribution; the 50th percentile; the point that divides the group into halves.

Mental age (MA). The age for which a given score on an intelligence or scholastic ability test is average. It is the average age of individuals making the average score on the test.

Modal age. The ages or age range most typical of pupils in a specified grade placement.

Mode. The score or value that occurs most frequently in a distribution.

Multiple-choice item. A test item in which the individual's task is to choose the correct or best answer from several choices presented.

Multiple-response item. A special type of multiple-choice test item in which two or more of the choices presented may be correct.

N. The symbol commonly used to represent the number of cases in a sample or distribution.

National norm. A norm based on nation-wide sampling.

Nonverbal test. A paper-and-pencil test, usually used with children in the primary grades, in which the test items are symbols, figures, and pictures rather than words; instructions are given orally.

Normal distribution. A distribution of scores or measures that in graphic form has a distinctive bell-shaped appearance and is symmetrical about the mean, with cases concentrated near the average and decreasing in frequency the further they depart from the average, in accordance with a precise mathematical equation.

Norms. Values that describe the performance of various groups on a test or inventory. Norms are only descriptive of existing types of performance and are not to be regarded as standards or as desirable levels of attainment.

Objective test. A test that can be scored in such a way that no matter who scores it the results are the same. Scoring keys or stencils are used.

Ogive curve. A type of curve obtained by plotting cumulative frequencies or percentages of a distribution. Also called the S-shaped curve.

Omnibus test. A test in which items measuring a variety of mental operations are combined into a single sequence and from which only a single score is derived.

Parallel tests, *see* Equivalent form.

Percentile. A point score in a distribution below which falls the percentage of scores indicated by the given percentile. For example, the 30th percentile is the point below which 30 percent of the scores fall.

Percentile rank. The percentage of scores in a distribution equal to or lower than the score corresponding to the given rank.

Percentile score. The score representing the percentage of persons who fall below a given raw score.

Performance test. A test usually requiring manual or other motor response by the individual instead of the responses called for by a paper-and-pencil test.

Personality inventory. An instrument intended to appraise or measure one or more of the nonintellectual aspects of an individual's mental or psychological make-up.

Point scale. A test in which each item responded to correctly contributes one or more points to the individual's score. The standing of the person being tested is based on the total points he obtains.

Power test. A test intended to measure level of performance rather than speed of response; hence, one in which there is either no time limit or a very generous one.

Practice effect. The influence of previous experience with a test on the later administration of the same or a similar test. The term is usually employed when the practice effect is not itself what is at issue, but is something to be eliminated or allowed for.

Probable error (PE). An indication of the variability of a measure; the extent to which an obtained value deviates from the measure in question; a measure of the error in sampling. In a normal distribution, half the deviations from a measure of central tendency fall within a range of 1 PE above and below that measure. The PE is .6745 of the standard error.

Product-moment coefficient. The most widely used correlation coefficient for linear relationships. Also called Pearson product-moment coefficient of correlation; symbolized by r.

Profile. A graphic presentation of the results of an individual's performance on a group of tests.

Prognostic test. A test used to predict future achievement in a specific subject or field.

Projective technique. A method of personality study in which the subject responds freely to a series of stimuli such as inkblots, pictures, unfinished sentences, and the like. In this free-response situation the subject "projects" into his responses manifestations of personality characteristics. Also called projective method.

Quartile. One of three points that divide a ranked distribution into four equal parts. The lower quartile Q_1 or 25th percentile; the upper quartile Q_3 or 75th percentile; the middle quartile Q_2, or 50th percentile, is the median.

Quartile deviation (Q). A measure of variability defined as one-half the score distance between Q_1 and Q_3. Also called the semi-interquartile range.

r, see Coefficient of correlation.

Random sample. A sample so drawn that every member of a population has an equal chance of being included in it.

Range. The distance between the highest and lowest scores in a distribution.

Rank-order correlation (rho, ρ). A method of obtaining a correlation coefficient by assigning ranks to each score of all individuals, and determining the relationship between them. Also called rank-difference coefficient of correlation.

Rating scale. A device whereby a rater can record the estimated magnitude of a given trait or quality being measured. Commonly indicated as descriptive, numerical, or graphic rating scales.

Raw score. The original, untreated result obtained from a test or other measuring instrument. Usually the number of right answers, or points on a point scale.

Readiness test. A test that measures the extent to which an individual has achieved a degree of maturity or acquired certain skills or information needed for beginning some new learning activity. Most frequently used with preschool children to determine their readiness for entering school.

Reading age. An age-equivalent score assigned to the average score on a reading test for individuals at a given age.

Recall item. A test item that requires a person to supply the correct answer from his own memory or recollection, as contrasted with a recognition item. Also called supply item.

Recognition item. A test item requiring an individual to recognize or select the correct answer from among two or more choices presented.

Reliability. The extent to which a test is consistent with itself in measuring whatever it does measure.

Reliability coefficient. The coefficient of correlation obtained between two forms of a test (alternate-form or parallel-form reliability); between scores on repeated administrations of the same test (test-retest reliability); between halves of a test, properly corrected (split-half reliability); or by using the Kuder-Richardson formulas.

Response set. The tendency for an individual to follow a certain pattern in responding. For example, "acquiescence" set is a set to respond true in a true-false test; "evasiveness" is a set to respond "undecided" or "don't know" in a personality or interest inventory.

Scattergram or scatterdiagram. A double-entry chart used for plotting the scores on two tests, or variables, for each individual in a group. It gives a graphic indication of the relationship between the two variables.

Scholastic aptitude, *see* Academic aptitude.

Semi-interquartile range, *see* Quartile deviation.

Sigma, *see* Standard deviation.

skewness. The tendency of a distribution to depart from symmetry or balance about the mean.

Sociogram. A chart or diagram that graphically illustrates interactions, usually those desired or not desired, among individuals in a group.

Sociometry. The determination of the social or interpersonal relationships among members of a group.

Spearman-Brown formula. A formula stating the relationship between the reliability of a test and its length. The formula permits prediction of the reliability of a test that is lengthened or shortened by any amount. It is used most frequently for estimating the reliability of an entire test from the correlation between halves of the test, as in split-half reliability.

Special ability. A term used for such abilities as mechanical, clerical, musical, artistic, etc., as distinguished from general ability.

Speed test. A timed test in which the speed of performance or response is considered the major variable.

Split-half coefficient, *see* Coefficient of internal consistency.

Standard deviation (SD, s, σ). A measure of the variability or dispersion of a set of scores. The more the scores cluster about the mean, the smaller the standard deviation. In a normal distribution, approximately 68 percent of the scores fall within the range of 1 SD above and below the mean; approximately 95 percent fall within a range of 2 SD's; and practically all the scores fall within a range of 3 SD's.

Standard error (SE). An estimate of the magnitude of the "error of measurement" in a score, i.e., the amount by which an obtained score differs from a hypothetically true score. The standard error is an amount such that in approximately two-thirds of the cases the obtained score does not differ more than 1 SE from the true score.

Standard score, z score. A score in which each individual's score is expressed in terms of the number of standard deviation units of the score from the mean.

Standardized test, standard test. A test that has been given to various samples or groups under standardized conditions and for which norms have been established.

Stanine. A standard score with a mean of 5, a standard deviation of approximately 2, and a range between 1 and 9. It is one of the steps in a nine-point scale of normalized standard scores; hence its name, derived from *standard-nine.*

Stem. The introductory part of a multiple-choice test item that is to be completed by one of the responses following it.

Stencil key. A perforated scoring key which, when positioned over an answer sheet, either in a test booklet or on a separate answer sheet, permits rapid identification and counting of the correct responses.

Strip key. A scoring key arranged so that the answers for any page or any column of the test appear in a strip or column that can be placed alongside the individual's responses for easy scoring.

Subjective test. A test that is often scored on the basis of attitudes, opinions, and idiosyncrasies of the scorer.

Supply item, *see* Recall item.

Survey test. A test that measures general achievement in a given subject or area and is more generally concerned with breadth of coverage than with specific details or discovery of causal factors. It is most frequently used for screening large groups of persons.

T score. A standard score with a mean of 50 and a standard deviation of 10; usually used to convert raw scores on two or more tests into comparable scores for ease in interpretation.

Test battery. Usually a group of several tests standardized on the same population, so that results on the several tests are comparable.

True score. The score that would be obtained if we had a perfectly reliable measuring instrument. If it were possible to measure an individual over and over again with the same test, without any changes in the individual, the average of all his test scores would be an estimate of his true score. True scores are never obtained, but rather are considered hypothetical values.

Validity. The extent to which a test measures what it is supposed to measure. Validity is defined on the basis of different purposes; different kinds of evidence are used in defining types of validity. The most common types of validity are: *content validity,* which describes how well the content of the test samples the class of situations or subject-matter about which conclusions are to be drawn; *concurrent validity,* which describes how well test scores correspond to measures of concurrent criterion performance or status; *predictive validity,* which indicates how well predictions made from the test are confirmed by evidence gathered at some later time; and *construct validity,* which indicates the degree to which certain explanatory constructs or conceptualizations account for performance on the test.

Verbal test. A test in which results depend to some extent on the use and comprehension of words, as in most paper-and-pencil tests.

X, Y. The symbols used in measurement to designate raw scores.

x, y. The symbols used in measurement to indicate the deviation of a score from its mean, i.e., $x = X - M_x$, $y = Y - M_y$.

z score, *see* Standard score.

Index

Format by Jeanne Ray Juster
Set in Linotype Electra
Composed by Brown Bros. Linotypers, Inc.
Printed by The Murray Printing Company
Bound by The Haddon Craftsmen, Inc.
HARPER & ROW, PUBLISHERS, INCORPORATED